Praise for *Divining,*

"This amazing memoir tracks one woman's connection with trees, with the natural world, with home and place. It is deeply personal and informative, intimate and well-researched, tender and science-based. Those contradictions make it both relatable and important in this time of climate crisis when the value of vigorous forests (and individual tree species) cannot be overlooked. Each chapter spirals around a central tree, from the maple to the crepe myrtle. Dunphy uses each species as both framework and also deep metaphor for life growth. As Dunphy explores how trees relate to her life, the light shifts from places where the trees thrive to threats from invasive fungus and nonnative insects to the hard-core realities of development. Threaded through all of her places are luminous moments of connection, her life history, and love of the trees."

—Anne-Marie Oomen, author of *As Long as I Know You*, winner of
AWP's Sue William Silverman Award for Creative Nonfiction

"I've read all of Maureen Dunphy's books with interest and consider her an important voice in Great Lakes literature. With *Divining, A Memoir in Trees*, she gives us an intimate, honest, and highly original view of the complexities of human life as seen through nature's lens."

—Jerry Dennis, author of *Up North in Michigan*
and *The Living Great Lakes*

"In *Divining*, Maureen Dunphy creates a voice that weaves poignant lyricism, the observational objectivity of a scientist, and the warmth of a welcoming conversation on the front porch. As we listen to her story, we once again want to climb that old maple in the backyard, only this time we will listen to the language of the leaves."

—Jack Ridl, author of *Practicing to Walk Like a Heron* (Wayne
State University Press, 2013), co-recipient of the gold
medal for poetry from Foreword Reviews

"*Divining* is a carefully constructed journey with one of Michigan's most talented writers. It does not pretend to include every tree, or every detail about the trees who appear in the book. Instead, it uses trees as anchors in deep waves of story. As she describes trees she has known from the Great Lakes to the central mountains and ocean coastlines, Maureen Dunphy connects a lifetime of memories to needles, leaves, seeds, bare branches, moist breath, bare roots, and remnant rings of ancient stumps. Each chapter folds over an origami-like idea centered on a species of tree but is really about the relationship between people and the trees they often forget to see. History, science, social systems, ceremonial requests, and the power of trees to heal are all part of the conversation. In her 'memoir in trees,' Dunphy urges readers to listen more carefully to the Standing Nation, but she also models listening to our own younger and older selves as we consider roots and branches."

—Margaret Noodin, author of *What the Chickadee Knows*
(Wayne State University Press, 2020) and *Weweni*
(Wayne State University Press, 2015)

"In *Divining*, veteran writer Maureen Dunphy brings her carefully honed prose to this personal genre. In sixteen essays, she explores different species of trees that have touched her life, a mixture of botanical information and her personal remembrances. She captures the moment, the short-lived foliage, and the eternal, the deep roots reaching to an ancient past. These narratives—both profoundly personal and enormously universal—are a rich and joyous read."

—Aaron Stander, host, *Michigan Writers*
on the Air, Interlochen Public Radio

Divining, A Memoir in Trees

Made in Michigan Writers Series

General Editors

Michael Delp, Interlochen Center for the Arts

M. L. Liebler, Wayne State University

A complete listing of the books in this series can be found online at wsupress.wayne.edu.

DIVINING

a
MEMOIR
in
TREES

Maureen Dunphy

WAYNE STATE UNIVERSITY PRESS
DETROIT

ISBN 978-0-8143-4842-0 (paperback)
ISBN 978-0-8143-4843-7 (e-book)

Library of Congress Control Number: 2022945947

Publication of this book was made possible by a generous gift from The Meijer Foundation.

Cover design by Lindsey Cleworth.

Wayne State University Press rests on Waawiyaataanong, also referred to as Detroit, the ancestral and contemporary homeland of the Three Fires Confederacy. These sovereign lands were granted by the Ojibwe, Odawa, Potawatomi, and Wyandot nations in 1807 through the Treaty of Detroit. Wayne State University Press affirms Indigenous sovereignty and honors all tribes with a connection to Detroit. With our Native neighbors, the press works to advance educational equity and promote a better future for the earth and all people.

Wayne State University Press
Leonard N. Simons Building
4809 Woodward Avenue
Detroit, Michigan 48201-1309

Visit us online at wsupress.wayne.edu.

In memory of the beech grove,
those trees who once rose
from the north bank of the Red Run and
later graced my neighborhood—
all massacred members of the deep-rooted community
that included the one American beech
who today still shares land and air, sun and shade with me
And with gratitude to Craig,
with whom I moved into the magic of the beech grove

Contents

Preface

I did not start out to write a memoir. And, if I had, these stories might not have been the ones I would have envisioned telling.

In 2015, when my Great Lakes island book was in the process of being published, I was feeling like I wanted to write about something new. Not knowing what that might be, I started keeping an "idea journal," logging one question a day relating to things in the world about which I wondered. Questions about trees kept showing up.

The 381-page first draft of this project—titled *Listening to the Murmurs of Trees: Engaging with Your Standing-Nation Allies for a Healthier Self, a Healthier Planet*—included sixteen chapters of information about trees, the result of me wanting to know more about some of the so many trees I love and have loved. The essay in each chapter was tucked away under the subheading "Tree Ambassador" with the purpose of bringing personal narratives about trees I have known to an otherwise educational enterprise, to show you why I wanted to know more about these particular species of trees.

But in the end, the essays contained their own logic and took me in a different direction, telling the story—not chronologically, but instead in a way resembling the rings of a tree, each essay containing an independent chronology of time and connection—circling the intersections of one human life with the lives of members of sixteen different tree species. Hence the "accidental" nature of this memoir.

You can find more information about each of these sixteen species in appendix A. Additional information related to each of these species—as well as other interesting tree-related material that answered many of my initial questions about trees—can be found at maureendunphy.com by clicking on *Divining, A Memoir in Trees*.

Introduction

The Norway maple tree has been gone three weeks now. Since long before we lived here, this "barrier" tree stood guard adjacent to the front sidewalk, providing a boundary between those who dwelled in our house and the cars, the amblers (with or without dogs), the power-walkers, the runners, the bicyclists, and the sun. The tree was girdled by its own roots, scarred by two large frost cracks in the bark on the west side of its trunk, where winter's afternoon sun touched, and dying of verticillium wilt even while canopying the well-walked sidewalk and our driveway. I could no longer put off making the hard decision. The tree's trunk was stripped of its limbs and then brought down, chain-sawed into logs for winter fires a year hence. The stump was ground into what appeared to be the remnants of a bomb blast.

When my dad died, my circle of six dear women friends brought me baskets filled with a generous meal of comfort to share with my mother and husband. Tucked into the accompanying sympathy card was a gift card to be used toward planting a tree in my dad's memory, a tree to honor him. I already had scheduled the Norway maple's demise, so I knew where this tree would be planted. But now I had a greater challenge to solve—greater than choosing my words of eulogy on tearstained leaves of paper—the question of leaves on what kind of tree. The sixteen tree species I wrote about in this book had picked me. What would be the right tree to pick for my dad?

My first thought was a flowering crabapple tree. We'd had one growing in the side yard of the house I grew up in. In the morning, my dad would kiss my mom good-bye at our side door, walk to our car parked in the driveway, and head downtown to work. At dinnertime, he returned, swinging his briefcase as he strode back up the side walkway. Every weekday, morning and evening, he passed the crabapple tree he and my mom had planted. This tree was unique, the first flowering tree we were aware of planted in our new neighborhood. At the time, the neighborhood was a treeless piece of sodded suburbia, still transitioning from a field of yawning basement holes, wiping away all memories of former farmland. The crabapple tree was beautiful in spring, summer, and fall.

I called landscape architects for their counsel. Initially, no one returned my calls—customers were making up for last spring's pandemic lockdown. But then one showed up. As Tim stepped out of his Jeep, I felt immediately happy, filled with certainty that he would know just what was needed. He said, "Evergreen," and I knew he was right. How had I thought I could face the shedding of leaves, bare branches, an annual death? Then, as he walked toward the empty, too-bright space left by the maple, Tim said, "Fir."

"Fir?" I asked, scrambling for what I knew of fir trees. "Balsam fir?" In my childhood, we had always selected a fragrant balsam fir for our Christmas tree. My dad loved Christmas and especially loved decorating our Christmas tree. In many other homes, in many cultures, Christmas has long been celebrated with a fir tree—known as the Tree of Light—as in pre-Christian times, when the winter solstice was celebrated as the time of the sun's rebirth, the return of light.

"No," Tim replied. "Not balsam. Concolor—white—fir."

Of the twenty-five species of fir worldwide, ten grow in the United States. The Arbor Day Foundation guidebook *What Tree Is That?* simply states of the white fir, "The most beautiful of the firs some would suggest." In the Midwest, the white fir may reach sixty-five feet in maturity. Its needles are long—two to three inches—and soft, not prickly. When they are crushed, the needles release a citrus scent. My dad told the story of receiving a most wondrous gift one Christmas when he was a boy: the gift of oranges. The pinecones of fir trees grow upward on the branch, like the candles on the Christmas trees of my dad's childhood.

Over the centuries, a white fir has come to symbolize

- Honesty
- Forthrightness
- Friendship
- Truth
- Hope
- Determination
- Endurance
- Renewal
- Promise

These traits associated with the white fir tree also exactly described my dad, Bill Dunphy. Could there be a better tree with which to remember him?

Perusing a tree book published over one hundred years ago, I learn that "in the gardens of Europe and of our Eastern states this [the concolor fir] is a favorite fir tree, often known as the 'blue fir' from its pale bark and foliage." My dad's favorite color was blue. If you were fortunate enough to have known him, you may well recall that when he was listening to you—which would be the case *whenever* you were talking—he would be looking directly into your eyes with those very blue eyes of his.

A month after we mark the first anniversary of his March 13th death, my dad's fir tree will be planted, flanked by two lilac bushes. The scent of lilacs always propels me back, deep into early childhood. I am outside a house I do not remember ever visiting before or after this evening in late spring. A group of children, none of whom are familiar, are playing around me outdoors within a large loose circle of folding chairs occupied by grownups. The house—filled with distant aunts and uncles, church congregants, or maybe both, and tables laden with food—is surrounded by towering bushes. As lamplight begins to shine out of the windows of this white house, emanating warmth, the bushes turn into dark shapes of shadow. Suddenly, my dad appears, so tall above the children, hoists me up, and holds me close in his arms, his presence already the most constant comfort in my life. At the same time, and for the first time, I notice being wrapped in a fragrance rising out of the descending dusk, a fragrance that for the rest of my life will always evoke happiness. Several years later, when my mom planted this species of bush right outside our suburban side door, I would learn to call this scent of happiness and comfort "lilac." That night with my dad was redolent with it.

In this memory, which I have been always able to call up like it was yesterday, my dad remains as vibrant, attuned to others—such a warm welcoming smile he had—and as loving as he was throughout my entire life, throughout the lives of so many people his life touched. His eyes would light up just at the sight of you coming toward him. How very lucky I was to have Bill Dunphy as my dad.

This week, as I started thinking about writing my dad's eulogy, I found myself listening to a band of raucous crows that had recently descended upon our neighborhood. Yesterday, four, then six of the birds bobbed and swayed from their perches in my neighbor's giant silver poplar, eyeing me and scolding my companion cat while engaging in their own loud conversations.

This morning, the crows brought their cacophony back to the trees with whom I share land, called out these memories, shook these stories free.

1
TREE

The ground moves.

My FOOT *is swallowed.*

I am sliding DOWN *to* DARK.

MOMMY *says,* "OOPS!" MOMMY *props me* UP *on the hard again.*

I look over the hard.

I am looking UP *at* SUN.

MOMMY *says,* "LOOK, DADDY." *In* SUN, DADDY *is walking on the sidewalk.*

"BYE-BYE, DADDY," MOMMY *says.* MOMMY *is waving my hand.* "BYE-BYE, DADDY."

DADDY *is not* HERE.

SUN *is coming in the room.*

I am watching LITTLE *drift in the tunnel of* SUN.

MOMMY *is watching me.* MOMMY *waves her hand.*

The LITTLE *dance. They are taking me* THERE.

I GO *to a place not* HERE.

MOMMY *is making the happy sounds.* "When the red, red robin comes bob, bob, bobbin' along, along."

I come back HERE.

"When the red, red robin comes bob, bob, bobbin' along, along." Her finger points. MOMMY *says,* "LOOK." *She lifts me* UP *in her arms.* MOMMY *says,* "LOOK. LOOK, OUT *the window.* LOOK DOWN."

An other falls DOWN *on the ground.*

"Robin. ROBIN. *When the red, red* ROBIN *comes bob, bob, bobbin' along, along.* ROBIN. ROBIN."

ROBIN *moves.*

MOMMY *looks at me.* MOMMY *makes the happy mouth.*

ROBIN *hops, moves its head, points down in the grass, hops.*

"When the red, red ROBIN *comes bob, bob, bobbin'."* MOMMY *looks at me.* MOMMY *makes the most happy sound.*

Some other is HERE.

MOMMY *says,* "LOOK. *Squirrel.* SQUIRREL."

SQUIRREL *looks* SOFT *like* LAMBY. LAMBY *does not move except for* MOMMY. SQUIRREL *moves.*

SQUIRREL *runs and stops. Runs and stops.* SQUIRREL *goes* UP. SQUIRREL *goes* UP *the other. The other is bigger than* MOMMY.

MOMMY *says,* "*Tree.* TREE."

SQUIRREL *is* UP *in the arms of* TREE.

ROBIN *goes* UP *behind the hands of* TREE.

Suddenly SUN *is not* HERE.

MOMMY *points* UP. MOMMY *says,* "Cloud. CLOUD."

SUN *is not* HERE.

I LOOK DOWN.

SQUIRREL *and* ROBIN *are not* HERE.

TREE *is* HERE. TREE *is* BIG. TREE *is bigger than* DADDY.

I am looking at TREE. TREE *is* HERE.

TREE *is looking at me.*

TREE *is taking me* THERE.

I GO *to a place not* HERE.

I GO *with* TREE.

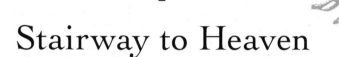

2

Stairway to Heaven

The American Sycamore

(*Platanus occidentalis*)

The first time we saw our house-to-be in Royal Oak, Michigan, the most noticeable feature of the yard surrounding it was a large, very unusual-looking tree smack-dab in the middle of the front of the house, a tree that towered above the rest of the surrounding canopy. The family selling the house told us that this tree, which was clothed in multi-color patches of bark with bare areas of creamy white showing through, was a sycamore tree. My mom predicted it would be a "messy" tree, recalling the sycamore near her Grandma Bateman's house in East Cleveland.

At the time the deed of the house changed hands and it became ours, ten steps—each constructed from two wooden wedges with a foot-length of two-by-fours connecting them—were screwed into the trunk of this tree, with a slight curve in their progression up toward the tree's crown. One of the first stories Mrs. Irwin, our elderly new neighbor, shared with me was about how—worried about the health of the tree—she "nearly had a heart attack" when she watched the dad of the family screwing these steps into the trunk to build a ladder up to the tree's lowest branches—a good ways off the ground—for his young daughter Maddy to climb.

Was this a Saturday project? What preceded the building of this ladder? Discussion, surely. Measuring? Sawing the two-by-four pieces below the tree's crown, between the house and the tree on the turnaround portion of the driveway? Was it a hand or power saw? Did a soft pencil mark off the measurements on the tree? Was a power screwdriver used?

Was the sycamore aware of the discussion going on beneath it? Did the sycamore feel the measurements being taken against its trunk? The pencil pressing against its trunk? The screws grinding through its bark? Through its phloem, cambium, and sapwood? Into its heartwood?

One sunny Thanksgiving Day, before we gave thanks at the table, my niece and nephews, under my brother-in-law's supervision, climbed all the steps to the lower branches of the tree's crown. Over the years we've lived here, my husband has removed most of the lower steps. But the support wedges that held the steps remain. The same arborist who misidentified the tree as a London plane tree told us not to attempt to remove the wedges, as the empty screw holes would leave the trunk exposed to invading wood decay pathogens, and so the tree is growing around and over the wedges, much like the trunk of the honey locust tree across our driveway is subsuming a flagpole holder. From my study window today, I can see the top two steps of the stairway, the only ones that remain screwed into the trunk of the sycamore.

Sometimes what a tree does best is inspire questions, first about itself. These have been mine over the years about this tree:

- What is the relationship between sycamore trees and London plane trees? How to tell them apart? Which species is this tree with whom I share land?
- The leaves of this tree resemble gigantic maple leaves. Is there a relationship between the sycamore and the maple?
- What is with the smaller branches striking out at such odd angles? And catching on to other branches—called "danglers"— when they break from the tree and fall? Does this process provide the tree with some advantage?

● In late spring, segmented brown balls—small, light, and hard—
fall from the tree over a short period of time. Larger, softer
balls become evident in the summer, falling over the winter and
sometimes into the next spring. What's with the two kinds of
fruits/nuts/seeds? Are there really two? The hard balls look like
those vintage leather knot buttons (aka leather braided buttons).
Are the hard little buttonballs an earlier version of the big, soft,
downy-filled ones?

● Why does the tree shed its outer bark and how does this shedding happen?

Maybe, though, a question more important than any of these is:
What did young Maddy see from this tree? Once up the ten steps,
how far into the crown, using the branches that stick out like a spiral
staircase, could Maddy climb, branch by branch? Some of the tree's
branches are very thin, even now, more than fifteen years after Maddy
moved to Virginia, but I'm guessing she could have gained another
six or eight feet of height beyond the steps her dad installed. Maybe
eighteen or twenty feet off the ground. Most important: How did she
feel to be up in the midst of the tree's wide rustling canopy, having
gained a bird's-eye view?

One can only imagine. But I am qualified to make a good guess.
I climbed up into two different tree house platforms multiple times
when I was in elementary school. One was the tree house Noël's dad
built in the large weeping willow in their backyard on Hillcrest Street.
For a while in elementary school, Noël and I were best friends, which,
outside school, involved riding our bikes together and climbing—with
me clutching my new transistor radio in its black faux-leather case—up
into her tree house, high above a little streamlet, to talk and to sing
along with the top 40 hits on WKNR, Keener-13 Radio. "Moon River"
was a favorite. Our view of the world was curtained by the tree's pendulous branches weeping downward toward the ground.

My best tree house memories, though, are from the "tree house" in The Field behind my house. The tree that held it stood alone, no longer on The Creek's bank once it had been rerouted. From our house, the tree was the distance away of the width of our corner lot's side yard, the dead-end side street, and four or five backyards west toward my elementary school. This tree house was nothing fancy. Today, understanding how development in Southeast Michigan has affected wildlife and judging from my memory of how and where the platform in the tree was built, I'm guessing it may have originally been built to serve as a hunting blind when the tree was surrounded by farmers' fields, even though no deer grazed in The Field after our subdivision was developed. But for us, it had always been a tree house. I wondered whose.

The tree in which the structure was built rose above and just west of the circle where we rode our bikes up the high creek bank and down, around and around. This was the lone large tree in the west that could be seen rising above The Field's wildflowers from the side door of our house, blazing orange with the sun setting behind it in the autumn. Could it have been a maple? I don't remember the tree releasing keys, the "helicopter" seeds that would have given it away as a maple. Looking at a photo of the May 3, 1949, aerial view of the township of Livonia's section 16, showing the farmland that was to be replaced over the next decade by the subdivision I moved to, I'm pretty sure I can pick out that tree standing alone, even then on the opposite side of The Creek—which was yet to be redirected or put underground—from the three cottonwoods I knew so well. Maybe the tree house tree was a cottonwood, and the setting sun blazing behind it colors the memory orange.

From above, on the east side of the tree, the bike-riding circle path lay below, worn through the white pinwheels of Queen Anne's lace, the chicory flower we called "dusty soldiers" in their blue coats, white and yellow sweet clover with their drowsing bees, and the purples of red clover, thistle flowers, and asters, depending on the season. We climbed up the far side of the trunk. Each step was a rusted rectangle of iron, bent at midpoint into a ninety-degree angle, nailed on one side into the tree trunk and sharp on the two outer corners of the step.

The first step was very high off the ground. In the beginning, before we neighborhood kids had gained the requisite height, we had to give one another a good boost up to the first step. That meant the tallest was left to navigate the first step on her own. I was usually the tallest. We all had to be careful not to catch a shin on the edge of the steps. A year or so after our first climbs, when we had reached the necessary height, we could stretch a leg to reach a foot up to the first of the three steps, all of which were best navigated while wrapping widespread arms in a hug around the tree's rough trunk. From the last step, the climber needed to stretch up and fold over a board platform, leaning forward onto her stomach and then hitching a knee over the edge of the platform while sliding her own trunk securely onto the platform's center. During this last maneuver, for a minute the climber's legs hung over the edge, into thin air, before she could be pulled onto the platform. Then finally, one was rewarded by being able to sit up to appreciate the spectacular view, high above the Earth. Room to sit or stand, but not to lie down, was available. The platform had sufficient room for three kids at most—maybe once, giggling, we got four packed in—but it was better for just two. I personally thought it best for just one: me.

I remember being up there, above the rest of The Field, alone, dangling my legs down on the side away from the stairs and surrounded by leaves. One board nailed between two of the three parts of the split trunk that rose from the crotch into which the platform was nestled provided something to lean forward against, farther out into space. Such a pleasure to be up so high. I could see everything spread out below: the dots of flowers in The Field, the movement of their attendant butterflies and bees. I felt the definition of euphoria. Yet at the same time, leaning the back of my head or a cheek against the furrowed bark of the tree was very grounding. The leaves twisted in the breeze and rustled. I was up too high to jump. The fact that I might not survive a fall was centering, focusing my thoughts on what I was doing when I shifted position.

I had already been diagnosed with "generalized anxiety" by my pediatrician a couple of years before I was big enough to climb the tree and twenty years before "generalized anxiety disorder" became an actual diagnosis. What is difficult to explain is how or why the thoughts I had in that tree seemed mine alone, and different than the thoughts I had on the ground. Maybe the height gave me a different perspective as well as a feeling of immunity. Heaven—the birds in the see-through blue sky, the clouds we were learning to identify in school—appeared so much closer. The challenges of dealing with family and friends, having all been left below, seemed smaller. When I came down from time spent alone in the tree, I felt refreshed, renewed, reset somehow.

Some evenings, before my mom leaned out the side door and rang the dinner bell, the wall lamp between her painting easel and our dining table would be turned on. In the fall, when twilight came earlier, I could see the small square of light at the window above the table infused with the red of the calico print valance my mom had made and hung at that window. That small square glowed out warmth, food, love, home. When I was away at college and occasionally homesick for childhood, it was the view of that window from the distance of the tree I visualized, even though we had left that home bordering the beloved field a long three and a half years before I'd left for college.

The first time I smoked marijuana I was a second-semester freshman at Oakland University—that would have been in the winter of 1972. Given the times, I might have been considered developmentally behind in this respect. One of the two roommates in the neighboring dorm room, Laurie, a pre-med sophomore, had never gotten high before either. Joe, Laurie's roommate's boyfriend, set up this event for us. Laurie had talked to Diane. Diane had talked to Joe. Joe had talked to his roommate Ziggy. I had talked to only Laurie, but now we both had an appointment to keep with Ziggy.

Joe was planning to have some alone time in Laurie's room with Diane, and during it, we had a specific time on a Friday night to be at Joe and Ziggy's room in Pryale House. On the appointed cold night, we walked out of Hill House (the all-girls' dorm, then known as "The Virgin Vault") and made our way around to one of the three small two-story dorms that were situated together on a circular drive. We entered the intimate warmth of Pryale and climbed the stairs, past the shadowy landing where a light was always burned out, to the second floor. We were punctual, but as we approached his door down the long hall, I was hoping Ziggy had gotten distracted, forgotten we were coming, was out, or wouldn't answer our knock.

Only thinking back now do I realize just how neat his room was. Ziggy had certainly set things up for us to have the optimal experience. He had a lava lamp lit, a stick of incense burning, and a Led Zeppelin album riding his turntable. I didn't know Ziggy at all, really, except by sight. I thought he was cute in a longhair, hippie, "stoner" sort of way, but more important, I trusted him. Which was critical for this event. He was the sweet kind of guy you suspected must have been raised with sisters.

Ziggy offers us a seat on his bed, which is neatly covered with a striped Mexican blanket. Laurie and I lean back against the cool cement block walls, our shoulders close together, our legs sticking out over the side of his bed. Ziggy pulls his desk chair out from his study alcove and sits down on it backward, leaning over the back of it, in front of one of his stereo speakers on which the lava lamp is bubbling. I am so nervous that I feel freezing cold and quickly jump up from the bed to grab my parka from Joe's bed and wrap it around my shoulders. It doesn't do much to stop my shaking.

We watch Ziggy roll a joint using Zig-Zag rolling papers, getting his weed out of a Ziploc sandwich bag. He licks the edge of the paper, smoothing it down with much precision, and then inserts the entire joint in his mouth, twisting it around, then pulling it back out to let it dry and shrink tight. He is very good at rolling joints. From what I've heard, this came from a lot of practice. I swallow hard to keep my teeth from chattering.

After some small talk between Laurie and him to fill up the drying time, Ziggy eventually lights the joint up with a wooden match, taking a quick toke from it as he does so. Then he hands it to Laurie, who often smoked the occasional cigarette with a shell of beer[1] at Knapps. (Despite being teenagers, because our peers are being drafted to fight in Vietnam, we are legal consumers of alcohol.)

After Laurie takes a hit and passes the joint to me, she walks me through the mechanics of smoking. The sucking in, watching the glow at the tip of the joint intensify in the dim room, holding in the smoke until I can feel my lungs, and then a slow, steady release. Interrupted by coughing. We pass the joint around our small circle three or four times, during which time I stop being afraid of what being high is going to feel like, is going to do to me, and start worrying that this just isn't working for me. For some reason, it appears that I'm not going to be able to get high. Nothing is happening. Absolutely nothing.

Then, sometime shortly after I have that absolutely thought, I notice that I am staring at the incredible grain of the dark wooden beam that stretches across the dorm ceiling. The pattern of the wood grain is amazing. No, *really* amazing.

And now my thoughts are slowed down enough that I can somehow be inside them, intensely enjoying the sensory experiences that are generating them, like recognizing the beauty of the wood's grain while also savoring my amazement at it. Someplace, at a distance, Laurie and Ziggy are talking, but I am totally alone inside my head.

---

1   A regional expression that some trace to the Detroit area, meaning a small, straight-sided glass of beer or, more specifically, a 6.5-ounce glass of pilsner.

And then Ziggy reaches over and turns up the volume of the music that previously had been in the background. Jimmy Page's opening guitar notes of Led Zeppelin's "Stairway to Heaven" make their way into my ears, and just after they find an opening in my brain, wood flutes join in from somewhere in my soul, a location I'd not been sure of until now. And then the lady in the lyrics—the one who's sure "all that glitters is gold" and who's "buying a stairway to heaven"— appears.

At that point, I'm pretty sure I am high. The feeling is nothing like I have ever experienced or imagined.

And a new day will dawn for those who stand long,
And the forests will echo with laughter.

I don't recall any laughter; it appears I was a very serious person when high. After what felt like a very long—but not unpleasant—period of being in my head, Laurie and I put on our winter outerwear, learning to move all over again, and went outside. I remember stopping midway on our way across the long arching bridge that spanned Beer Lake, totally blown away by the blazing stars, larger than I'd ever seen them before in a wide navy dome of sky, before briefly getting lost in the reflection of the walkway lights on the lake. But what I remember most vividly, over fifty years later, is how the music felt, how the lyrics spooled out story in my head, how I suddenly had a different relationship with what was going on in my brain.

The experience of smoking marijuana made me feel the same elation as being up in the branches of my childhood tree house tree. High. Up in the tree everything was recognizably what I saw when I was down on the ground, but the perspective was unusual and much more interesting. It was removed, distant enough for studying, for the careful consideration that was harder to do down on the ground, in the midst of it all. Somehow, being high in a tree or high on marijuana soothed me, smoothed out the anxiety-laced background babble of my thoughts that I still occasionally mistake as being me.

Many decades later, I have learned how to get from here to there most days with a mix of ritual and writing. Some might call it a "natural high," but it doesn't happen naturally. I am still prone to be fraught with a low-level anxiety much of the time. This makes writing challenging until I am able to stop thinking about outcomes, relax my expectations, and turn down the perfectionism. Ritual is what transports me through this process until I can focus on what is before me, until I get into the flow. I begin my daily writing period with a pre-writing ritual that puts me in a different space and opens me to trust what's happening in the here and now.

I work my way toward writing in eight or nine simple steps:

1. Get "off the grid" (close both of my email accounts and turn off my cell phone or set it to "Do Not Disturb"), so there are no outside prompts to distract me.
2. Fill up my water pitcher and drink my first hourly glass. I don't like water, but I do understand it's good for my brain as well as my body. And if it doesn't really make my thoughts flow, at least I've earned a bit of self-righteousness in drinking it.
3. Clean my aromatherapy burner, fill the top with water, add one to three essential oils, depending on what I imagine to be needed. Today's mix is: Sweet Basil for "aiding in concentration"; Frankincense for "dispelling fear"; Clary Sage for its "warming, relaxing, uplifting, calming, euphoric" contributions. Then I light the tealight beneath it. I've found that once I get to this step, there's no going back.
4. Write down at least three things I am grateful for at the moment in a journal I keep handy on my desk exclusively for this purpose.
5. Meditate for ten to twenty minutes. During the pandemic, as I began a regular daily session of Loving-Kindness meditation,

the form of meditation I'd been doing successfully for years, I experienced a panic attack, complete with chest pain. Then and there, in the throes of the panic, I switched to using short, guided meditations on my phone offered through the Headspace app. I find it easier to follow directions given by another voice, rather than having to quell my anxiety on my own.

6. Start playing the soundtrack I've selected for my current writing project. For this book, it has been Ösel's *Medicine Buddha Mantra* (2012).

7. Ask a question related to where I am in my project, what I expect to be working on that day, what I'm afraid of, or what I'm hoping to encounter.

8. Draw a card from the Hallowquest Arthurian Tarot while thinking about my question in step 7 and look up the card's meaning. Am I a big believer in the tarot? No, not in the traditional way, but the description of a card's meaning works even better than an inkblot in bringing to the forefront of my consciousness what I already know.

9. This is the optional step. If I've been going through a rough patch of writing, I text the person who has agreed to serve this purpose and to whom I confirm I've completed my ritual and am about to start writing.

After performing all of these steps, turning to write feels automatic, and the turn, because of the way it has been executed—by ritual—offers a much better chance that I will be able to reach below the surface of the anxious chatter in my brain to find ideas to investigate, words that work, and sentences that stick, oftentimes accompanied by the reward of pleasure. On very good days, a bit of euphoria drifts onto and may emanate off the page.

What I have learned, where I have landed, all makes perfect sense to me. Climbing a tree, smoking a joint, and engaging in a daily writing ritual and writing practice have all led to similar feelings of being comfortable in my skin, my brain, my current life circumstances. Having left the first two of those experiences in the past, I've discovered that while writing involves more work and comes complete with its own set of sharp edges to run into, it brings with it more reward, providing me with countless opportunities to follow even more intriguing wood grain.

During the over fifteen years we've lived in the house, the sycamore is the tree I have come to love best from among the many trees in and bordering on our yard. I'm not the only one. At least two years in a row, a pair of robins have chosen this tree as home to raise their family in. Last year a tiny hummingbird nest decorated one of its zigzagging branches over our driveway, visible from our kitchen table, and its creator returned this year. Growing in plain view of my desk, Sycamore has become an ally of sorts. When I meditate before writing, I visualize sending roots from the soles of my feet down into the ground to intermingle with its roots, and when I imagine myself contained in an egg of light, I hang the egg from the tip of one of the tree's southern-reaching branches.

I like to imagine that any resulting feelings of sanctuary and/or inspiration, of grounding and/or centering in young Maddy were well worth the wounds made by the screws in the trunk of my dear friend.

Here are the "smoke-laden" questions: What did the tree feel, know? After the stairway was in place, could Sycamore feel the weight of the young girl climbing? Did this tree experience positive or negative, neutral or no feelings about holding a human youngster in their[2] arms? We may not yet learn enough about trees' sentience to answer those questions in my lifetime.

---

2 Sycamore trees are monoecious, bearing both female and male flowers, hence my use of "their" as a nonbinary (singular) possessive pronoun.

What I do know, however, is that while I love Sycamore in all seasons, I especially love their bare bones thrust up against Michigan's lake-effect clouds come late fall. On some nights in November after the sun sets, Sycamore holds the waxing Frost Moon high in their arms. Fireside, I imagine being held up in Sycamore's branches, myself, a masthead on a ghost ship, singularly and solely present.

3

The Boundary Oak

The White Oak

(Quercus alba)

The only time, in my sixty-five-plus years, that I'm sure I've felt the Earth move was as I lay alone, flat on my back, under the massive spread of The Boundary Oak. This spot served as a particularly fine place to look through leaves and branches to clouds moving across the depth of a blue sky. The slightly damp soil between the feet of The Boundary Oak barely cupped my back and cooled my limbs that were spread for balance, but that tenuous contact was enough to keep me attached, grounding me sufficiently, so I could feel the Earth rotating on its axis as it revolved around the dizzying sun.

The lower grades were not allowed to venture off the school's asphalt playground during recess, but the older students at Roosevelt Elementary School were allowed to cross the black grate of the iron pedestrian bridge over The Creek to the school's athletic field. During grass-growing season, this wide field running east and west between Melvin Street and Henry Ruff Road was mowed, south to north, between The Creek and the woods of the park. We were allowed to go just as far north on this field as The Boundary Oak, which stood sentinel, surrounded by playing fields before the wooded park began. This field is where our gender-role socialization advanced daily at recess and over the lunch hour: the boys played baseball on the baseball diamond or threw a football around, and the girls, walking or sitting, talked about boys, other girls in our grade, boys, our futures, and, well, boys, the subject we often circled back to.

On this particular day, I was sitting on the sun-warmed bench of a picnic table with a group of three other fifth-grade girls, talking. We were a short distance from, still under the watch of, The Boundary Oak. Celia, Anne, and I were on one side of the table, Loretta on the other. This day, a fifth presence was between us. On the green-painted wood of the picnic tabletop was a prominent four- or five-inch carving of the four-letter word that begins with the letter "F." We all knew it was a bad—a "dirty"—word. I knew not to speak that word out loud, although it was reverberating through my head as our talk drifted to a stop and we silently considered it together.

It was not a word that had been explained at the fifth-grade meeting "Becoming a Young Woman," attended by mothers and daughters, which had featured the animated film *The Story of Menstruation*, produced by Walt Disney Studios. The word certainly wasn't in the "Very Personally Yours" Kotex booklet on menstruation, which had been the text for the meeting and currently waited on my closet shelf under a yet-to-be-opened box of Kotex sanitary pads. We were still a year or so away from our junior high health class that would include six weeks of "sex education," during which we'd be separated from the boys for that class period, held every other day. But despite being given enough clues to sort of figure out sexual intercourse during those six weeks, that word wouldn't be mentioned then either.

The four of us seated at the picnic table that day were all serious students. Each of us liked to read—which surely made us prone to well-developed imaginations—but we also were four of the only five girls—the fifth being Cathy—placed in the highest-level math group. In addition to indicating that we were relatively intelligent, this may have also been proof that we were lagging behind in terms of our socialization. Celia was the prettiest of us. Anne tended toward chubby and, as the only girl and the youngest sibling in her family, having three older brothers, she possessed a great sense of humor. Celia and Anne had been best friends since kindergarten, and both were well-liked by their peers. Loretta was the adopted only child of older parents. She dressed in babyish, old-fashioned dresses that I suspected her working mom sewed from patterns other than the Butterick patterns my mom used to make my dresses. That day, she was wearing a red-and-white-checked gingham dress with puffy short sleeves that ended in too-tight bands on her upper arms. At her waist, she wore a thin, tight black patent leather belt. The ensemble did nothing to minimize her height or disguise her large-boned frame.

Loretta was definitely not a social leader in our class. But as we focused on the word before us—none of us daring to finger the deep-cut letters that looked as if a one-inch chisel and a lot of time had been devoted to the task—Loretta confided she knew what this word meant because her mom had explained it to her. Her translation of that explanation was: "Men put their thing in women." (All of us at the table except Loretta had at least one brother, but none of us would have introduced the word "penis" into this or any other conversation.) Perhaps the most outrageous part of this revelation was that Loretta claimed to know that the youngish choir director at her church and his wife actually did this F-thing. I couldn't imagine such knowledge coming to light at one of my church choir practices, but then our choir director was a woman. Anne, for once, had no response at the ready to make us laugh.

I remember the quiet that followed Loretta's comments, during which, I suspect, we each used our well-developed imaginations to process this new information. I immediately came to the conclusion that Loretta's definition of this word—because of what a serious person she was—was most likely true. On the heels of that recognition came the instant realization that the definition of this word was definitely more than I wanted to know. With this revelation on that warm spring day, something in my world shifted, and I momentarily felt physically ill, like I might throw up.

Life had taken a turn recently to include other such disquieting moments. Earlier that week, I had gone shopping with Grandma Klotzbach, coming home with my first "training" bra, an item I had very urgently wanted so I could be more like the other girls in my class, of whom I was the youngest. I had put it on for the first time when I got home, admiring how I looked in my dressing table mirror before I went downstairs to practice piano. Sitting on the hard piano bench in our cold living room, warming up with scales, I suddenly, desperately, wanted to go back to who I had been before the longed-for purchase.

At the picnic table that day, I could feel the straps of this new bra on my shoulders and the unrelenting stretch of it across my back, unfamiliarly binding me and making me much more aware of my new breasts than I wanted to be. Now, possessing this new, just-a-few-minutes-before-unimaginable information, I turned away and stared off into the near distance at The Boundary Oak, willing it to ground me, to return me to who I'd been before we'd crossed the field, sat at the picnic table, and focused our attention on the stupid word carved into it. The comforting image of the spreading Boundary Oak on that particular day is still with me today.

But, when I return more than a half a century later to Roosevelt Park to visit The Boundary Oak, I am stopped in my tracks by what is strikingly missing, gone. Several groupings of colorful polyethylene plastic play structures are scattered across the mowed field where once the oak had spread, had separated playfield and woods, had connected ground to sky, had grounded me. At the edge of one of these play-scapes, next to a narrow asphalt walk, is a hummock rising up from this field, where it appears a very large tree stump has been removed. Today, The Boundary Oak lives only in memory.

Deeply sad, I walk to the edge of woods that now marks the end of the playing field. Here is a stand of cottonwoods, showing their shade intolerance by growing at the outer perimeter of the woods. Growing up, I did not know any of the cottonwoods in this park intimately. These cottonwoods are certainly tall enough to have been here when I was in elementary school, but cottonwoods are fast growing. With a lifespan of fifty to two hundred years, it makes sense these cottonwoods might have been here then and may still be here when I am long gone, unless a chain saw or a wild wind of a storm becomes involved. But without the oak in the foreground, it is difficult to tell what might have been here before. Everything looks off without the familiar landmark—truly a "marker of land"—of The Boundary Oak.

When we sat under its canopy, in its shade at recess, with a huge clearing in front of us and the woods at our backs, this particular oak certainly must have been at least a century old. Maybe several centuries. How old do oaks grow? A long time, apparently:

An oak can be very tough if it doesn't have any competition. Consider open spaces . . . oaks growing near old farmyards or out in pastures easily live for more than five hundred [years].

White oaks, which can live 600 years, are said to be 200 years growing, 200 years living, and 200 years dying.

Quercus [the oak's genus name] belongs to the long-lived trees; the life of some species is believed to reach one thousand years.

Windsor Great Park . . . contains one of the largest collections of oaks in Europe, including several that are more than 1,000 years old.

Before leaving the park, I walk back to and circle around what I am now thinking of as The Boundary Oak's gravesite. Some of The

Boundary Oak's roots must still be there, underground remnants; surely, they would have spread farther than a grinder could have ground. But I can't find any of The Boundary Oak's feet, between which I felt the Earth move.

Several weeks after visiting the former site of The Boundary Oak, I pick up Peter Wohlleben's *The Hidden Life of Trees: What They Feel, How They Communicate—Discoveries from a Secret World* in a bookstore and open to the first chapter, which begins:

> Years ago, I stumbled across a patch of strange-looking mossy stones in one of the preserves of old . . . trees that grows in the forest I manage. . . . I stopped and bent down to take a good look. I . . . noticed that the remaining "stones" formed a distinct pattern: they were arranged in a circle of about five feet. What I had stumbled upon were the gnarled remains of an enormous ancient tree stump. All that was left were the vestiges of the outermost edge. The interior had completely rotted into humus long ago—a clear indication that the tree must have been felled at least four or five hundred years earlier.

Wohlleben's initial belief that he was looking at moss-covered stones made me think how a *stump* circle might be like a *stone* circle. The outer edges of Wohlleben's great tree stump had become "stone" and now marked the circle of forest that that had been taken up by the ancient tree. Like the great stone circle Stonehengé had marked—what?

Theories abound, but scientists and historians still don't know the reason(s) why Stonehenge and the other over three thousand stone circles, standing stones, and megaliths that dot Great Britain, Ireland, and northern Europe were constructed. Current debate centers around whether the stone rings were built to assist in viewing astronomical bodies or events, such as the summer solstice; as a means to demonstrate a community's power; or as places for ritual and to commemorate the dead of the Neolithic communities.

In my imagination, I try out the idea of the stone circles commemorating the dead but not the *human* dead of the Neolithic community. What if stone circles marked where ancient trees had stood? Maybe stone circles were built to memorialize a great tree, a protector, a tree who was a fine leader, an important teacher, who had lasted for generations of human families—perhaps an oak.

After all, didn't people worship trees once upon a time? With that thought, a cascade of questions followed: Weren't those tree-worshipping people called druids? Or did druids serve as the priests of the people who worshipped trees? What exactly did druids do? *Did* they worship trees? Did they commune—that is, communicate—with trees?

According to some etymologists, "druid" comes from the Celtic compound "dru-wid," or "strong seer," from Old Celtic "derwos," or "true," from the Proto-Indo-European root "deru," meaning "tree," especially oak, plus "wid," or "to know"; hence a druid—"dru-wid"— was literally an "oak-knower." Druids were *they who know the oak.* What exactly did druids know of the oak?

Unfortunately, we will never have any means of discovering what druids knew of the oak because the single thing that we *do* know about druids is that learning how to be one happened via the *oral* tradition. Did the druids of old know—as we do today—that their oak trees, like all trees, are able to solve problems—that is, possess intelligence? Did the druids know that their oak trees are capable of learning and communicating and are endowed with memory? Did druids know that their oaks, like all plants, have all of the five senses that humans do: sight, hearing, smell, taste, and touch . . . plus at least fifteen other senses? As plant neurobiologist Stefano Mancuso has shown:

Plants use their senses to orient themselves in the world, interacting with other plant organisms, insects, and animals, communicating with each other by means of chemical molecules and exchanging information. Plants talk to each other, recognize their kin, and exhibit various character traits.

The business of—the secrets involved in—being a druid and exactly what druids knew of the oak were not left behind in writing. No authentic Celtic text has been or is going to be found to translate and study. No words. A dead end. We can only imagine.

Just as I can only imagine what human lives the life of The Boundary Oak intersected with over the centuries—members of the Potawatomi band who lived in the area that is now Livonia, Michigan? the European-descended settlers who arrived from New York to farm the area two centuries ago? the generations of children who attended Roosevelt Elementary School?

Who else remembers this magnificent tree? Who else looked to it for help in a time of need? Who else felt the Earth move beneath its branches?

4

Another Notable Night

The Eastern White Pine

(Pinus strobus)

Before graduating to the Great Lakes the summer following sixth grade, I grew up vacationing at the Driftwood Resort, a series of log cabins on Houghton Lake, one of Michigan's many inland lakes. Houghton Lake is south of the 45th parallel, but nonetheless was considered "Up North" by my family. One vacation in the early 1960s particularly stands out because my maternal grandparents came with us. I spent most of the week practicing pumping my legs on the big swing hung between two telephone poles at the beach's edge, playing in the lake's shallow water alongside the boat dock, fishing for pan fish, cheering Grandpa on at horseshoes after dinner, and appreciating sunsets over the lake, bonfires after dark, and the catch and release of fireflies. It was a summer of gaining important new skills: learning from Grandma Klotzbach how to braid using beach grass; practicing blowing bubbles of Coca-Cola-flavored bubblegum that came in a paper straw, mentored by my mom; learning to whistle, courtesy of my patient dad; figuring out how to row a rowboat with Grandpa Klotzbach's help; and graduating to reading chapter books on my own. (My dad still kidded me after I reached adulthood about how I cried over the dog book *Beautiful Joe* by Marshall Saunders that summer.)

That year, like every other, my family made our annual pilgrimage to several spots near the lake: to pick wild blueberries down two-track lanes in the woods nearby, lanes also frequented by black bear, which we saw at the dump at dusk; to Prudenville's bakery for molasses cookies with jelly centers; to feed the herd of albino deer at Johnson's Rustic Tavern Resort on the lake's east bay; to Sea Shell City and the Call of the Wild Museum on Old U.S. 27 Highway in Gaylord. That one year we also visited Hartwick Pines State Park in Crawford County, just north of Grayling, the largest state park in Michigan's Lower Peninsula, established in 1927.

Today, Hartwick Pines is a 9,762-acre recreation area including four small lakes, a campground, and a network of four-season trails for hiking, mountain biking, and cross-country skiing, some of which run along the east branch of the Au Sable River. What makes the park unique, however, is its 49-acre forest of old-growth conifers, primarily eastern white pines and red pines but also some hemlocks. Accessible on the 1.25-mile paved loop of the Old-Growth Trail from the Michigan Forest Visitor Center, this is one of only a dozen places in Michigan's Lower Peninsula where you can experience old-growth forest.

The heart of the everyday definition of an old-growth forest is one that has never been "directly impacted by humans. . . . These forests often contain a well-developed structure, including large trees, multiple-aged trees, and abundant downed wood." Significant disturbance in a forest is most often caused by lumbering. Take what happened in Michigan, for instance:

> The earliest lumbering in Michigan was done by the French in order to build forts, fur-trading posts, and missions. The British, and later the Americans, used Michigan's hardwoods to build merchant and war ships. Beginning about 1855, white pine became the most desired tree species by the lumber industry

of the Great Lakes states. Navigable rivers and extensive pine forests formed the basis of a flourishing pine industry in Michigan's Lower Peninsula until 1895, and about 10 years longer in the Upper Peninsula. . . .

The pioneer settlers of the 1820s found a land covered by dense stands of virgin timber; scarcely 50 years later, Michigan was the leading lumber producer in the nation. The clear-cutting was so extensive that by 1910, the once-abundant forests had almost completely vanished. . . .

Many [had] felt that the huge forests of Michigan would last for many, many years, yet within a 20 year period, 1870 to 1890, most of the trees were cut. . . .

The pine grew primarily as pure stands, on sandy, dry soils in the northern two-thirds of the state. . . . [At the time,] many white pines were over 200 years old, 200 feet in height and five feet in diameter.

The few old-growth forests we have left exist because they have been preserved. Hartwick Pines is no exception. In 1927 Karen Hartwick saved a small patch of primeval forest to memorialize her military-man-turned-lumberman husband Major Edward E. Hartwick, who had died nine years earlier from the spinal meningitis he had contracted in France during World War I. The Hartwick Pines grove of white and red virgin pines and hemlocks originally covered an eighty-five-acre parcel of land. Almost half of this remaining speck of old-growth forest was destroyed by a November windstorm—another cause of significant disturbance—in 1940. Today, the pine trees remaining in the stand at Hartwick Pines are between 350 and 500 years old.

That summer when I first visited Hartwick Pines, I don't remember knowing that I was visiting an old-growth forest or even understanding what an old-growth forest was. I just knew I had never seen trees as big as these before. At the time, my dad was still a Baptist minister. My family prayed and attended church together, but we didn't talk much about God or religion. Entering the stand felt like being ushered into a different denomination of church, one I might look forward to attending regularly.

On Saturday, April 1, 2017, "A Night for Notables," the Library of Michigan Foundation's Twentieth Annual Notable Books program was held in the Library Rotunda to celebrate twenty notable titles published in 2016 that highlighted Michigan people, places, and events. Accompanied by my husband and my parents, I was in attendance with my 2017 Michigan Notable book, *Great Lakes Island Escapes: Ferries and Bridges to Adventure.*

One of my fondest memories of the lovely evening is of meeting Carl the eastern white pine, a representative of the species that is Michigan's state tree, who is growing in the courtyard of the Library Rotunda of the Michigan Library and Historical Center building. According to the Library of Michigan's tour card for the first-floor rotunda, Carl was a gift, transplanted when they were forty-seven feet tall from Novi, Michigan in December 1986.[1] Carl was lifted by crane into the glass-enclosed first-floor courtyard before the rest of the building was built. Above the first floor they rise into the open air of the courtyard.

Carl was named after Lansing native Carl D. Johnson (1926–2010), the prize-winning, internationally recognized landscape architect and professor of landscape architecture in the University of Michigan's College of Architecture and Urban Planning. Carl Johnson's firm, Johnson, Johnson and Roy, was the landscape architectural firm contracted for the Michigan Library and Historical Center building.

Naming Carl the white pine after Carl the architect was a nice gesture. However, since eastern white pine trees, along with the majority

---

1   As conifers are mostly monoecious, "they" and "their" are used as nonbinary (singular) pronoun and possessive pronoun, respectively, for Carl.

of other conifers,[2] are mostly monoecious—with both male and female flowers present on the same tree—a non-gender-specific name, like Finley, Riley, or Skyler, might have been a better choice. But "Carl" is the name by which this pine tree is known.

At one point in the evening, following the official program and during a break from book-signing, I stood alone on the one side of the window wall, looking out at Carl, who, frankly, didn't appear particularly happy, at least not at their first-floor level. They looked like they could use a forest vacation. The month before my island book was published, I had started feeling like I might want to write another book, and with that feeling came the inkling that maybe my next book was going to have something to do with trees. Almost a year later, then and there, with the noise of celebration swirling around me, feeling happy that I'd achieved my original three-pronged 2012 goal in writing my island book[3] and gearing up to set another writing goal, with Carl as my witness, I committed to writing a book about trees.

I had the occasion, when I was on a 2017 three-library tour—one of my Michigan Notable Book responsibilities—in between Devereaux Memorial Crawford County Library on June 8 and Boyne District Library on June 9, to make a return visit to Hartwick Pines. While I could barely recall my earlier visit to this special place, its most salient feature came back to me as soon as I entered the hush of the old-growth section of forest. What one notices—even more than the amazing height of these one-hundred-foot-tall pines—is quiet. An

2 Conifers include evergreen trees and shrubs of the class Coniferinae, including pine, fir, spruce, and other cone-bearing trees and shrubs, as well as yews and other trees and shrubs that bear drupe-like seeds.

3 My 2012 writing goal was to write a book that would help readers fall in love with the Great Lakes so they would be more likely to contribute to protecting them by: (1) providing them information to visit one or more of the 136 Great Lakes islands accessible by ferry or bridge; (2) publishing the book with Wayne State University Press; and (3) succeeding in having the book recognized as a Michigan Notable Book.

intensity of quiet with which, despite being a person who is naturally drawn to quiet, I'm not familiar.

When we were leaving the Library of Michigan, my husband gave me a slice of small tree trunk, two and a half inches across, with the shapes of the five Great Lakes painted in blue in the center, over the growth rings. He'd purchased it from the Michigan History Museum gift shop while I was otherwise occupied. The souvenir proved a perfect symbol of my transition from islands to lakes to trees. The magnet affixed to the back of tree trunk slice has held it to my metal desk lamp over the intervening few years while I worked on a middle-grade book about the Great Lakes before returning to fulfill the promise I had made to Carl. How grateful I feel to have been given the impetus that night to spend the next few years learning more about trees while writing down my memories involving some of the tree allies of my life.

And that very sentence was intended to conclude this essay—but between introducing Hartwick Pines as one item on a list of Houghton Lake pilgrimages made in my childhood and defining old-growth forest, suddenly, eleven other Michigan old-growth forests "flashmobbed" my intent.

Yes, I knew about the old-growth forest at Hartwick Pines, having experienced it as a kid. But who knew that—despite "old-growth forest having dwindled from close to 70% to under 10% of the Great Lakes landscape"—there are still a dozen places to experience old-growth forest in Michigan? It's true! (You can learn more about these Michigan forests in appendix B.)

"Downstate" (in the lower half of Michigan's Lower Peninsula):

- Newton Woods
- Warren Woods Natural Area
- Toumey Woodlot

"Up North" (in the upper half of Michigan's Lower Peninsula):

- **Roscommon Virgin Pine Stand**
- **Hartwick Pines**
- **Interlochen State Park**
- **South Manitou Island**
- **Colonial Point Memorial Forest**

In Michigan's Upper Peninsula:

- **Tahquamenon Natural Area**
- **Estivant Pines Nature Sanctuary**
- **Sylvania Wilderness**
- **Porcupine Mountains**

And without warning, my imagination took flight toward forests. I suspect that the conversation my husband and I had just had the previous week—about four months after COVID-19 arrived in Michigan and related to its arrival—about the wisdom of investing in a camping van gave it a boost. Despite having owned two cottages over the last twenty-five years, at heart, I'm more of a camper than a cottager. My husband and I had talked about getting a VW Bus at the beginning of our relationship. In fact, my husband had once owned one, but he'd sold it before I met him and took him on his first actual camping trip.

The U.S.-Canadian border was closed for almost seventeen months during the pandemic; we were unable to visit our cottage on Ontario's Pelee Island in Lake Erie in 2020 and for most of the 2021 season.[4] In July 2021, with the border still closed and after we'd not had

---

4 The border to Canada finally reopened August 9, 2021, during a fourth COVID surge, over four months after we suddenly, and rather unexpectedly, had sold our Pelee Island cottage, furnished. We crossed the international border and the Western Basin on September 13 to remove our personal effects.

power for fifty hours due to a thunderstorm, we got up the morning of Day 3, purchased three bags of ice during "Senior Hour" at the local grocery store, threw one bag in our refrigerator, one in our freezer, and another in a cooler, and drove three and a half hours to Mears State Park on Lake Michigan, the first place we'd ever camped together in September 1976. This was where we made the decision to spend five months of 1977 backpacking in Europe. This decision necessitated the other big decision we made that short weekend: to move in together.

We carried through on both of those decisions, finding a lovely upper flat on West Margaret Street, across Woodward Avenue from Detroit's Palmer Park by October, and then subletting it the following April through October for nineteen weeks, while we backpacked through nine Western European countries—Germany, Austria, Italy, France, Spain, England, Wales, Ireland, and Denmark—and took a week tour to Leningrad and Moscow in what was then still the Soviet Union.

But we have never followed through on the idea to get a camping van. We continued tent camping when our daughters came along. Our oldest accompanied us on her first camping trip on a Father's Day weekend at eleven weeks old.

The first time we put our Pelee cottage up for sale, a few years ago, we talked about getting a vehicle that could pull a classic teardrop trailer on visits to the national parks. We also talked about getting a condo within walking distance of our grandchildren in North Carolina. But when the cottage didn't sell, we took it off the market. Once we'd paid off the Pelee cottage, I didn't want another house to worry about. But parking a camping van in our oldest daughter's driveway? That could work. And being able—during what I suspected would be a long time before we flew without fear of contagion—to drive to our younger daughter and her husband's house in Denver, Colorado, camping on our way. What's not to like?

Last night, as I was starting down an old-growth-forest-remnants-in-Michigan research rabbit hole, it struck me—wouldn't that be fun? To visit all the old-growth forests in our state? Although I've visited all of the Great Lake islands accessible by bridge and ferry and written about them, I didn't get to camp except on one of those twenty-seven trips to 136 islands—on South and North Manitou Islands—because I was trying to highlight the accessibility of these Great Lake islands. Although many of the islands have campsites, you can spend a night on most islands without camping, except for North Manitou. And my second book, one written for kids about the Great Lakes called *All about the Great Lakes*, involved going no farther afield than my desk. But just about all of the old-growth forests in Michigan have campgrounds located near them, so these destinations tantalize with the allure of road trips, camping, and writing.

Today, I opened Google Maps in three separate tabs and started plotting, envisioning three long trips to all of Michigan's old-growth forests, dividing them up geographically: the lower half of the Lower Peninsula (three), the upper half of the lower Peninsula, aka "Up North" (five), and the U.P. (four). Perhaps I'll write something on these trips in the yet-to-be-purchased camping van. Something titled: "Michigan's Dozen Vestal Virgins."

This evening, happy to have another subject to explore bestowed upon me, I was dreaming about breathing in the quiet of old-growth forests and imagining the pleasures of writing about them: another notable night.

5

Twin Volunteers Host a Murderer

The Eastern Redcedar

(*Juniperus virginiana*)

Alone in my yard on a drizzly spring day, I suddenly stumble back in alarm before I can process what I am seeing. Great blooming fluorescent-orange gelatinous tentacles!

That was not my exclamation of fright or surprise. That was an apt description of what I was seeing, and whatever it was, it was like nothing else I'd ever seen in nature before. Very colorful but also over-the-top sinister-looking.

I came across this surprise while stroking an unidentified evergreen branch, trying to determine what made it feel so prickly. When I caught sight of this psychedelic blob deep into the branches, snuggled up to the evergreen's spindly trunk, my first thought was: What trickster has placed it here? And then (gulp), could it be alive? I hadn't a clue what it was, where it had come from, or how it was going to complicate things on this tiny piece of Earth of which I serve as steward. A quick search yielded more psychedelic blobs on the interior of the small evergreen tree, as well as some on its neighboring twin.

I don't know how these twin evergreen trees came to be in my yard. I suspected a bird (or birds), on its way to or from my feeder, planted the seeds as it relieved itself, a theory their original location suggested. I had come across the two of them under an ancient overgrown deciduous bush at my neighbor's drive while I was weeding and trying, yet again, to make something of the southwest end of the front-yard sidewalk bed. When I first noticed them, they were two small middle fingers of bristly blue-green stem pointing directly skyward, in the general vicinity of each other. They were surrounded by a few scattered clumps of Stella D'Oro daylilies, some green and gold hostas, and a small shrubby spirea bush with bright green leaves and purple flowers. I thought I might give the baby evergreen trees a better chance by transplanting them away from the encroaching myrtle to the edge of the English ivy bed, letting them become a defining factor at the northeast edge of the bed instead. So I moved them to the other end of the same sprawling ivy bed, near our driveway. In the process, I unthinkingly planted them too close together, inadvertently creating a very narrow hedge, cramping each of their fast-growing individual selves.

When I had transplanted them, I recalled that somewhere in the immediate vicinity another unidentified evergreen tree had once grown, one that I always imagined had been planted to block the view of the mailbox. By the time we became stewards of the yard, however, it had grown beyond its usefulness in that respect as all of its lower limbs had been trimmed to the trunk at the bottom of the tree. By that time, too, the tall evergreen tree was leaning over the driveway, reaching out for sun from under the shade created by the spreading crown of the Norway maple. It was slanting in the direction that I imagined the west wind could help push it. I feared that someday it might topple and fall across both our and our neighbor's driveways.

Or did I just disapprove of its slant? I wonder about that now. I defended my action of having it cut down to the neighbor on the other side, Mrs. Genevieve Irwin (may she rest in peace)—who I suspect felt then the way I feel about trees now—by saying I didn't want to create an issue with my other neighbor should the evergreen tree fall on her car. But in reality, cars are never parked at that end of her circular drive. I was working full-time at Volkswagen's headquarters then as an instructional designer. Much of the year, I left and returned in the dark. Did I just not know where the neighbors parked their cars then?

At any rate, Davey Trees removed it. I remember thinking the view from the house and street was an improvement, so maybe I wasn't so concerned with my neighbor's car after all. Only now, at least a decade later, do I consider that this evergreen tree was the first tree I was ever responsible for killing.

I don't even know what kind of evergreen it was. All I recall is that it was a needle-leaf conifer, not a scale-leaf conifer like a northern white-cedar is. Using Stan Tekiela's *Trees of Michigan Field Guide* and the process of elimination, I'm guessing it was a spruce. It was not any kind of pine because its needles were single, not clustered, and it certainly was not a soft-needled eastern hemlock, a distinctively coned balsam or Douglas-fir, or a prickly eastern redcedar. That leaves spruce. It was not blue like a Colorado spruce, but whether it was a white, black, or Norway spruce, I can't be sure. If I had to guess, I'd say a white spruce.

The first few years after the unidentified leaning evergreen tree was cut, I set a large pot of geraniums atop its stump during the growing season, but today the decade-old stump is buried under a thick spread of English ivy. This morning, I became curious about what the circumference of the evergreen tree had been, at least at its base, the only part of it left, and I went out to search for it. The stump was easier to find than I expected because when I looked at the area where I thought it should be, I noticed the twelve-inch-high ivy sloped up into a mound at least three feet across. It took a bit of time and effort with a heavy-duty hand pruner to get to the stump.

As I cut the thick covering of ivy from across and around the stump, the rich smell of humus rose up toward the already-steamy, last-day-of-June mid-morning sun. Tucked into the crevices of the twining ivy root and ringing the stump were: dead ivy leaves, dried red oak leaves from my neighbor's tree, a sycamore leaf the size of a luncheon plate from my own dear front-yard friend, a couple handfuls of sweetgum fruit balls from the tree across the yard, their spikes softened from the moisture, and a number of Norway maple keys from the dying tree whose branches now canopied over the stump.

The stump measured a foot across from the southwest side to the east side closest to the drive and thirteen and a half inches on the wider southeast to northwest side. While the side of the stump on what was the "inside" of the tree's slant rose three inches straight up from the ground, the outer slant stretched in a slope beyond the inner wood another eight to twenty-two inches. Here was visual proof of something I'd recently read: that a leaning tree's root system will grow to accommodate off-center weight distribution. So maybe a west wind couldn't have blown it over. All the tree had been trying to do— and apparently in a safe way—was to reach more sun.

The southeastern third of the stump was covered in what I would come to identify as a white fungal growth, specifically "white-rot fungus." In the center of the stump was a two-inch soft circle that was decomposing at a faster rate than the trunk around it.

I set the yard-waste can filled with ivy strands atop the stump, took my tape measure, and had a look at the twin volunteers I'd transplanted just a few feet away. The two trees, their trunks only two inches in circumference, were growing just thirty-four inches apart. The taller of the two trees was just over six and a half feet; the other one was shorter by about two inches. The shorter one was wider, measuring four feet at its widest branch spread.

Both had a few brown needles. Cutting those out was a prickly job. Today neither tree held any sign of harboring the flamboyant "Jimi Hendrix creature" that had startled me so in April when I had come up with the pandemic plan of cleaning a few square feet of yard a day.

That plan had lasted exactly a day, a day ended by my discovery. After I recovered my composure—trying to get over the feeling that the horned gelatin beings were watching me—I went inside to my computer to figure out what strange alien from another planet had landed in my at-that-point unidentified evergreens.

Judging from the images I pulled up on my computer monitor, I had just made the acquaintance of *Gymnosporangium juniperi-virginianae*, aka "cedar-apple rust." Rusts are fungal diseases that will not kill their hosts; in fact, they need their host to be alive. However, the word is that "repeated infection of this pathogen can seriously weaken and destroy the health of susceptible plants . . . [which] will also lose any ornamental value."

But wait, there's more! This fungus is biotrophic; it depends on *two* species to develop and spread. One is a variety of juniper, often the eastern redcedar but sometimes other varieties of juniper. The fungus has five different kinds of spores, which develop in the late fall on young juniper branches as a reddish-brown gall (which I wasn't looking for last fall). With spring showers, the galls grow and release spores, which are carried by wind to infect apple and crabapple trees. On the fruit trees, they develop into a disease that causes red spots to occur on the leaves and that can deform the fruit:

> The damage done to the leaves greatly affects the apple trees' ability to gather sunlight and nutrients from the air, damaging its health and fruit production, and in some cases causing death. [Fortunately,] the fungus cannot be transferred from apple tree to apple tree, or from juniper to juniper. [But] the following year, spores are released from the apple trees that, in turn, infect the junipers. The disease is extremely prolific during wet years.

Which is when the galls swell and grow telial horns that turn bright orange in the rain.

This is exactly what I had seen: telial horns. It had already been a rainy spring, it was even raining the day I was starting my cleanup, and we continued to have a very wet spring. But I don't have any apple trees, nor do any of my neighbors. Looking at pictures of the affected leaves of the apple trees, I realized I'd seen similarly orange-spotted leaves on the largest hawthorn tree by our walk down to the beach on Pelee. Turns out there is a cedar-*hawthorn* rust. Was that the cause of the spots on the leaves of one of our hawthorn trees in our Pelee yard? There, I'd transplanted an even smaller and bristly "baby finger" similar to my twin volunteers. This tree had come to me on Pelee Island in a three-ounce Dixie paper cup filled with soil and identified as the island's native eastern redcedar (which is a variety of juniper, not a true cedar tree), a favor from the writer Margaret Atwood's Spring Song celebration of birds and Canadian authors. That was about a decade before I found these two mainland twin volunteers. That tree is now taller than the twins.

Given the pandemic, I am not likely to be on Pelee Island for some time, but what about the hawthorn on the driveway of my neighbor to the west? Are these twins, who were actually much closer to this ancient hawthorn tree before I transplanted them, carrying a fungus that is stressing it? The hawthorn was prolifically adorned in white blossoms this June, and today I can see the morning sun glinting off its (currently) shiny green leaves.

What is the solution to a problem I wasn't yet sure I had, but which I certainly could be inviting? "When possible, avoid planting Eastern redcedar and other junipers within several hundred feet of apple or hawthorn trees. However, the two hosts can infect each other from a quarter mile away." Cedar-hawthorn rust can also affect pear, serviceberry, and quince trees. What about the two pear trees we purchased from the city and had planted on our park lawn some years ago? Time to do some more measuring.

My neighbor's hawthorn is about forty feet from the transplanted evergreen twins; the closest of the two pears trees is not much farther. Both the hawthorn and the pears form a triangle with the twin eastern redcedar volunteers and, in fact, did so before they were transplanted, when the eastern redcedars were at the west point of the triangle, as they now were at the east.

So it is clear these two stalwart soldiers have been luxuriating in hours of morning sun and rising, measure by measure, next to my mailbox, forming a smaller second triangle with the red-stem variegated dogwood bush and a thick border of purple echinacea that began blooming this last week of June (and which now desperately need thinning). This second triangle involving the eastern redcedars has impeded the airflow, with the trees forming a tiny windbreak of their (and my) own making against the west wind. I imagine that this is what's responsible for the mildew I smell every day as I reach over from the driveway to open the mailbox.

These young eastern redcedars clearly need to be moved for not just one (the hawthorn) but three (plus the pear trees) reasons. But where to transplant their prickly selves? This morning on my walk I noticed, for the first time in a decade, although I take this walk regularly, a more mature eastern redcedar growing on the boulevard about a mile away. Its branches had been trimmed up about two feet to allow a trunk with a circumference of fourteen and a half inches at its base.[1] Despite its height of ten or twelve feet, its overall appearance leaned toward a bluish-gray palette and a scraggly habit.

I decided to have a G&T, with the emphasis on the gin—courtesy

---

1 Circumference is not how dendrologists or timber merchants measure tree trunks. Nor are tree trunks measured at their bases. Instead, the *breast height diameter* (DBH) is used. DBH is specifically defined as a point around the trunk at 4.5 feet (1.37 meters) above the forest floor on the uphill side of the tree. Several different measuring instruments can be used; the most common is a diameter tape. Special rules apply to measuring trees that have trunks that are not "normal" or straight, such as trunks that fork below the DBH, multiple-stemmed trunks, a straight tree on a slope, a leaning tree, or a tree with a swelling tree base.

of the berries of junipers other than mine[2]—to help me work through this conundrum.

Sipping my aromatic cocktail while reading, I discovered that, in fact, neither eastern redcedars nor common junipers should be planted in the vicinity of *any* member of the Rosaceae family—and pear trees and hawthorn trees are both members of the Rosaceae family. Could these fungal creatures have also caused the problem from which my Knock Out rosebush suffered this year? This rosebush had been given to me by members of my husband's office and was transplanted from its pot in May 1999 to our Ferndale park lawn as a memorial planting for my dear Grandma Klotzbach, was subsequently moved with us to our yard in Rochester Hills, and then was finally transplanted in our Royal Oak yard. It has thrived, until this year. For the first time, the rosebush's leaves had small discolorations on them, much like the spots I'd noticed before on the Pelee hawthorn's leaves.

Surely, there must be a way to have both: the eastern redcedars and the members of the Rosaceae family growing in the same vicinity. I was determined to figure out how. Turns out there is no cure for cedar-hawthorn rust, but here is the suggested two-pronged strategy for preventing its spread:

- Spray the hawthorn tree with either chlorothalonil or mancozeb until the fungicide drips from the branches.
- Spray the junipers with a Bordeaux fungicide mixture every two weeks beginning in midsummer.

Before deciding which two of the three treatments in which to invest, I paused to consider if these fungicides posed any risks to other nearby life. Being raised in the Christian faith, I had learned at a young

2   Gin is vodka flavored with juniper seed cones, called "juniper berries"—and other natural botanicals like coriander, citrus peel, cinnamon, almond, or licorice. Although gin is considered England's "national spirit," the Dutch made it first.

age in both Baptist and Presbyterian Sunday schools that one of my responsibilities as a human being was to look after the Earth, to be a good steward, so I thought the least I could do was a little research on any probable consequences of how I was planning to look after my small piece of the planet.

Chlorothalonil is an organic compound used as a broad-spectrum fungicide, sold under the product names of Daconil, Echo, and Bravo. Chlorothalonil is a "recognised irritant . . . moderately toxic to birds, honeybees and earthworms but considered to be more toxic to aquatic organisms." In terms of human health, in addition to being a skin, eye, and respiratory irritant, Chlorothalonil is a probable human carcinogen, responsible for causing endocrine issues as well. More specifically, given my dreams of increasing my pollinator garden beyond my burgeoning echinacea borders:

> Chlorothalonil exposure was found to have an effect on 1) honey bee resistance and/or tolerance to viral infection by decreasing the survival of bees following a viral challenge, 2) social immunity, by increasing the level of glucose oxidase activity, 3) nutrition, by decreasing levels of total carbohydrate and protein, and 4) development, by decreasing the total body weight, head width, and wing length of adult nurse and forager bees.

If nothing else, a decline in the honeybee population alone was enough to strike the use of that "organic" compound from my list of possible "looking-after" actions.

What about "mancozeb"? Sold as Penncozeb, Trimanoc, Vonozeb, Dithane, Manzeb, Nemispot, and Manzane, mancozeb is a combination of two fungicides, maneb and zineb. While mancozeb apparently poses little threat to our bee population—its toxicity to honeybees is low—it has been shown to negatively affect mammals, including humans:

The widely used fungicide mancozeb has been shown to cause hypothyroxinemia ["defined as a normal maternal thyroid-stimulating hormone (TSH) concentration in conjunction with a low maternal free thyroxine (FT4) concentration"] . . . and other adverse effects on the thyroid hormone system in adult experimental animals. In humans, hypothyroxinemia early in pregnancy is associated with adverse effect on the developing nervous system and can lead to impaired cognitive function and motor development in children.

While I'm beyond my childbearing years, mancozeb is also highly toxic to fish and aquatic invertebrates, and moderately toxic to birds and earthworms.

Okay, so what about the "Bordeaux mixture"? Maybe I could just treat the evergreen trees. Bordeaux mixture (also "Bordo Mix") is a combination of copper sulfate, slaked lime, and water that is used as a fungicide. Although it is approved for "organic use," it has been found to be moderately toxic to birds and honeybees, fish and aquatic plants, livestock, and—due to potential buildup of copper in the soil—earthworms. I have no fish or livestock, but I do have a cat, and in addition to wanting to support our bee population, for both altruistic and selfish reasons, I am partial to earthworms. Then I learned that the Bordeaux mixture was used by the United Fruit Company in Central America to control Sigatoka, an airborne banana pathogen.

A nickname for a Bordeaux mixture-stained [banana] was *perico*, or "parakeet"; [workers became] as brightly colored as the common tropical bird. . . . After a few months of exposure, workers could no longer scrub the blue tint from their flesh. They'd lose their sense of smell and their ability to hold down food. Then they died.

In the end, I chose the hawthorn tree in my neighbor's yard and the two pear trees on our park lawn, as well as Grammy Klotzbach's Knock Out rose, over the eastern redcedar twin volunteers. On a sunny bright Sunday, I donned thick gardening gloves to protect my hands from the prickles and sawed through both of their two-inch-circumference trunks at ground level. Then I pruned off all their branches from their trunks, stuffed them into two yard-waste bags, and put them out for Monday's pickup.

And what might these transplanted twin volunteers—who certainly through no fault of their own were serving as a host for a fungal rust that threatened the nearby hawthorn, the pear trees, the Knock Out rose bush—have felt as I sawed through their slender trunks?

While we humans learn more every day about the beings with whom we share this planet, we apparently have yet to reach a consensus on whether plants feel pain, as three distinctly different answers have been given just in the last year:

Given that plants do not have pain receptors, nerves, nor a brain, they do not feel pain as we members of the animal kingdom understand it.

The simple answer is that, currently, no one is sure whether plants can feel pain. We do know that they can feel sensations. Studies show that plants can feel a touch as light as a caterpillar's footsteps.

Itzhak Khait and his colleagues at Tel Aviv University in Israel found that tomato and tobacco plants made sounds at frequencies humans cannot hear when stressed by a lack of water or when their stem is cut.

Did the twin evergreen trees cry out as I cut through the base of their trunks?

Only today, scrolling through photos of my yard during 2020's early pandemic days, do I wonder for the first time whether these twin volunteers were actually common junipers or eastern redcedars. Both species are just two of the sixty-three identified species of junipers, *Juniperus*—the largest genus in the family Cupressaceae (the cypress family)—which includes a total of 130 to 140 species of junipers and redwoods.

The common juniper, *Juniperus communis*, is the variety best known for its contribution to the flavor of gin, while the eastern redcedar (*Juniperus virginiana*) is the variety known best for the aromatic cedar oil, which acts as a moth repellent, as in cedar chests and cedar closets, and whose wood, once upon a time, was responsible for wonderful-smelling cedar pencils. The production of such pencils ended sometime between the 1920s and the 1940s because the supply of eastern redcedar wood dwindled and, compared to other wood that could be used for pencils, became more expensive. (Today, you can purchase cedar pencils to appreciate the fragrance, although these are now made from California incense-cedar trees [*Calocedrus decurrens*], another species in the Cupressaceae family.)

In Tekiela's *Trees of Michigan*, only the eastern redcedar—not the common juniper—is featured, and the gifts of both taste (gin) and smell (the scent of cedar) are ascribed to it there. Other sources note that the main difference between the two species of junipers is that the common juniper is usually a bush and an eastern redcedar is generally tree-shaped. Regardless of the type, junipers have made contributions both to humans' forgetting of the past, via gin, and to humans' yearning for the future, via hope chests.

I can still remember struggling up the tall stair risers of the narrow, cold, dark staircase, which smelled faintly of mothballs, to the second floor of my paternal grandparents' house in Detroit's Brightmoor neighborhood. In the guest room, my cousin Kathy and I lifted the heavy lid of Grandma Dunphy's hope chest. The fragrance of cedar, pungent and resinous, rose in the cold air of the shut-up room, aproning us in its mysterious smell. Was this the smell of hope?

Six decades later, when so much of what I'd hoped for as a young girl, and more, has come true, I occasionally enjoy sipping a summertime gin and tonic on our front bench atop the low rise overlooking the rest of the front yard, where the shape and shadow of the twins' miniature windbreak survive now only in my memory.

6

The Shade

The Northern White-Cedar

(Thuja occidentalis)

When I was little, "going on vacation" meant driving three hours to Houghton Lake. Houghton Lake is located in the Roscommon State Forest Area of Michigan, just below the 45th parallel. On one vacation when I was very small (and on another when I was older), Grandma and Grandpa Klotzbach came with us. As a part of this first shared trip, I remember the strange sensation of sleeping with a pillow for the first time—because of a neck injury at birth, I was not supposed to do so until my fourth birthday—which means this memory must be from the summer before I turned four.

At Houghton Lake, on the low ridge just above the sandy beach, two heavy, worn-smooth board swings hung from long lengths of heavy chain bolted into a horizontal pole between two telephone poles. The structure was painted white; the swing seats were a faded porch-paint blue. In this memory, I am still a couple years away from being pushed on those sunny swings while my dad recited Robert Louis Stevenson's poem "The Swing." A couple more years would pass before I would pump my legs to rise the highest I have ever risen from the Earth under my own power, before or since, while belting out songs from the soundtrack of *The Sound of Music* that we were listening to on the newfangled high-tech silver and white reel-to-reel tape recorder my dad had borrowed from work that year to bring to our rented-for-a-week lakeside log cabin.

But before those years of the big swing, in that summer of 1957, an old metal swing set had also been there, in the shade. Made entirely of heavy metal and painted dull red and dark blue, it had two seat swings and a trapeze hanging from it, as well as a ladder on one end of the set. The set was erected in front of one of the five lakefront cottages, adjacent to the walk-through that allowed the renters of the back-lane cottages to access the lake. Perhaps the Braunschweigers, who owned Driftwood Resort, had erected the swing set in the shade of several evergreen trees so children would not get burned on sun-heated metal.

Stepping into the shade that sheltered the swing set meant not being able to see clearly for a few minutes after leaving the sun, meant cold damp earth against my bare soles and cool air raising the hairs on my forearms, meant, especially, steadying the tender arches of my feet on the vast network of sinuous white-cedar roots that ridged the ground. That summer, a number of times, I was placed on the swing closest to the lake and farthest from the dark trees by my parents or grandparents, warned to hold on tightly, and gently pushed. The chains cut into my hands, and balancing was a hit-or-miss struggle against the invisible force attempting to tip me off the seat.

In a memory that has vividly remained with me for over six and a half decades, Grandpa Klotzbach, a box camera hanging from his neck, is nearby, watching me, just outside the shade. When this memory revisits me, it is always about the shade, the quiet of the trees, the roots, and something else I have never tried explaining before, have never been able to explain to myself. All I am sure of is this: my grandpa was out in the sun looking in, but another presence was much closer to me there in the shade. The other presence was somehow related to the trees. And there in the shade, while I was negotiating the crossing of the white-cedar roots, something else seemed to be transpiring.

I know this memory involves communication of some sort. Scrolling through this memory's still frames, it feels like I am receiving a message. What was being transported in the meeting of the bark of the tree roots and the skin and nerves of my feet? On what breath, via what synaptic lightning, was this message crossing? What was the nature of this transaction? With what purpose, for what result? I know the message was not at all threatening; it did not feel like a warning in any way. Instead it felt like I was acquiring an understanding, one that, in the replay of this memory, always feels like I was receiving some sort of reassurance.

Trying to decipher this memory, one of my most intense memories—and certainly the oddest one—of my early childhood, I wonder why I have retained it. Perhaps because of its strangeness; it definitely wasn't like any other memory. I have never been able to figure it out, to assign it to a place of understanding. But also, I think, I've retained it because of the sense of total familiarity I felt at the time, which I have always been able to recall, viscerally, in my body. At the time, I felt familiar with, had an understanding of, what was transpiring that I have never understood since. Was I remembering another language, another way of being? Were those trees telling me something through their roots, in their shade, via transpiration from their scaly needles? I'm grasping at air here. Northern-white-cedar-scented air.

Had I experienced this feeling of communing before in my earlier years? I also know it—whatever it was—involved remembering something from some other time and place that came before that particular time, that specific place. Was this the last time I knew where or what that place was? I know it is a place I have peripherally revisited in dreams, at least in dreams I had in my youth. Could that be why the memory of something transpiring in the shade of the northern white-cedars has stuck with me—because I don't go there anymore?

In considering this memory, trying to tease sense from it, to make it adhere to some structure of reason—and thinking about moments

I've witnessed with my four grandchildren over the six years I've been a grandmother—I wonder if it had something to do with the notion that as I matured, becoming more human, the less communication I could have with nonhuman life.

That's when I imagine that what I felt in the shade might have been the trees reassuring me that everything was going to be all right, despite our imminent parting. Perhaps they were saying good-bye.

7

Bones and Skeletons

White Ash, Green Ash

(*Fraxinus americana, Fraxinus pennsylvanica*)

A gray day of snow being washed away. Outside my study window, the bare branches of the sycamore are shiny, slick with rain. Sweetgum's dried fruit bristles out into the abyss of winter sky, and the raindrops fatten the architecture of the red maple's crown a few houses west. But it is the bare bones of the sycamore that are particularly beautiful at this time of year, at least on this kind of day.

Although I am surrounded by such beauty, this February day evokes thoughts of loss. The people we have lost to time, of course, and especially those, in this past year, we have lost to the pandemic.[1] Now, the loss of our nation's unity in another pandemic, one of stark political division, culminating in the insurrection and deaths at the United States Capitol Building, breached at 2:30 p.m., Wednesday, January 6,

---

1 The first U.S. death definitely attributable to COVID-19 occurred on February 6, 2020, in Santa Clara County in California, before the virus had been given the official name of COVID-19 and before the pandemic had been declared. (Four U.S. deaths in January 2020 may have also been caused by the virus.) By February 6, 2022—with less than 64 percent of the U.S. population fully vaccinated (per the Centers for Disease Control and Prevention) and the Omicron variant (BA.1) surging—that number, provided by the Johns Hopkins Coronavirus Resource Center, had risen to over 919,000.

the day between the day I first revised this paragraph and the day I revisited it.

Awash in a mix of feelings in response to these losses while considering the arms of the sycamore reaching heavenward through a somber sky propels me to consider other great losses that our planet has borne. One such casualty is the loss of entire tree populations due to arboreal pandemics: the American chestnut tree, the American elm tree, and all North American species of ash trees.

A *tree* pandemic? How does that happen? A primary cause of economic and ecological loss in both forest and urban ecosystems, tree "pandemics rely on the introduction of a non-native pathogen that exploits well-developed interactions between native non-aggressive organisms and insects associated with trees." The introduction of alien species (for example, a non-native pathogen) ranks second only to habitat destruction as one of the major threats to our native ecosystems.

Deforestation, whether caused by tree pandemics or by clearing and replacing forests with farmland, "creates the conditions for a range of deadly pathogens—such as [COVID-19]—to spread to people." Outbreaks of new human diseases are often linked to destruction by humans of the natural habitats of wild animals: "When forests or grasslands are razed to graze cattle, to grow soy or to build roads and settlements, wild animals are forced ever closer to humans and livestock, giving viruses an opportunity to jump ship."

I have never seen an American chestnut tree except in vintage photographs or paintings, but at one time the American chestnut was known as a dominant member of the American forest. American chestnut trees used to be so common along the East Coast of the United States that it was said "a squirrel could travel from Maine to Georgia on chestnut tree branches alone without ever touching the ground."

The demise of the American chestnut trees began with a pathogen accidentally introduced to southern U.S. ports on plant material carried from Asia in the early 1800s. The results of the introduction of this fungus-like organism, *Phytophthora cinnamomi*, was called ink disease and is also known as phytophthora root rot (PRR). PRR steadily killed the chestnut in the *southern* portion of its range.

But it was the chestnut blight (*Cryphonectria parasitica*), a fungus imported from Japan around 1904 and spread by wind-borne and rain-splashed spores, that finished off the entire population—4 billion—of our country's American chestnut trees in less than forty years.

Forty years is not even a human lifetime. It is less than half of the ninety-six years my paternal grandfather lived. The forty years that the chestnut trees were dying of chestnut blight are the years between Grandpa Dunphy's fourteenth year, when he lived in a Catholic orphanage in Peekskill, New York, and four decades later, when he was raising teenagers himself in Detroit's Brightmoor neighborhood and working at Ford Motor Company. In 1944, my dad was seventeen, my uncle Maurice would have been fourteen—the same age my grandpa had been when chestnut blight arrived in the United States—and my aunt Muriel, their half-sister from my grandpa's first marriage, would have been long gone from home and living in North Carolina. Forty years—in the space of one generation—4 billion American chestnut trees dead.

By the time I was born, only a few groves of American chestnut trees remained, and all of these were outside of the chestnut's natural range in Michigan and Wisconsin. Today, "there are only 100 or so" American chestnut trees that remain, resistant to blight.

I am old enough to remember the American elm trees at Grandma and Grandpa Dunphy's house. In a black-and-white "Kodak moment" for which I still recall posing, toddler-me stands at the broad base of an elm trunk near my grandparents' driveway with my older cousin Ronnie, my "first love," who was visiting from North Carolina. My dad later said my grandparents had the tree cut down because of "its proximity to their driveway." Were they worried about hitting the tree with the car?

Or the tree falling on the car? Or perhaps it produced what they considered "a mess" atop their white American Motors (AMC) Rambler?[2]

In a nook of Grandma and Grandpa Dunphy's backyard was another elm that was boxed in by the drive, the narrow cement walk from the drive to the back door, and two walls of the house, one the outside wall of a pantry-like room where Grandma set her pies to cool. The other wall was that of the cool, shaded back bedroom, where we children, as babies and toddlers, napped after long summer Sunday dinners. In that nook of the yard, under the branches of the guardian American elm, was a large sandbox Grandpa Dunphy had built for us grandchildren. The cold sand never appealed to me, but being close to the trunk of the elm did. The tree was huge and very friendly.

One summer afternoon, Grandma sprayed my cousin Kathy and me with a nasty-smelling and apparently potentially poisonous insecticide while we were playing in the sandbox. Surely she meant well, but what was she repelling? It had something to do with the tree. Were there mosquitoes in the shade or ants around the tree? Maybe it was just preventive, in case something untoward did appear, but when our mothers discovered what had happened, we had the insecticide washed off us, including out of our mouths, with a harsh soap. For a moment, I can recall the signature smell of sickly sweet bath powder in my grandma's pink-tiled bathroom, where this washing took place, almost as well as I can still feel the soft coolness of that majestic backyard elm's shade on my skin.

Before the blight, countless elms had been planted as American street trees. Perhaps yet another elm grew on my grandparents' park lawn of which I have no memory. Conceivably, at one time, between sidewalk and curb, broad trunks rose into vase-shaped crowns,

---

2 Several American Motors Corporation Ramblers took their turn parked in the driveway following Grandpa's retirement from "Ford's," as we call it in Michigan. Perhaps my Dunphy grandparents were attracted to the name of the model, Rambler; they were big on Sunday drives and annual road trips.

fountaining up and out to meet in a cathedral arch over Blackstone Street.

Dutch elm disease is caused by a fungus, *Ophiostoma ulmi*, spread by European and native elm bark beetles. This fungus was first reported in the United States in 1928, the year after my dad was born. The European elm bark beetles are believed to have arrived in logs shipped from The Netherlands to Ohio furniture makers, who were importing European elm logs to make veneer for cabinets and tables. Quarantining and sanitation efforts kept them within the New York City area until World War II "loosened" those efforts. The first case of Dutch elm disease reached the Detroit area in 1950, three years before I was born. As American elms were stricken by Dutch elm disease, they were cut down. Of the estimated 77 million elms in North America in 1930, when my parents were toddlers, over 75 percent had been lost by 1989, a year after my youngest daughter was born. Within two generations. More have been lost since.

Two summers ago, after a bike ride on Pelee Island, my husband and I sat out on the deck of the Anchor and Wheel Inn under a large handsome tree I'd never noticed before, who was holding out to us a heavy mass of dark green leaves. When I asked Mark, the owner of the establishment who came out to wait on us, what kind of tree it was, he confidently replied that it was an ash.

I was pretty sure he was wrong.

We had already had to have all three of the ash trees on our island property removed several years prior, when each had been killed by the emerald ash borer, probably carried to the island—an hour and a half ferry ride from the mainland—on firewood brought over by campers. The majority, if not all, of the ash trees on the island, as well as most of Ontario and Michigan, had been several years dead, the result of the emerald ash borer larvae scrawling their signature serpentine lines beneath the bark of each tree. The mature beetle leaves a D-shaped emergence hole in the bark when it flies away from its nursery. To add insult to injury, the adult emerald ash borer eats ash tree leaves.

Today, the skeletons of ash trees rise above the hackberry and haw-thorn trees on the island and stand over small woodlots along the highways on the mainland.

While drops of condensation formed on our bottles of cold Labatt's Blue in the shade of the tree, I pulled out my cross-folded, laminated, tree-identifier leaflet from my backpack. This tree's leaves looked nothing like an ash's opposite, compound leaves. Instead, they looked like the simple, alternate leaves of an elm, with coarsely toothed margins, uneven leaf bases, and leaf blades three to six inches long. The ridges of the tree trunk's bark, which I leaned over to press my palm against, fit the description of "corky." The more I considered this tree, the more exotic it looked.

We sat happily in the tree's green coolness, watching, above the crowns of more distant trees, swallows glide through the roiling smoke clouds of high-altitude fishflies.[3] As the light shifted in the sky and the sun set over Lake Erie, our companion tree served us up an earlier twilight.

Turns out, our companion that evening is not portrayed on my tree identifier, which is a guide to the "Upper Midwest" trees. It is an elm—but a rock elm (also known as a "cork elm")—a lesser-known cousin of the American elm. The rock elm's range in Michigan only reaches into the Lower Peninsula, and even here it is not considered common. Of course, Pelee Island, in Lake Erie's western basin, is south of all but fewer than ten miles of the Lower Peninsula. Landmark Trees of Ontario first put me on the rock elm's trail with this remark: "A concentration of [rock elms] is found in Ontario's deep south on Pelee Island." At least one is.[4]

Of course, there have been other tree pandemics, introduced in similar ways, both here and abroad, since the early 1800s when the United States began to engage in foreign commerce, which led to non-native

3 "Fishflies" are what residents of Michigan and Ontario call burrowing mayflies.

4 Because I was unable to cross the U.S.-Canadian border at the time this essay was written due to the COVID-19 pandemic, my island friend, naturalist Ron Tiessen, confirmed my identification of the tree's species.

pathogens hitchhiking on foreign goods and swimming in the ballast of the ships that carried them. Other tree pandemics include:

- **Beech bark disease (BBD)** has been killing American beech trees in eastern North America since the late 1890s. The disease is initiated by the feeding of a European beech scale insect, *Cryptococcus fagisuga* (first introduced to the continent in Nova Scotia around 1890 and first found in the United States in Massachusetts in 1929), which leads to the development of small fissures in the bark, into which one of two fungi, *Neonecctria ditissima* or *Neonecctria faginata*, enters and kills the tree's phloem and cambium as it invades.

- **Cypress canker** is caused by the fungus *Seiridium cardinale*, which was first reported in California in 1928, its geographic origin unknown. It was also responsible for spreading the pandemic to the Mediterranean area.

- **Oak wilt** is caused by the fungus *Ceratocystis fagacearum*, believed to have originated in Mexico or Central or South America and first reported in the United States in the Upper Mississippi River Valley in the 1940s. It can be carried by beetles in the family *Nitidulidae* and affects oaks, particularly oaks in the red oak group, in a manner similar to how Dutch elm disease affects elms. The fungus enters the water-conducting vessels of the sapwood through fresh wounds, carried by sap-feeding beetles or through roots connecting healthy and diseased trees, and prevents water transport through the tree. An infected tree is killed *within a few weeks*.

- **Butternut canker** is caused by the fungus *Sirococcus clavigignenti-juglandacearum*, believed to have come from Asia and first documented in Wisconsin in 1967 on butternut trees, a species of walnut.

- **Pine wilt disease**, which affects Scots, Austrian, jack, mugo, and red pines (and, less commonly, white pines), came from Japan, where it was first reported in 1971, to Missouri in 1979, and is spread by the pine wood nematode (*Bursaphelenchus xylophilus*), a microscopic worm transmitted by pine sawyer beetles (of the genus *Monochamus*).

Do you count any beech, cypress, oak, pine, or butternut trees among your arboreal friends? In addition to American chestnut, American elm, and any North American species of ash, all these species of trees are currently threatened by a pandemic.

Every part of the world has experienced a loss [of trees] so traumatic that it's left a permanent scar on the public consciousness.

Tree pandemics can also be initiated by insects alone. Are you fond of and/or do you take care of any fruit tree or an oak, sweetgum, linden, willow, birch, alder, box elder, hawthorn, hemlock, ash—or any other hardwood tree, for that matter? If so, you may want to know more about these insects and their relationship to trees:

- **Japanese beetle** (*Popilla japonica*), which came from northern Japan to New Jersey in 1916, feeds on about three hundred species of plants, including eating the foliage, flowers, buds, and fruit of fruit trees. My Knock Out rosebush, planted as a memorial to Grandma Klotzbach, has suffered a Japanese beetle infestation twice since 2000.
- **Gypsy moth** (*Lymantria dispar dispar*): its larvae/caterpillars eat tree leaves in the spring, including oak, sweetgum, linden, willow, birch, apple, alder, box elder, and hawthorn.
- **Hemlock woolly adelgid (HWA)** (*Adelges tsugae*), native to Japan and first observed in Virginia in 1951, attacks North American hemlocks.
- **Asian long-horned beetle** (*Anoplophora glabripennis*), currently

causing infestations in Massachusetts, New York, and Ohio, threatens hardwood trees in the United States and "has the potential to do more damage than Dutch elm disease, chestnut blight and gypsy moths combined."

● **Emerald ash borer (EAB)** (*Agrilus planipennis*), fatal to all North American ash (note: the mountain ash is not a true ash and is thus not an EAB target), was first discovered in the United States in the Detroit area in 2002 and is believed to have entered the country on wooden packing materials from China. Since 2002, EAB has killed more than 30 million ash trees in southeastern Michigan alone.

In the yard of our cottage, we lost all three of our magnificent ashes—hybrids of white ash and green ash, as most ash trees were on Pelee Island[5]—to the emerald ash borer. Three large stumps in the yard remain among the hackberry and hawthorn, three birches, an American basswood, and a scattering of purple leaf plum. Corresponding to the stumps are huge chunks of sky, holes in the canopy.

We had the arborist cut the ash trees when we were not on the island. I knew I could not bear the soul-chilling sound of the chain saw. On our next trip over, after we'd pulled up in our parking space and I saw our backdoor guardian was gone, I cried. The canopy of this ash tree, not far from the roadside door, had filled the sky of our backyard. Every year, through a number of generations, a pair of tree swallows had nested in the wooden birdhouse I'd mounted on the ash's trunk. There, the swallows laid their clutch of eggs, hatched their hatchlings, and nurtured their nestlings. We'd watch the fledglings learn to fly the

---

5 Ron Tiessen, naturalist and founder and former director of the Pelee Island Heritage Centre, responding to my request for an identification of trees no longer in existence to identify, shared this observation with me in an email of January 8, 2021: "To my knowledge we have no record of Black Ash on Pelee. We have Blue Ash in the alvars and the hybrid of White and Green (and Red?). I believe the latter are difficult to identify of those saplings left."

couple of yards between the tree and the low telephone wire strung on the other side of the walkway from the tree. Two more ash trees had reigned supreme in the front yard between cottage and lake. Each of these three trees was larger than any other tree around. Every year, now, suckers burst forth from one stump—the one that, despite its proximity to the lake, we fed in a desperate attempt to keep it alive. The suckers haven't survived over the winters well, but every spring new ones sprout.

Eventually, the stumps, all that really remains of these grand ash trees, will be ground up, their holes filled in. The next year, or maybe the next, mushrooms will rise through the loose circle of soil, a cluster of memorial stones for a friend of the birds, and of ours, a friend who welcomed us home to where we really belonged.

8

From Royalty to Immigrant

The English Oak

(*Quercus robur*)

The January 10, 2017, entry from my journal reads:

A mere ten days separates today from the day Donald J. Trump is to be sworn in as president of the United States. Many things scare me about this president-elect, but perhaps what angers me most are his feelings with respect to immigrants, as displayed in his statements about Mexicans and Muslims.

Every single human being in the United States is either an immigrant or the descendant of immigrants, except for members of the native tribes, from whose ancestors our immigrant ancestors stole all the land, all the land over which, apparently, Donald J. Trump is about to govern.

Even "The Donald" himself is only a second-generation American on his Trump side (and a first-generation on his mother's side). Donald Trump's paternal grandfather was Frederick Trump (or possibly Friedrich Drumpf), who was a German immigrant sometime toward the end of the nineteenth century.

> *Despite being the grandson—and son, on his mother's side—of*
> *an immigrant, Donald Trump is xenophobic, believing entire eth-*
> *nicities and any follower of Islam should be barred from immigrat-*
> *ing to the United States.*

My next day's journal entry, under the scrawled title "Invited to the
Soil," reads:

> *While I was swimming laps this morning, my watery thoughts*
> *floated around ideas about being an immigrant and then eddied*
> *about what is perhaps one of our most basic inherited tasks as*
> *Americans—given that most of us are of immigrant lineage—the*
> *role of inviting immigrants to the table. No argument that this*
> *country has been built by the contributions of immigrants over*
> *the last 240 years.*
>
> *As my laps added up, it was a leisurely crawl to considering the*
> *recent story I'd learned about my city of Royal Oak "inviting"*
> *the English oak, also known in Europe as the "common oak," to the*
> *soil of our community. The English oak was invited "to our table"*
> *as an immigrant for some interesting reasons, some of which I*
> *suspect may have involved gain of one sort or another. Regardless*
> *of the impetus for the invitation, imported English oak acorns were*
> *nurtured until they were strong enough and then were planted in*
> *Memorial Park to honor the young men of Royal Oak who lost their*
> *lives in service to their country during World War II. Interesting*
> *to note that this "immigrant" (non-native) species who came to*
> *honor our soldiers of a later war originated in the very country with*
> *which we went to war to declare our independence. These English*
> *oak acorns were immigrants to our soil. We nurtured them and*
> *treasured the resulting trees, using them to memorialize our heroes.*
> *Who's to say that the child of one of our nation's immigrants*
> *won't be the next Barack Hussein Obama? (Who, it shouldn't need*

pointing out, was a natural-born citizen.) Or, just as likely, an immigrant's child may be the next successful business tycoon (hopefully, one with a stronger character and better ethics than Donald John Trump). It will, mostly likely, be immigrants or descendants of immigrants who solve our greatest challenges in the future. Because, after all, immigrants and descendants of immigrants are those who have solved our greatest challenges in the past. We are mostly all the descendants of forefathers and foremothers who arrived on this soil sometime in the last century and a half.

The acorns of the English oak put down their roots in our American soil and flourished, providing us shade and beauty—and meaning, reiterating what we stand for.

We need the diversity and all the different approaches immigrants bring to the table to solve our challenges. When we invite immigrants to our land, treasure and nurture them, we receive their contributions back.

Seems pretty simple, an obvious formula.

Why did these particular thoughts bob to my consciousness that particular morning? Because of several currents of thought coming together in the pool in the early mornings, as they often do.

Current #1: Today, I live in Royal Oak, Michigan, a city that is named after a particular tree, not a particular species of tree—the Royal Oak—an individual tree of the English oak species that grew in England and was given its title over 370 years ago.

Following the execution of King Charles I in 1649, the king's eldest son made an attempt to regain the throne. In 1651 his hopes were dashed at Worcester in the final conflict of the English Civil War, and the young Charles was forced to flee for his life. Initially, the future King Charles II had set out to cross the River Severn into Wales, but his way was blocked by Oliver Cromwell's Roundhead patrols. So he sought refuge at the Boscobel House—a very secluded house, built in the thick Shropshire woods by the Giffard family about thirty years earlier, which contained hiding places for Catholic priests, who were persecuted during this time in England. Charles hid first in the crown of an English oak tree, the tree that was to become known as the Royal Oak. England's Royal Oak was located in a meadow behind the Boscobel House. The tree that grows there now is a descendant of the original Royal Oak that hid Charles II in its branches.

One hundred and sixty-eight years after Charles II hid in the Royal Oak, history claims that in 1819—while trying to disprove land surveyors' 1815 assertions that the territory of Michigan was swampy and uninhabitable—Lewis Cass, the governor of the territory, standing under a large oak amid dense underbrush, marshland, and a preponderance of swamp oaks, supposedly remarked, "Ah, this truly is a Royal Oak."

What possessed him to say this? Was he familiar with a painting or a carving that portrayed the scene of Charles II hiding in the Royal Oak? Given that it was unlikely Cass was being pursued, why would he be feeling the need to hide? Was his remark intended to contrast a particular white or northern red oak with the prevalent swamp white oaks in the region he was exploring and surveying? We do know the tree he was exclaiming over at that time could not have actually been an English oak, a species that is not native to Michigan or to the continent.

The thirty-six-square-mile township in which the tree that Cass remarked upon was growing, according to one Royal Oak historian, Owen Perkins, was surveyed in November 1818 and established as what would become Royal Oak Township on January 23, 1819.[1]

---

1   Another Royal Oak historian has written, "When Royal Oak was first being settled, it was actually part of Bloomfield Township. In 1827 it became part of Troy Township and finally Royal Oak Township in 1832" (Bob Muller and Ted Vickers, "History of a Piece of Land in Northern Royal Oak: Tenhave Woods," 2016, https://www.romi.gov/documentcenter/view/665).

Oakland County, the county in which the city of Royal Oak is located, had been established eleven days before Royal Oak was recognized as a township, on January 12, 1819. The Village of Royal Oak was established on March 18, 1891, and the City of Royal Oak was incorporated in 1921.

Current #2: In 1935 or 1936, depending on the account, the City of Trees Committee, a civic tree-planting group, was formed by order of the City Commission in Royal Oak to study suitable tree types and promote their planting. This was between the two world wars; houses were being built, resulting in more trees being cut. This was after the swamp that extended north from 7 Mile Road had been drained and the forest surrounding it lumbered. After the clear-cutting, farms had filled the township, the same farms now being sold off to developers. The committee decided to offer trees to homeowners at a reduced rate to plant on their park lawns, the strip of land between sidewalk and street.

One member of the City of Trees Committee—Floyd J. Miller, publisher of the local newspaper, the *Daily Tribune*—asked Walter H. Millgate of London, a special correspondent for the *Detroit News*, to "get the story" about the Royal Oak at Boscobel House, in which the future king had hid, and if possible to also get some acorns from the tree (which was most likely a descendant of the original tree). What possessed the members of the committee sometime between 1935 and 1937 to carry through on acquiring acorns from the descendant of the Royal Oak? Was the local newspaperman simply interested in a good story? The acorn project did get a fair amount of publicity. Might this story have been a catchy kickoff to interest prospective residents in the vision of Royal Oak as a "Tree City"? In 1930, according to the census, Royal Oak's population had begun to plateau at 22,904 residents. By 1940, population was heading on a steep uphill climb, peaking in 1970 at 86,238, an increase of 277 percent. Planting trees on the former farmland and land cleared for development was a big focus during these years. The story of the Royal Oak acorns is still being told today.

In response to the City of Trees Committee's interest, acorns from the descendent of the Royal Oak (the number varies according to the account—fifty, sixty, or seventy-four acorns) were transported by ship in a package bearing the personal seal of Sir Charles Arthur Mander, mayor of Wolverhampton, England. Numerous accounts report that some of the acorns sprouted en route.

The history of this event is a little hazy eighty-five years later (details differ slightly among sources), but in the version I most trust, the acorns arrived at the Detroit Zoo in 1937 and were nurtured first in pots, then transplanted to prepared soil in 1939, and finally planted out in the open on the zoo grounds in 1940. In spring of 1949, forty-seven of the saplings were transplanted in Memorial Park to honor the 102 men from Royal Oak who died serving in World War II:

MEMORIAL PARK & ENGLISH OAK GROVE, Woodward Ave. and 13 Mile Road. Twenty-five acres with athletic and picnic areas. In 1949 the 47 young trees from the acorns (planted in 1937) of the Royal Oak Tree of England located near Wolverhampton, England were transplanted to this site as a living memorial to the men from this area who gave their lives in military service. This site is known as the "English Grove." Twenty trees formed the outer circle and the entrance path to the Great Oak Circle. The inner circle was planted with the other twenty-seven oaks. Dedications, June 26, 1936, Sept. 2, 1941, March 8, 1948 & Sept. 19, 1960. Named: October 22, 1945.

These trees known as "English oak" are also called "common oak" (in Europe), "European oak," or "pedunculate oak." While the English oak has a particular historical connection to the City of Royal Oak conveyed by Governor Cass, members of this "immigrant" (non-native) species came from the very country with which we went to war in order to declare our independence from it.

One of the original English oaks—this oak species is distinguished from other oaks by its relatively small leaves and long acorns—is still growing on the zoo grounds in its own small area between the Aviary and the Penguinarium. The metal plaque identifying the tree reads:

Quercus robur

English Oak

Still a Kid!!

This tree was cultivated from an acorn brought here from England in 1935. English oaks can live for hundreds of years and grow to more than 100 feet in height which means this tree is still in the early stages of its life.

At a Royal Oak City Commission meeting during the time Royal Oak was involved in a $100,000 downtown development plan, city watchdog Ron Wolf claimed that there was another of these Royal Oak immigrants in front of city hall that was about to be bulldozed by the razing crew. But local historian and naturalist Bob Muller said, no, that tree was a native American, a black oak. Around that time, one of my neighbors discovered what might have been one of the English oaks in Marais Park (aka Bicycle Hill) marked with a blue bull's-eye to be removed, as it appeared to be dying. A year later, it was gone.

Most recently, in July 2021 the Royal Oak Historical Society (ROHS) reported:

Two historic oak trees are now found on the [Royal Oak Historical Society M]useum's lawn. One was given away in honor of

Oakland County's bicentennial and is a Swamp White Oak. The other is a great-grandchild of the "Royal Oak" at the Boscobel House in England that Charles II took shelter in after his defeat at the Battle of Worcester in 1651. ROHS president Bob Muller raised this tree from acorns picked up at the English Grove in Memorial Park.

In 2020, Royal Oak achieved a status that it shares with only one other municipality in Michigan (Adrian), that of maintaining its "Tree City, USA" designation for the previous forty-four years, every year since the Michigan program began in 1976. Retaining this status means meeting the program's four requirements:

- Creating a tree board or department: The Royal Oak Environmental Advisory Board, the Royal Oak Garden Club, and South Oakland County Board of Realtors partner to fulfill this stipulation.
- Having a tree-care ordinance: Royal Oak Tree Ordinance and Policy Recommendations of June 12, 2017, realizes this requirement.
- Having an annual community forestry budget of at least $2 per capita: Royal Oak, with a population of 59,461 in 2018, should have spent $118,922.
- Having an Arbor Day observance and proclamation: Even during the COVID lockdown in 2020, while no observation could be held, a proclamation was released.

At the time Royal Oak was approaching the anniversary of its forty-second year as a Tree City, USA, the *Oakland Press* in January 2018 reported that Royal Oak had a tree canopy cover of just over 30 percent. The last survey done of the city's 11.8 square miles, in 1999, showed that the city had 26,794 trees. But a city report in 2017 revealed that 1,800 trees had been removed from the rights-of-way, parks, and other public areas in the city in the preceding three years alone, while only 250 were replaced in these areas.

The Royal Oak Parks and Forestry Division of the Department of Public Services is responsible for fifty parks and playgrounds (in a combined area of over 310 acres) and for over twenty-three thousand trees, including those in the parks, the central business district, parkways and easement areas of roads, the municipal golf course, the Royal Oak cemetery, and other city-owned open spaces. While one of the six 2019 goals of the Royal Oak Parks and Forestry Division addresses trees—"To improve the urban forest"—the city's adopted budget for the fiscal year 2019–20 projected planting only two hundred additional trees. This year I noticed that at least two of the trees they planted, one on a boulevard and the other on a park lawn, were Japanese tree lilacs (*Syringa reticulata*), native to eastern Asia. So here we have trees, both native and not, forming an arboreal community that mirrors our human community made up of both those born in the United States and those transplanted to our soil as immigrants.

As Trump continued tweeting xenophobic slurs and signing executive orders targeting immigrants, I reactivated my ancestry.com membership and dug deeper into the roots of my own family's immigration to the United States and then farther into who the descendants of my immigrant ancestors—my grandparents—were to me.

All four of my paternal Grandpa Dunphy's grandparents were born in Ireland and died in New York. My great-great-grandfather James Dunphy, born in 1831, came from Ireland with his two brothers. My grandfather Bernard Joseph Dunphy, born in the Greenwich Village neighborhood of Manhattan, was the son of Michael Francis Xavier Dunphy and Margaret Soden, who met on the dance floor. His mother abandoned at least two of her three children when her husband Michael was injured roofing and could no longer work. I don't know what happened to their older sister Mary, but the brothers, my grandpa Dunphy and great-uncle James, grew up at the Third Order of St. Francis St. Joseph's Home in Peekskill, New York, a Catholic orphanage on the banks of the Hudson River that, at that time, housed over a thousand residents.

Grandpa Dunphy, whose first wife was part Cherokee and died in childbirth, rode a train with his two-year-old daughter, my aunt Muriel, to Detroit to get work on the Ford Motor Company assembly line. The family story is that during the train ride, he fell asleep and his toddler daughter wandered off. When he awoke and went looking for her, Grandpa found her sitting up in first class on the lap of Henry Ford, playing with his pocket watch. Henry Ford gave my grandpa a business card and told him to come to the factory the next day and ask for Harry Bennett, Ford's right-hand man, a union buster and general enforcer. Thus, my short and slight grandpa—who, judging from photographic evidence, was possibly at one time arrested as a member of the New York City Hudson Dusters, a street gang involved in election fraud, among other things—apparently became part of Ford's security department. But he moved out of that role soon enough.

In 1927, when Ford opened up a new toolroom at the Ford Rouge Plant, Bernard was in the position of ordering all the materials for the tool and die room. By the time he retired at sixty-five on November 30, 1954, after thirty-three years with Ford (thirty-one of those years as a supervisor), his position was that of transportation services analyst. In the following year, 1955, he received a Suggestion Award check for $230.96 for suggesting "the use of IBM sheets to simplify summarizing and charge billing."[2]

The great-grandfather of my paternal grandmother, Luella Alena Pierce, emigrated from County Conath, Ireland, in 1803 to Canada.

---

2 The year 1955 happened to be when IBM introduced the IBM 608 transistor calculator, "the first all solid-state computing machine commercially marketed" (IBM Archives, "1955," https://www.ibm.com/ibm/history/history/year_1955 .html; accessed 1/06/22).

Some of the family settled and remained in Ontario. However, my grandma Dunphy's father immigrated to the United States on November 20, 1890, probably the most recent of my family to arrive in the country. My dad was named after this man, his grandpa Pierce: William Arthur. As boys, my dad and his brother, my uncle Maurice, left Detroit annually to work on the Ontario farm belonging to their aunt Maggie (Mary Margaret "Maggie" Pierce) between the Memorial Day and Labor Day weekends. Aunt Maggie's farm was still in the family when I was a child (kittens in the barn!), until she died in 1970.

My grandma Dunphy was the youngest of three sisters. Her father left the family twice for Columbia, South America, for a total of almost ten years to work, as family history has it, "in lumber." However, in the 1900 U.S. Census he is listed as a "Stationary Engineer," and in 1930 his occupation was "Engineer" in the industry of "Odd Mining Works."

My grandma Dunphy was nine years younger than my grandpa. She was on her way to being what then was called an "old maid" at the age of twenty-three. He was a widower, with a toddler, looking for a wife. My Catholic grandpa's boarding-room landlady had suggested he attend the Baptist church, where Luella's mother introduced her to Bernard as her youngest, her baby, whereupon he said, "Some baby!"

My maternal grandfather was Howard Zimmerman Klotzbach. His mother, Hattie Zimmerman, and father, August Klotzbach, were both of German descent. Grandpa Klotzbach grew up in the German section of Cleveland, Ohio, and worked for Glenn L. Martin Company, an American aircraft and aerospace manufacturing company, before he started working for General Motors' Chevrolet Division, from which he retired.

His dad, my great-grandpa Klotzbach, was an architect who grew up in the German Methodist Orphanage Asylum. His mother, my great-grandma Zimmerman, who I met in Cleveland when I was three, was a first-generation American whose parents came from Baden-Baden, Germany, after forty-five days at sea. Great-grandma

Zimmerman was able to read tea leaves, a divination tool (aka tasseo-graphy or tasseomancy) used to explore the past, present, and future.

My maternal grandmother, Madaline Venette Bateman, was the daughter of a Welsh coal miner who immigrated to Pennsylvania, had nine children, kept a small family farm, and worked as a miner in his adopted land before moving his family to East Cleveland, Ohio, where he became a school janitor.

Grandma Klotzbach's mother was Agnes Showers, who was from the branch of my family that stretches the longest way back in the United States—back at least six generations through her mother, Louisa Edmonds, whose maternal grandfather, Frederick Hoenig Haney, was born in 1769 in Pennsylvania, a part of what was then still known as the "United Colonies." Historic evidence places him at Fries's Rebellion of 1799, the last of three American tax revolts, where farmers in eastern Pennsylvania, some dressed in their Continental Army uniforms, were led by John Fries, an auctioneer and a local Revolutionary War hero, in an uprising in opposition to a direct federal property tax that was being collected for an anticipated war with France. The participants in Fries's Rebellion "re-engaged Revolutionary ideals in an enduring struggle to further democratize their country." Forty-five men were arrested and tried. Haney and Fries were two of the three or four insurrectionists con-victed of treason and sentenced to be hanged. All three were pardoned by President John Adams two days before they were to be executed.

From the time I was born, I was fortunate to have my four grand-parents as my only babysitters on the rare occasions when my parents went out in the evening. The Klotzbachs lived ten minutes or less from us, the Dunphys only twice as far. As I grew up, I was very close to three of my four grandparents and did a number of interesting projects with them, beginning when Grandma K. ordered a subscription of *Jack and Jill* magazine for me, her only grandchild at the time, to be sent to her house. I hadn't started school yet when we regularly read the newest issue on the glider in her sunroom.

Grandma D. taught me, her third of five granddaughters, simple hand sewing when I was seven, and Grandpa D. taught me how to cane chair seats when I was in college.

I inherited my photographer's eye from Grandma K., and Grandpa K. taught me darkroom skills in my pre-teen and teenage years. Grandma K. taught me to knit in elementary school and how to make a dress with a sewing machine in junior high. Grandma and Grandpa K. bought me my first full-size bicycle, a white and pink Schwinn with a metal grid seat on the rear-wheel cover to carry a passenger; my first camera, a Kodak Brownie; a rock tumbler, and a microscope. I played word games with Grandma K. and my mom after the big delicious Sunday dinners my grandma prepared. Grandma K. taught me the scrambled eggs recipe I made for my daughters and now make for my grandchildren today; served me "French tea" made with half Red Rose tea and half milk; and bought me new school clothes before the start of every school year.

I sometimes catch a glimpse of Grandma Klotzbach in my face when I glance in a mirror these days. In my mind, she was the perfect grandmother, and I try to emulate her in building a heart connection with my own grandchildren. She was always fun to be with. Here's a story of her having fun that I'd like to know more about. Born in 1903, Madaline Bateman—one of my two short and slight grandparents whom I surpassed in height during elementary school—as a young woman, despite her small stature, became known as "Shooter Bateman" for her prowess on the basketball court. She did have brothers. But still.

One of the scariest things I overheard as a child was a conversation Grandma and Grandpa Dunphy had downstairs after my brother and I had gone to bed. I wanted to sleep, but their voices floated up the open staircase outside my bedroom door. Grandma, who was prone to *tsk*-ing even at good news (but who, in all fairness, was raised by a very dour-looking Mennonite woman and had lost her own first baby, "Baby Bernard," to scarlet fever at age three), initiated the discussion. She was telling my grandpa about something she was reading in the

Reader's Digest about communists and the possibility of nuclear war. Today, I suspect this may have been during the Cuban missile crisis.

Other than this conversation between these two grandparents, I do not recall politics ever being discussed in our family. The news was on the TV in our family room, but I mourned the loss of JFK, who died five days after my tenth birthday, alone. Was my family silent because he was a Democrat? A Catholic? Or was it just not polite to talk about politics (any more than it was to talk about religion)? If the adults had talked about the sad and scary things happening in the world while I was growing up, would it have made the sad and scary things happening now any less so?

The 2020 presidential election took place today amid a third surge of the COVID-19 pandemic. What's at stake hits home harder than ever with COVID-19 cases and deaths on the rise after seven and a half months of our country living and dying with the pandemic . . . and the almost certainty that one side or another of our polarized country will be in the streets within the week. This week, in working on my family tree of immigrants and with the election front and center, I've become more curious about President Trump's family:

● President Trump's third wife, Melania Trump (née Knavs), a Slovenian model born in what was then Yugoslavia, arrived in the United States in 1996, received what is known as the "Einstein visa," reserved for "individuals with extraordinary ability" (hers would be in modeling; one can imagine Einstein rolling over in his grave), in 2001, and became a citizen in 2006.[3]

---

3   A photo taken in the first month of Trump's presidency at an Edinburg, Texas, demonstration protesting his immigration policies, posted on Facebook, captures a young woman wearing a hijab holding up a hand-lettered sign that reads: "⅔ of Trump's wives [have been] immigrants . . . proving once again we need immigrants to do the job most Americans wouldn't do." Trump's first wife, Ivana Trump (née Zelníčková), was also an immigrant; born in Czechoslovakia, she became a naturalized U.S. citizen in 1988.

- Donald J. Trump's great-grandparents are, on his father's side, all German.

  The first Trump to come to the United States was Donald J. Trump's paternal grandfather, Friedrich Trump, who immigrated in 1885, at age sixteen, from Kallstadt, Palatinate (which was a part of the kingdom of Bavaria when he was born, a part of the German Empire by 1871). After working as a barber and traveling to the Yukon Territory during the Klondike gold rush to run a restaurant and a brothel for Canadian miners, he returned to Kallstadt to marry. The story there was that he had immigrated to America in order to evade the military draft; following an investigation, the Bavarian government stripped Trump of his citizenship and permanently banished him from the country. Back in the United States, while working as a barber and a hotel manager, he began acquiring real estate in Queens. Trump's ancestors had already changed their name from Drumpf to Trump; Friedrich Trump changed his name to Frederick in 1892 when he became a U.S. citizen.

- On his mother's side, all of Trump's grandparents are Scottish. Trump's mother, Mary Anne MacLeod, was Scottish and emigrated from the Hebridean Island of Lewis to the United States in 1930, becoming a naturalized citizen in 1942.

Large-scale emigration from Scotland to America began in the 1700s. By 1850, immigrants arriving anywhere in the United States were, like my own ancestors, almost exclusively from Ireland and Germany, except for immigrants from Mexico arriving in California. In 2018, the top five countries of birth for immigrants were:

- Mexico (25 percent)
- China (6 percent)
- India (6 percent)

- Philippines (4 percent)
- El Salvador (3 percent)

Trump's family has not been on American soil all that long. Certainly not as long as many Mexicans who have become citizens, those immigrants Trump described, based on their nationality, as "rapists," those against whom he has attempted to build his wall. Certainly not as long as many people who voted for him or many people who didn't vote for him. But his family's newness to the country did not prevent him from becoming president of the United States. Nor should it have.

About two weeks after the 2020 election was successfully certified, Matthew Continetti, a fellow at the American Enterprise Institute who focuses on the development of the Republican Party and the American conservative movement, when asked about Trump's key legacy, responded:

> Donald Trump will be remembered as the first president to be impeached twice. He fed the myth that the election was stolen, summoned his supporters to Washington to protest the certification of the Electoral College vote, told them that only through strength could they take back their country, and stood by as they stormed the US Capitol and interfered in the operation of constitutional government. . . . If Donald Trump had followed the example of his predecessors and conceded power graciously and peacefully, he would have been remembered as a disruptive but consequential populist leader.

Despite his own feelings about immigrants, the fact that Trump is a son and grandson of immigrants has nothing to do with how he will be remembered. Nor should it.

Nature has its own ways of organizing information: organisms grow and register information from the environment. This is particularly notable in trees, which, through their rings, tell the story of their growth. Drawing on this phenomenon as a visual metaphor, the United States can be envisioned as a tree, with shapes and growing patterns influenced by immigration. The nation, the tree, is hundreds of years old, and its cells are made out of immigrants.

9

Pages from the Cottonwood Calendar

The Eastern Cottonwood

(*Populus deltoides*)

I turned away from the open windows and looked back toward the front of the classroom. The overhead fluorescent lights had been turned off to keep the room cooler, but my white short-sleeve cotton blouse with the Peter Pan collar was still sticking to my back. The light imprinted on my daydreaming eyes now appeared as mirages against the blackboard, and through them, I could barely make out the shadowy figure of our teacher.

By now, the sting of my first-day embarrassment in front of the class had faded. What would possess a sixth-grade teacher to begin the school year by reading Alfred Noyes's romantic ballad "The Highwayman"? What with "hell" and "breast" scattered throughout the stanzas; a gun physically bound to the landlord's daughter and she herself tied to her own bedpost; kissing of two varieties, passionate and sadistic; and the shot that both warns off the highwayman—that robber on horseback—from the trap set by King George's redcoats and actually shatters an honest-to-goodness flesh-and-blood breast—what were we supposed to do with all that? For Pete's sake, depending on gender, the members of the class were either just beginning to grow or just beginning to notice breasts.

But like the wind, "a torrent of darkness among the gusty trees," that the highwayman was "riding—riding—riding—" through, the poem's rhythm, the language, the imagery, the love story swirled through me and stirred some part of me to life. Suddenly, I very much wanted to do this.

Whatever exactly this was.

As Mrs. Houck put her finger in the book to mark the page and asked the very first question of the very first day of my last school year at Roosevelt Elementary, my hand—surprising no one more than me—shot up. Even more alarming, this teacher, whom I suddenly very much wanted to impress, immediately called on me, catching me midstream in my struggle to come out of the spell into which I'd been transported by her reading of the poem.

What had I done?

In an awful space of utter quiet, I attempted to mentally reconstruct what her question might have been. I had no idea. I wanted to undo what I'd set in motion by raising my hand, but I didn't know how. Most likely seeing the panic on my face, she repeated the question: "What sound did the horse's hooves make?"

Who had been paying attention to *the sound of the horse's hooves* in the midst of all the rest of it? Drenched, as we were, in narrative tension from the poem's sexually charged atmosphere to its bloody conclusion, who cared about the horse or the horse's hooves, let alone the *sound* of the horse's hooves?[1]

But in that classroom on the first day of sixth grade, the interminable stretch of silence following her repetition of her question was broken

---

1 Of course, it is the sound of the horse's hooves in "The Highwayman" that gallops readers to the poem's narrative's climax and then trots them to its resolution. The sound of the horse's hooves *is* of paramount importance. It was a great question, but I wouldn't understand that until a reconsideration decades later.

only by a wild waving of other hands around me, all motioning for this cool teacher's attention. Finally, knowing my answer wasn't right, my voice surely heavy with upward inflection, I choked out, "Clip-clop?" I wouldn't learn the word "mortify" until a few weeks later from a Friday advanced vocabulary list, but I have ever since associated that word with that experience. I was completely and thoroughly mortified.

Once I had heard the correct answer from one of my classmates, who'd begun waggling his hand a nanosecond after mine had shot up, I thought the wonderful thing about the sound the poet had invented to describe the sound of the horse's hooves in the poem—*tlot-tlot*—is how much more it evokes a galloping horse than the standard *clip-clop*, the sound of which suggests walking. However, I wasn't planning to volunteer that observation anytime soon.

I don't know how long it was, in fact, before I ventured to raise my hand in that classroom again, but I know it wasn't until after I'd begun writing poems in my spiral beige notebook journal. Mrs. Houck had each of us turn in such a journal weekly. This cool teacher liked my poems, gave them plus marks every week, and sometimes scrawled encouraging notes in red pen at the end of a poem. Maybe I *could* do this. Whatever this was.

I looked back to the windows. Through them, the afternoon sun was streaming into our classroom. My eyes squinted against the brightness. The heart-stopping blue of the June sky was interrupted with bits of white fluff. This almost-summer snow caught on the faintest of breezes in a graceful, aimless drift. How could this—a snowstorm in June and the feel of this end-of-the-school-year day—be translated into words and line breaks on paper? My fingers itched to lift up the lid of my desk, take out my fountain pen—my first, the one with the ruby-red cartridge barrel purchased from Leslie's Pharmacy with my allowance, the special pen that I used only for *unassigned* writing—open my spiral notebook journal to feel its scrawl, and try.

I knew from observation that those pieces of down came from the big trees growing wild around our school. The arrival of this "snow" announced—even more definitively than the happy smell of lilacs at the side door of our house, the annual arrival of the special anxiety spiraling toward my spring piano recital, or the bouncy feeling that accompanied wearing canvas tennis shoes to school for my long broad jumps at the annual Field Day—that summer was coming, that school was about to be over for the year.

I had discovered that each "snowflake" was actually a parachute made of a fine hair-like fiber transporting one tiny seed. I didn't know, however, that the seeds being transported by these skeleton parasols, which often got their fine ribs tangled together in clumping masses, would come to naught unless they landed in mud. In Livonia—former farm fields turned Detroit suburb—a lot of mud puddles developed atop the clay of The Field behind our backyards after spring showers. But some of the seeds apparently were coming to naught as I watched that day, as they clotted together on the screens of our classroom windows, which were open to the omnipresent smell of freshly cut new grass. This grass was growing where a different kind of grass—most likely alfalfa to be harvested as hay—had once grown and been windrowed on a settler's farm fields.

The trees from which the seeds were released by the thousands were the big trees, the only big trees anywhere around my home or school. The exceptions, the two other big trees with which I had more than a passing acquaintance, were The Boundary Oak that marked the end of the school field and the start of a wooded public park, designating how far from the school building we could go during recess, and the weeping willow with the tree house in my friend Noël's backyard.

All of the other trees in my world were small, pathetic-looking sticks of trees planted by either homeowners or the city once rolls of sod had been laid that divested our muddy clay yards of their boot-sucking ability. One year, just after the cottonwoods had let loose their fluff to snow down on us, an adult neighbor disparagingly identified the trees as "those messy poplars." But to my mind, these were truly majestic trees.

I had moved from a tame Detroit neighborhood, just ten miles away, where the only trees of any stature were those planted on the park lawn, the strip of grass between sidewalk and street. We had not even had a park-lawn tree growing in front of our 1929 brick bungalow, but I had become intimate in early childhood with the Bobrowskis' park-lawn maple tree next door, my mom and I watching it change through the seasons from my dad's second-floor study. When we went for a walk and its samaras—the maple's winged seedpod, also called "keys," but we called them "helicopters"—were falling, I enjoyed gathering them and throwing them up in the air to twirl down again. I had liked having that tree as a neighbor.

When we moved to Livonia, I was in awe of all the huge cotton-wood trees, apparently just growing on their own in the midst of what to me was still—at least out back in The Field that ran all the way to my school—an untamed, wild land. These cottonwoods formed the backdrop of my entire third-grade year when my classroom had a wall of windows facing east. Bored by the introduction of social studies into our curriculum, when I wasn't inventing more made-up stories to share during Show and Tell, I imagined scenes out of Laura Ingalls Wilder's books, about her pioneering family, taking place in The Field amid the cottonwood trees.

In fifth and sixth grade, for forty-five minutes before and after school, I worked as an aide in my school library. Cathy Stewart was the other fifth grader given this honor after both of us went through a two-round hiring process. First, members of a large applicant pool, all girls, completed a written application. The top ten or twelve applicants were then to go through an in-person interview with the school librarian, Mr. Hamer. Thrilled as I was to see my name posted on a typed page taped on our classroom door, as the youngest in my grade and painfully shy, the idea of an interview with the librarian, a man I had never spoken to before, alone in his office with the door closed, was so terrifying that I have absolutely no recollection of the event.

Along with two sixth graders who had also been hired, Cathy and I shelved books, stamped the day's return cards, repaired damaged books, changed the display on the library bulletin out in the hall, and performed all of the other tasks necessary to keep our library happily humming. Which is what I was usually doing when I was working in the library—happily humming, at least to myself in my head. While the rest of the girls in fifth and sixth grade served as members of the Service Squad, spending much less time corralling the children in lower grades into and out of their coats and into order, I would gladly have spent even more time in the library—if only our janitor, Mr. Bates, had unlocked the exterior doors earlier in the morning, or had he locked them up again later in the afternoon. Being a student library aide—my first job, other than babysitting—was the best job I've ever had, other than my occupation for the past decade of facilitating writing workshops and coaching individual writers. While I did not get paid in money, the dividends of this first job were invaluable to my sense of self, my education, and my writing, even today, almost sixty decades later.

One afternoon in late winter, when I was the last student aide preparing to leave, Mr. Hamer asked me to come into his office. On his desk was a box of books I had delivered to him that morning, which he had just slit open. He took out the book on top and handed it to me. The book's unblemished dust jacket was a dark blue with three sets of green concentric circles, each set containing the figure of a person in white. An embossed gold medal seal was affixed to the upper right corner of the cover, adjacent to the top of the circles. The title was in white, too: *A Wrinkle in Time*.[2] Mr. Hamer asked me if I would take the book home to read and tell him what I thought of it. He had never

2 Published in 1962, Madeleine L'Engels's book *A Wrinkle in Time*, a children's science-fiction book, one of the first featuring a female protagonist, Meg Murry, won the Newbery Award in 1963 for the year's "most distinguished contribution to American literature for children." The original cover (along with over a thousand other book covers in her career) was created by Ellen Raskin, herself a Newbery Award winner (in 1979 for *The Westing Game*).

asked a library aide to do this before. The hardback book was a naked newborn. It was pristine: no protective plastic-film yet placed on the cover, no manila circulation card pocket pasted on the inside. Tingling, I carefully placed the precious book in my plaid school satchel and walked home full of excitement.

I started reading the book as soon as I got home, crouching down in front of the heat register in my room with a blanket draped over me, a favorite reading position of mine. I read all 211 pages that night. (This feat may have involved an under-the-covers flashlight in the later hours.)

I left early for school the next morning, before Cathy Roth, one of the two sixth-grade library aides, appeared from over the other side of The Creek, walking fast down the long length of Lori Street, before she could spot me and call out to me to wait. Even before I had removed my coat, I shyly knocked on Mr. Hamer's office door. He looked up expectantly and I, still lost in the story, handed the book back to him, blurting out that it was the best book I'd ever read.

The spring I completed sixth grade, Mr. Hamer invited me, my parents, and my brother to his house on Hoy Street for dinner. I was honored. Those days of working in the library, with the cottonwoods standing sentinel outside the windows and thousands of books lining the library's interior walls, their bindings containing millions of pages, both nurtured and satisfied a hunger in me. As I wheeled the wooden library cart of books to the start of the fiction or nonfiction section and began adeptly decoding the Dewey Decimal labels and adroitly shelving the books, I often felt as if I were in a dream.

I didn't know then that the cottonwood, while classified as a hardwood tree, has one of the softest woods, producing high-grade pulpwood particularly suitable for making paper. When I paused in shelving books or stamping due-date cards to consider where the cottonwoods and I were situated, I imagined that The Creek—which I now know to be a part of the Bell Branch of the Upper Rouge

River—running between me and the trees out the window was the very same creek where the cows that produced milk for a city boy, raised in Detroit's Brightmoor neighborhood and who was to become my dad, had once quenched their thirst on lazy summer days. Which most likely was exactly what they did.

Those big trees, eastern cottonwoods (*Populus deltoides*) are in the genus *populus*, as are all poplar trees. Growing along The Creek, they were showing their family affiliation as willows (*Salicaceae*). The eastern cottonwood's range is centered in the Midwest. These trees are attracted to waterways in the Great Lakes basin, from tributary to marsh to beach, and then trail across the Great Plains, where towering poplars indicated water and provided shade for the native people and later, the European pioneers heading west. Had these eastern cottonwoods in The Field, or their ancestors, signaled to travelers from the East to stop and set down roots here?

I wondered then if the grasshoppers taking wild leaps up into the open from the vegetation in The Field and the crickets singing in the dark below my window at night were the descendants of the grasshoppers and crickets that had, respectively, leapt and sang at the farm where my dad's family had brought their milk. I was amazed by the story of the city boy who went with his family "out to the country" to buy milk from cows that grazed on the very property on which he someday, after becoming my dad, would have a house built. I never really wondered about what had happened to that farm until decades later—who had called that farm home, who else might have appreciated those particular cottonwood trees on the banks of The Creek.

All that was left of the farm when I was growing up was the grand old white farmhouse with gingerbread decorative millwork framing the top edge of the porch and decorating the corbels under the eaves above the second-story windows. This one-of-a-kind house was set up on a hill in the deep shade of mature evergreen trees. Other large deciduous trees grew on the land around the house. From my house, this farmhouse on Middle Belt Road was across The Creek and south the distance of two streets running parallel to ours on the other side of The Field. In our car, my family passed it, a house like none I had ever seen before or since, on our many trips to and from church, to my Monday evening piano lessons, and on weekend trips to the Wonderland Shopping Center. I had no idea who had built the house or who was living there when we drove past. On some level, I sensed that their loss of farmland was responsible for our gain of being able to live in such a nice house in such a fine neighborhood with access to The Field and The Creek, and having the cottonwoods in view from my bedroom window.

Nonetheless, without fail, just a quick glance at this farmhouse up on the hill caused an odd instantaneous shift somewhere inside me to what felt like another time and place. It was as if I stumbled into another life. I would not have been able to explain the feeling adequately then, had I thought to do so, even to myself because what I might now define as "strange" feelings related to place and time were not unusual occurrences in my childhood. I still experience these feelings sometimes as an adult. The closest I can come now to explain how I felt when I looked at the farmhouse is that it was like experiencing a waking dream, the subject of which was completely foreign, but somehow comforting. This phenomenon, with respect to the farmhouse, persisted throughout the portion of my suburban childhood when we lived on the edge of The Field. I experienced a similar feeling when I was across The Creek from the family of three cottonwood trees rooted to its banks.

We know from the accounts of the first European-descended settlers—who came west for the rich land—that when they arrived at the thirty-six-square-mile area that would become Livonia Township in 1835, the Bodéwadmi (aka Potawatomi) inhabited the forest there (and before them, the Woodland Indians). The pioneers who cut this forest to get at the rich soil were primarily from New York.

Because, some accounts report, many of them were eastern European, they named their township after a town 357 miles east in western New York: Livonia. In New York in 1808, the name had been borrowed from a onetime region on the eastern side of the Baltic Sea inhabited by the Livs, a Finno-Ugric people. The region of "Livland"—or Livonia—had been so named in the twelfth century by Germans. According to subsequent records, for the first one hundred years after settlers arrived with axes in hand, the Livonians of Michigan grew vegetables and grains, planted orchards, raised sheep and dairy cattle, and established dairy farms. All of those activities, of course, involved the cutting down of a number—a number not left in any record—of individual trees.

In 1976, the year after I graduated college and had already spent my last night in my family's subsequent home in that city, in a subdivision called Birchwood Farms (no birch, no farms—no surprise), Livonia established the Greenmead Historical Park. As I was thinking about my cottonwood friends on the bank of The Creek decades later, I wondered if such a complex of historic buildings might include a historical museum where I could find out more about the grand white farmhouse on whose acreage my childhood home had been built, perhaps discovering to whom those particular remaining cottonwoods might have meant as much, in an earlier time, as they had to me. I had grown up with these distinct individual cottonwoods as beloved neighbors for eight of my most formative years, and now I imagined other people must have had relationships with them. Who were those people and what had those cottonwoods meant to them? From 1960 through 1969, the shadowy silhouettes of the three massive cottonwoods—growing on the far bank of The Creek, across The Field bordering the south side of our backyard—were the last sight I took in at night from my second-floor bedroom window, the first I saw in the morning. Sometimes, even now, this trinity of trees appears in my night dreams.

My dad was born in 1927, so I figured he would have been going with his parents to buy milk from that farm in the 1930s. In an attempt to learn more about the people who lived in the farmhouse and sold their land with some trees remaining, I located a 1936 Livonia Township map. In the southeastern part of section 23, in the acreage bounded by Middle Belt and Merriman and Five Mile and Schoolcraft Roads, I could make out the names: A. Wolfrom and Wolfrom Brothers. Plugging "Wolfrom" and "Livonia" into my search engine, I was asked if I meant "*Wolfram* brothers." I guessed I did. The list of hits that followed filled two screens with both Wolfroms and Wolframs.

Late one rainy night—still troubled by what it must have meant to the Wolfrom or Wolfram family to sell that land—to see the trees that had once surely been extended family members in the large farmyard and those trees that had served as sentries and shade at the edges of pastureland and orchard cut down to be replaced by at least three subdivisions—I entered "Wolfram farm" and "Greenmead," wondering if Greenmead held a collection of historical records, not just historical buildings. The "Greenmead Farms" Wikipedia entry previewed with this intriguing piece of a sentence: "The *Wolfram* familty [*sic*] lived in the house until the 1980s, when it was donated to the city and moved to . . ." Wait, what?!

The full Greenmead Farms Wikipedia entry begins:

> Greenmead Historical Park, also known as Greenmead Farms, is a 3.2-acre . . . historic park located at 38125 Base Line Rd., Livonia, Michigan. It includes the 1841 Greek Revival Simmons House, six other structures contributing to the historic nature of the property, and *additional buildings moved from other locations* [emphasis added].

The entry gives a short history of how the City of Livonia acquired the Simmons family farm, originally called Meadow Brook, and later named it Greenmead, for use as a park. What follows is a description of the original farm complex on the site. Next comes a listing titled "Other structures moved to Greenmead." None of them sounded like anything resembling the grand, old white farmhouse on the hill and surrounded by trees that I recalled from my youth.

But the last building listed of the eleven structures moved to Greenmead caught my eye. What specifically attracted my attention was the thumbnail photo of a bright yellow house rising up from the treeless, snow-covered ground against an eerily teal sky. It is listed as "mid-19th century," certainly before my dad or even my grandparents were a twinkle in anyone's eye. But then in the description column I found:

> This structure was built by Judge Alexander Blue, who served as Justice of the Peace from 1846 to 1874. The Blue house, originally located on Middlebelt Road, had a number of decorative Italianate flourishes. The Blue family lived in the house until 1915, when it was sold to Fred and Frank Wolfram. The Wolfram familty [sic] lived in the house until the 1980s, when it was donated to the city and moved to Greenmead. The house has been restored to its 1880s appearance.

Oh, my. This is the *actual* house, the grand old farmhouse (no longer white), not just *information about* the farmhouse. Perhaps the most important human-constructed landmark near my childhood home, that magical house in the shady glen, had been the heart of the Alexander Blue farm before the Wolfram family lived there and ultimately sold off all of the acreage, on which had remained three very specific cottonwood trees, at least for the eight years I lived there. But the Blue House at Greenmead looked to be more than double the size I remembered the large farmhouse being in my youth. Was it really the same house?

On a mission now, I discovered *Livonia Preserved: Greenmead and Beyond*, an "Images of America" book. The book contains one drawing of the house, outbuildings, and surrounding orchard and farmland and five photographs of the Alexander Blue house in its original location. Another thirteen photographs show the house in the process of being moved to Greenmead on May 26, 1987, long after I'd moved from our second Livonia house to Rochester to Detroit to Ferndale, where I was raising my family. Eight more photographs depict the house at Greenmead. One shows a huge addition being attached in 2001, which included a large dining area, so that one hundred guests could be seated therein, and a kitchen equipped for catered events. That explained the how and why of the farmhouse's increased size.

The captions under the photos in the book explain that Alexander Blue moved with his family in 1832 from Oneida County, New York, at age fifteen. I imagine the family traveling on the south side of Lake Ontario, overland or via the seven-year-old Erie Canal; they would have passed north of Livonia, New York, on their journey west. Alexander's father, Daniel Blue—one of Livonia, Michigan's first settlers—had also purchased land for each of his sons. Alexander married his cousin Catherine Blue in 1843. Circa 1855, the couple built the two-story farmhouse with "many stylish Italianate details." (One hundred and four years later, my family moved into a house on a lot that had been a miniscule part of the Alexander Blue farm.) While living in the house, Alexander Blue went on to become a prosperous farmer and held several township and county offices—township assessor, township supervisor, and Elm postmaster—and was a member of the Elm School Board and the Wayne County Board of Auditors as well as serving for twenty-eight years as the first justice of the peace for Livonia Township.

The last of the historic pictures of the farm shows a woman and a young boy at a pump with an outbuilding in the background. The caption reads:

Fred and Frank Wolfram purchased the Blue farm in 1913. Fred's daughter Helen Matavia [*sic*], pictured above with her son Jimmy around 1955, inherited the property after his death. The Matiavias [*sic*] *sold some land to a developer in the 1950s and other acreage later on* but continued to live in the house until the 1980s. After Helen died, the property was sold with the understanding that the house was to be donated to Greenmead [emphasis added].

It must have been the Wolfram farm when my dad was a boy and drove out with his family to buy milk. Wolfram's grandson, Jimmy Matevia, looks to be maybe six or seven in the photograph. In 1955, I would have been approaching my second birthday, still four years from moving to the land on which I imagine Jimmy must have run free among the cottonwoods on the bank of The Creek, at least until the steam shovels began digging holes for basements. Once upon a time, did Jimmy Matevia love those trees—and perhaps others that were removed (some of which were left in a pile we called "The Stumps" between the tree house tree and the school) for the Algonquin Park subdivision my family moved to in 1959?[3] Might Jimmy have loved those trees as much as I did?

How old exactly had Jimmy Matevia been in 1955? Had he ever been in The Field at the same time I was? Did he consider The Field *his* field? How did he feel about those who cut the trees, built houses, and moved onto the land he had grown up thinking of as his home? Had he attended my elementary and junior high, passing me in the halls?

I felt flush with the prickly feel of obsession as I entered the Livonia

---

3 The subdivision name is a nod to those who lived on and hunted this land when it was forest, before the European settlers arrived to claim it as private property. The native people spoke the Bodéwadmi (Potawatomi) language, a Central *Algonquian* language spoken around the Great Lakes in Michigan and Wisconsin.

Civic Center Library to dig into the genealogical section. But even as I gave myself free rein to go down this rabbit hole for an afternoon, I knew in my heart that wanting to know more about the people who may have loved those cottonwoods as much or more than I was only a substitute for wanting to know more about the trees themselves. Knowing that the Matevias, Alton (an employee of Ira Wilson Dairy Company) and Helen Matevia (née Wolfram), had three children, that Jimmy was the youngest of three siblings—what difference did that make? This knowledge couldn't bring the trees back. I already knew as much about these cottonwoods as I ever would, and I had seen them for the very last time before I turned fourteen.

The people who were attached to the land on which those cotton-woods lived on the bank of The Creek—the Blues, the Wolframs, the Matevias—could be "known" and remembered through the paper records they left behind—now additionally available electronically, courtesy of fossil fuels, wind, or sun—documents related to their financial affairs and important life moments (births, baptisms, grad-uations, marriages, deaths), summed up in their obituaries, and their images frozen in photographs over the last century and a half. Not only could the cottonwoods not be conjured back, I could find no evidence of human sorrow, other than that residing in my own heart, which marked the loss of the cottonwoods.

On my desk resides a black-and-white photo taken by my grandma of Grandpa Klotzbach attired in a polka-dotted bow tie, felt hat, and dapper tweed overcoat, camera hanging from his neck, with one hand in his coat pocket and the other on my shoulder as I, with a shy but genuine smile, lean against him. I would have been seven or eight years old. In the background of this photo are the massive wooden double doors of the Kirk in the Hills Presbyterian Church in Bloomfield Township with black wrought-iron trim and surrounding limestone-block façade. Somewhere, I still have my own black-and-white photos taken of the Gothic-style church on that chilly spring day, my first photographic field trip, with my grandparents. Why hadn't I ever taken a picture of The Field, The Creek, and especially the cottonwoods with the Kodak Brownie camera that my grandparents gave me the year after we moved onto the former Wolfram farm acreage? Somewhere in a moldy album of fading photos kept by another family or in the archives of the city's planning department, does a photo of those three cottonwoods—landmarks of my childhood, those long-gone friends who helped me learn both to daydream and to pay attention—exist?

Jimmy's and my cottonwoods—next to The Creek, with other family members around the school and in the park beyond the school's athletic field's Boundary Oak—were tall and stately, their crowns wild, the bark on their trunks deeply grooved. The sunlight glinted off their reflective heart-shaped, coarse-toothed leaves. I always thought that in order to shine so, cottonwood leaves must be made of a different material than the leaves of other species of trees, but that's not true; the leaf stems—the petioles—of cottonwoods are flat and catch the slightest breeze, allowing the moving surfaces to flash back a Morse code of light.

In The Field, the landscape of my childhood and home to the three special cottonwoods, the farm's former grazing pastureland had gone wild with the native and non-native plants of disturbed soil:[4] Queen Anne's lace (the white flowers of wild carrot), dusty soldier (the blue flowers of chicory), red clover, white clover, white sweet clover, yellow sweet clover, goldenrod; scattered common mullein, cow vetch, crown vetch, daisy fleabane, and knapweed as well as the occasional milkweed, black-eyed Susan, and Canada thistle, all of which called to them happy bees and dancing butterflies.

---

4 Identification of the following list of plants in my memory of The Field was assisted by Jennifer Schlick, a teacher-naturalist and photographer living and working in western New York, whose blog *A Passion for Nature: WinterWoman's Observations* (no longer active) contains a posting, "Roadside Weeds," featuring helpful photographs and a listing of the plants.

My friends and I pedaled hard and fast on our bikes over a narrow-worn path through flowers and butterflies and up the backside of the western hill of The Creek's north bank.[5] Along this high bank, a massive, ridged web of cottonwood roots crisscrossed the path. I didn't know then that this root system was preventing the erosion of The Creek's bank. The cottonwoods glinted as if they held a secret. The secret was enticingly close as I pedaled hard on the packed path alongside The Creek over their entwined roots.

Riding a bike on the high bank was a happy place to be in summer's cottonwood leaf-dappled shade, the place to build up speed after the hard climb, and the sole way to the stomach-dropping thrill of the steep hill back down. A large circular path circumscribing the entire width of The Field between creek bank and our suburban backyards—overlooked by the tree house and topped by "big sky," a place to see the cloud types we were learning in school: cumulus, cirrus, stratus, nimbus—led the way back to the eastern end of our circuit. And back up. And down, my ponytail stiff in a summer wind created by the speed inherent in the joy of descent. We circled around to do it again, do it again, do it again. When we tired of that—some days after a hundred count of circles around—the cottonwoods stood silent witnesses to our games of hide-and-seek in The Field and baseball in Beatrice Street, the street that dead-ended at The Field and was adjacent to my house's corner lot.

One year, instead of being yanked up by the roots by my dad, as so many were, the "weed" of a sapling cottonwood, whose seed had taken root at the edge of our lot, was allowed to remain. This volunteer grew quickly, providing shade for the play-yard, an area in our

5 Both banks of The Creek were cut through in the early 1960s to allow the construction of a concrete footbridge, replacing the earlier plank bridge, over which schoolchildren from the subdivision to the south of The Field, also formerly a part of the Wolfram farm, crossed The Creek for easier access to Roosevelt Elementary School.

backyard surrounded by a hedge of currant bushes and filled with sand, where our swing set and sandbox were. This cottonwood came to mark the beginning of The Field at the southwest corner of our yard, across the dead-ended sidewalk from a telephone pole on our park lawn. The cottonwood grew so quickly that my brother Gregg was able to climb up into it, at least once.

Fifty years—half a century—later, the play-yard cottonwood is not there. It had been growing under the wires that ran to that telephone pole. I suppose Detroit Edison or subsequent owners of the property must have cut it down. I wonder how big it was then. Did it become stacked logs drying to be burned as logs in the fireplace of our former house or was it chipped to be used for mulch in the garden? How big would that cottonwood tree be now if it had been left to grow? Individual members of the Standing Nation—as native people have sometimes referred to trees—are as different from each other as individual humans are. Today I wonder: in any of our thousands of family photos, does the shape of that particular volunteer cottonwood tree growing in our play-yard on Lori Street exist in an image, an image magically imprinted on one specific day by the same rays of sun the cottonwood was using, at the very moment the shutter clicked, for photosynthesis, an image made permanent some later Friday evening by the alchemy of Grandpa Klotzbach's darkroom?

Likewise, none—not one—of the cottonwood trees growing in what we had called The Field remained after it was developed into two blocks of homes on Lyndon Street, the "half-mile street" between Schoolcraft and Five Mile Roads. But when I was growing up, every year, in the days of lengthening light, cottonwood fluff came down from the heavens like pure happiness, making nests against the curbs of after-supper streets.

By late August, the cottonwoods' summer-juicy leaves began to become dry. Even before they turned their signature fall yellow—so lovely against both September's blue skies and October's gray days—came the cottonwoods' rustle, a warning of the approach of the end of summer, a signal that triggered anticipation of a new beginning, the start of another school year.

The year I turned forty, I stole away from my own family, which included two daughters, to a rooftop retreat I had created at our Ferndale house to read Doris Lessing's *The Golden Notebook*. Lost in thought, I frequently looked up from the book, gazing at the familiar glint of the cottonwood's leaves at the Stoys' house next door without really noticing that I was. Nonetheless, twenty-five years later, the image of that cottonwood telegraphing its dots and dashes of light is what stakes that memory for me. And I apparently got the message: I applied to a graduate writing program, and by fall, as the rustle of the leaves began, I was off to a new life, feeling just as I had at the start of every new school year in my younger years, excited and full of hope, and now ready to do whatever exactly this is.

10

The Mother's Day Tree

The Ginkgo

(*Ginkgo biloba*)

The house we live in now, our fourth, and the Pelee Island cottage we have now, our second, each had a small ginkgo tree on the property when we purchased it. We learned in both cases, as the deeds exchanged hands, that both had been Mother's Day presents. Neither tree had grown very big when we assumed responsibility for their care, and each was growing decidedly crooked due to completely different causes.

Despite measuring nine feet tall when it was pulled upright, the ginkgo at our island cottage had been unmercifully bent east and beaten down by the westerly winds that blow pretty much year-round off Lake Erie. It rose less than half of its height off the ground in a position that ran more parallel to the Earth than any other tree I have ever seen. After staking the tree for a few years with no good outcome—staked, it was held taut against the wind's onslaught and could not escape by bowing low to the ground—we cut it down; it was too large to successfully transplant on the island. At the time, the ginkgo was only the second living tree I had been responsible for having cut down. In this case, I had the distinct feeling that we were putting the tree out of its misery.

The ginkgo at our mainland house was stretching west into the open space of our driveway, reaching out for sun from under the canopy created by a sugar maple and a honey locust, both planted on the same side of the driveway. Too much sweet shade. We had the ginkgo transplanted to an open sunny spot in the center of our front yard and staked by a tree service. After three or four years staked, the tree's trunk rose straight up, splitting off in a lovely pattern of sprawling branches. A most beautifully satisfying tree to look at, unique in every season.

I can gaze upon, study, this ginkgo in the middle of the front yard just by turning my head from my desk, as the tree now grows directly in line with the front window of my study. We are working adjacent to each other: me writing, it photosynthesizing. This ginkgo is doing its work completely surrounded by a circle of mature trees. The failing Norway maple and pear tree twins are to its south, the eastern white pine and sweetgum to the southwest, the hawthorn to the west, one honey locust to the northwest, another honey locust and the sycamore to the north, and the other member of the pair of sugar maples, under which it had been bending, to the east. In the center of this circle, despite the proximity of its neighbors, the ginkgo luxuriates in full sun for at least a few hours each day.

Compared to all of the mature trees around it, this ginkgo is still a little tree, the smallest of the trees we share land with, other than the newly planted Princess Emily dogwood establishing its roots in the backyard. The ginkgo's trunk is ten inches in circumference and the tree's height at the tip of its tallest flung-out branch is 14.75 feet.

Every year in November, before Thanksgiving, my husband holds a six-foot ladder alongside the ginkgo for me to climb up into its branches. Over the years, I have needed to rely more and more on the assistance of a lightweight plastic angle broom to extend my reach in arranging first one, then two, now three strands of white twinkly lights in a stylized "Z" on its branches. Some years the Z has more flourish than others. The year 2020 was not one of my better artistic displays of lights on the ginkgo, but I left the lights up until May in support of and to honor the sacrifices of our front-line and essential workers—especially healthcare workers and first responders—as more people fell victim to the novel coronavirus, COVID-19, as it multiplied in Michigan, the United States, and the world. I only took them down when all but a few lights in a short line had burned out, a lit hyphen in the increasingly longer days, when the pandemic's curve was, for the first time, showing signs of flattening in Michigan, for what we then thought would be for good. Given the outcome of that thought, I bought new lights in 2021, and for the first time, I just left the lights up on the ginkgo for sixteen months.

What I've wondered over the years is how it is that I've come to make decisions about two ginkgo trees bestowed as Mother's Day presents. Is a ginkgo a common Mother's Day gift? In the last century, this species, historically a symbol of longevity, has also become a symbol of resilience, hope, and peace. Not a bad thing to wish for one's mother, particularly on Mother's Day, especially given the holiday's historical roots.

In 1870, peace activist and suffragette Julia Ward Howe made her Mother's Day Proclamation, calling upon mothers of all nationalities to unite to promote "the amicable settlement of international questions, the great and general interests of peace." Mother's Day was first celebrated in 1908 at a memorial for Ann Jarvis, a peace activist who had cared for wounded soldiers on both sides of the American Civil War and created Mother's Day Work Clubs to address public health issues. In 1914, Woodrow Wilson signed a proclamation designating Mother's Day, to be held on the second Sunday in May, as a national holiday to honor mothers.

But it was an act of war, not peace, that put the ginkgo in the international spotlight. After the Great Kanto Earthquake of 1923, which, at a 7.9 to 8.4 magnitude, included extensive firestorms and a fire tornado, the Japanese noticed that the ginkgo, above all species, proved most resistant to fire, budding again after having been burned. The most famous ginkgoes, perhaps, are the six that survived the World War II blast of the first atomic bomb on August 6, 1945, unlike the estimated 100,000 to 150,000 people who immediately died. Growing just a mile from the bombsite at Hiroshima, Japan, the trees suffered extensive damage in the blast, but new buds soon emerged from their burned trunks. A total of approximately 170 ginkgo trees, within just a mile and a half of the bombsite, survived the blast. Hence, the ginkgo became a symbol of endurance amid great destruction and human suffering. To the Japanese, the ginkgo became the "bearer of hope."

In 2014, saplings grown from the seeds of these surviving ginkgoes were given to the city of Manchester, England, in recognition of its being the first city in the United Kingdom to become a nuclear-free zone on November 5, 1980. A young American woman, Dr. Randall Caroline Forsberg, the founder of the Institute for Defense and Disarmament, initiated the Nuclear Weapons Freeze Campaign in 1979 with her proposal paper "Call to Halt the Nuclear Arms Race." The goal of the movement was to secure an agreement between the U.S. and Soviet governments to halt the testing, production, and deployment of nuclear weapons.

I had been actively involved in the Nuclear Freeze movement during the Reagan administration, before my first daughter, Meagan Mná, was born on April 2, 1982. The act of circulating petitions for a referendum on a nuclear freeze became even more crucial to me with the birth of Meagan, who attended her first political demonstration with me at seven weeks of age in Lansing, Michigan, where we both appeared on a local TV newscast. I still have the photograph a friend took of us, me wearing Meagan in a front infant carrier, Meagan wearing a wide-brimmed white sunhat, and both of us wearing red Nuclear Freeze T-shirts bearing the motto "You can't hug your children with nuclear arms." The petition drive succeeded in garnering

375,000 signatures from Michigan voters, enough to put the issue on the ballot that November.

The Michigan Nuclear Weapons Freeze Initiative, Proposal E, was on the ballot in Michigan as an indirect initiated state statute. It was approved by 1,585,809 (56.6 percent) of registered Michigan voters who voted in the 1982 midterm election. Proposal E was new legislation calling for a mutual, verifiable nuclear weapons freeze between the United States and the Union of Soviet Socialist Republics. The proposal required communicating its content to U.S. government officials. The text of the transmitted proposal read:

> The people of the State of Michigan, recognizing that the safety and security of the United States must be paramount in the concerns of the American people; and further recognizing that our national security is reduced, not increased by the growing danger of nuclear war between the United States and the Soviet Union, which would result in millions of deaths of people in Michigan and throughout the nation; do hereby urge that the Government of the United States immediately propose to the Government of the Soviet Union a Mutual Nuclear Weapons Freeze, whereby both countries agree to halt immediately the testing, production, and further deployment of all nuclear weapons, missiles, and delivery systems in a way that can be checked and verified by both sides, and that Congress transfer the funds which would have been used for those purposes to civilian use.

This grassroots movement's scope was dramatically illustrated by the June 12, 1982, disarmament rally in New York City, in which an estimated seven hundred thousand to 1 million people participated, making it, at the time, the largest political demonstration in the history of the United States. In 1982, when the Nuclear Freeze campaign delivered its antinuclear petitions to the U.S. and Soviet missions to the United Nations, they contained the signatures of more than 2.3 million Americans.

Debates over the nuclear freeze dominated radio and television talk shows, as movie stars and celebrities, prominent intellectuals and scholars, bishops and reverends, and governors and congressional leaders lined up for and against the idea. Both houses of Congress debated the idea of an arms freeze, with the House of Representatives endorsing it in May 1983. The movement played a key role in curbing the nuclear arms race and, perhaps subsequently, preventing nuclear war.

So all things considered, a ginkgo tree seems like a fine Mother's Day gift. One year for my birthday, or perhaps it was a Mother's Day, the daughter who accompanied me to the Nuclear Freeze demonstrations gave me a pair of silver ginkgo-leaf earrings. On other occasions, she has given me a copper mobile of ginkgo leaves and a serving dish of three ginkgo leaves fashioned in silver. I am pleased by this connection between Mother's Day, the Nuclear Freeze, and ginkgo trees, a connection of which I was unaware until I sat down to wonder and write about ginkgo trees.

One more thing to appreciate about ginkgo trees: in the fall—on a single day, sometimes within just an hour or two—a ginkgo tree drops all his or her leaves *in synchrony*. If it is a windy day, the leaves may funnel off to one side. Often the tree in our yard decides to drop his leaves on a completely still day "neither to rain nor to wind / But as though to time alone." The vibrant yellow leaves shower down, creating a perfect golden ring encircling the base of the trunk, a trunk that, at the other end, flings his now empty and eccentrically angled branches out and upward, ever aiming for the sun.

11

The Flowering of 2020

The Silver Maple

(*Acer saccharinum*)

The silver maple was not one of the twenty-seven tree species I'd originally considered including in this book. But then the COVID-19 pandemic hit. While I was working on a second draft of this essay, the *New York Times* reported on December 27, 2020, that one out of every seventeen people in the United States had been infected and that 1 in 1,000 had died, a total of 332,000 people. Exactly two weeks ago today, on December 14, 2020, the first COVID-19 vaccine shots were administered in the United States, to healthcare workers. By now, over nine months after we first became aware that the pandemic had arrived in Michigan—although a woman living across the street from my parents still believes, as recently as last week, that it is all a hoax—most people have at least one COVID story, one they've heard or one that has happened to them. Many of these stories are heartbreaking.

And of course, many people by now have more than one story. In the first half of April, within a month of the lockdown, two very dear friends of mine lost their fathers.

On April 6, 2020, Ward Davis Peterson died at ninety-two in a rehab facility with respiratory symptoms, very likely not directly attributable to COVID but during the first weeks the facility was on lockdown.

One of his daughters suspects he may have lost whatever incentive he still had to keep going once the facility was closed to visitors. Peterson was a pioneer virologist, involved with the Salk polio and other vaccine trials. A mutual friend introduced me to Ward in the Pleasant Ridge Community Pool before I knew his daughter Kathy well. He had served as a member and as the president of the Ferndale Board of Education, and while both of us stood in waist-deep water in the pool, the sounds of happy children surrounding us, he offered me counsel as I began my tenure as a Ferndale school board member. Ward was the kind of man for whom the expression "The world is less for his loss" is apt.

I never had the pleasure of meeting my friend Lucinda's father, Robert Lee (Bob) Garthwaite Sr. An actor with a thirty-five-year career as an award-winning television producer, he died at ninety-five years of age on April 18 of what his daughter suspects was COVID because at the time, the virus was raging through his long-term care facility in New York.

Neither daughter could be with their father at the end—neither could hold her father's hand when he was on his lonely deathbed— nor could either daughter hold a funeral service for her beloved dad, at least not until well over a year later.

One of my writing workshop members had gone with her husband to Ambergris Caye, Belize—an island that won Trip Advisor members' awards in both 2013 and 2014 as the "best island" in the world to visit—for a second visit. They were on vacation but considering relocating there now that her husband had retired from General Motors. They both contracted the virus on their way home, en route from Belize City to the Dallas/Fort Worth International Airport. William Brinson Jr. died less than a month before his sixty-eighth birthday, alone in the hospital, while Dinah struggled with COVID at home. Now, at the end of the year, although Dinah has returned to writing, she has no sense of smell or taste and is still focused on recovery with the help of cardiac, respiratory, and neurological specialists.

These three men died within twelve days of each other, two in Michigan and one in Maine.

In January 2020, we had learned more about a new serious virus, first reported in Wuhan, China, in December 2019. By February we knew it had arrived in Washington State and on the eleventh day of the month it was given a name: "Severe Acute Respiratory Syndrome Coronavirus 2 (SARS-CoV-2)." My husband and I will probably never know if what we had in March 2020 was COVID-19.[1]

The virus was actually already in North Carolina a day before I flew to the Raleigh-Durham International Airport (RDU) on March 5, 2020, to visit my eldest daughter, who was pregnant, her husband, and my two Durham grandchildren. The previous day, a Wake County man was confirmed as having the first case of this new coronavirus in their state; he had flown from Washington State, where the first known cases of COVID in the United States originated, into RDU. Wake County, home of the airport, is the county adjacent to Durham County, where my daughter and her family reside. During my five-day visit, both of my grandchildren, Avery Grace and Caden Daly, four years and twenty-two months, respectively, had coughs left over from the influenza strain A, for which they'd tested positive, as well as stuffy, running noses, possibly from being infected with a cold virus. Nonetheless, I had a lovely visit, punctuated by discussion with my daughter and son-in-law, both scientists at Duke University, about the new virus.

When I landed back at Detroit Metro Airport on Tuesday, the 10th, I stopped at a busy Middle Eastern restaurant for a carryout dinner (waiting inside until my order was ready) to take home before going off to rehearse with a local community choir, in which I sang—*vigorously*—with over one hundred middle-aged and elderly people. During the rehearsal, an alto who sits next to me shared a text she had

---

1   CO = corona; VI = virus; D = disease; 19 = 2019.

received from a friend in the medical field. The text claimed that the first two cases of the novel coronavirus in Michigan, which happened to be local—one in the county in which I live and the other one county over—had been confirmed, but that this would not be publicized until the next day. Meanwhile, in-person voting in the 2020 Michigan Democratic presidential primary, which had begun at 7:00 a.m., continued through the evening until the polls closed at 8:00 p.m.

The next day, while the confirmation of the first two COVID-19 cases in the Detroit metro area was being broadcast on the news, I facilitated two writing workshops attended by a total of fifteen writers, the afternoon one in the local public library, the evening one in the local senior center. I engaged in my first, and last, elbow bump after a private consultation with a writer before the first workshop. Before each of the two workshops, I wiped down the tables' surfaces and edges and the backs of the plastic chairs. In the evening group, I arrived twenty minutes early and was able to distance the chairs around the narrow table to about three feet apart.

Not everyone was on the same page, however. The first writer to arrive that evening was a senior citizen, a male nurse still practicing in home settings. Entering our workshop room, he wrinkled his nose at the residual smell of the lemon-scented Clorox wipes I had used to wipe down the table and made a disgruntled sound.

I explained that although I myself have a negative physical response to chlorine, I felt using it was the responsible thing to do.

He countered by citing the number of people infected with that season's flu virus and the number of people who had died from it, adding, "We didn't do all this for *that* virus," implying that I, and anyone like me, was making far too big a deal about COVID-19. I, judgmentally, suspected I knew what television news station he watched and for whom he'd vote come November. Just several weeks later, this writer and his daughter who lived with him were both diagnosed with COVID. Fortunately, both had a complete recovery.

The next morning, Thursday, March 12, I had a 6:30 a.m. physical therapy appointment, my first—and it turns out my last—in a series. I was tired that morning, but I'm often tired the morning after facilitating my Wednesday writing workshops. Nonetheless, the exercise felt good. Afterward I went home for a 8:00 call with a professional coach, during which we discussed that I should be sure to get enough rest and hydration, given my recent history—in the last two years, I had typically come down with a virus, followed by some sort of bacterial infection, after visiting my grandchildren—because I don't sleep well there during my five-night visits and because I am exposed to the potpourri of viruses carried by my grandchildren, who attend the Little School at Duke three days a week with many other preschoolers.

During my call, without consciously thinking about it, I wrapped the shawl I keep on my desk chair around my shoulders and then eventually, recognizing that I felt chilled, pulled the afghan off the loveseat in my study to cover my lap.

My plan had been to spend the rest of the morning writing and then visit my parents, who were in their early nineties and lived independently in a condo about thirty-five minutes away by expressway. I started writing at 10:18, according to my writing log, and stopped shortly after noon. By then I was feeling like I was coming down with a head cold. I called my mom and asked her for their doctor's nurse practitioner's number to call and ask about visiting my parents, whom I hadn't seen in over a week. In the voicemail I left for Renee, I asked, "Could I visit them if I wore a face mask?"—an item I did not yet possess at the time.

That evening I was reclined on my bed reading *The Overstory*, Richard Powers's novel about trees, when Renee finally called me back. She said I most definitely needed to stay away from my parents. And that, in fact, given my recent travel, I needed to self-isolate from the rest of the world for fourteen days.

The first two days, Thursday and Friday, I felt like I had only a mild cold—scratchy throat, headache, and fatigue. I did wake up in the middle of the night Thursday, feeling pressure on my chest, which kept me awake for a bit trying to adjust my position in bed to ease it, but that I attributed to anxiety. The news about the coronavirus pandemic, which had been declared as a pandemic the day after I got home from North Carolina, was becoming more dire by the day. In the nine days I hadn't seen my parents, my mom had made three trips out to a store, only the last time taking any precautions against the virus. How were they to manage if I couldn't see them for two more weeks?

Saturday, with my cold symptoms oddly abating instead of getting worse, as I would normally expect to happen after two days, my husband and I agreed we needed to get out of the house and decided to walk to the mailbox, a block away at Main Street. Within the distance of a few houses, I realized that the pressure on and the tightness in my chest appeared to be connected to another symptom: I was breathless. Breathless enough to interfere with talking. It reminded me most of the case of altitude sickness I'd once experienced in Leadville, Colorado, when we went up into the mountains with my younger daughter and son-in-law to spend time with them at their mountain place. I even had a similar accompanying headache, but it was not as bad, nor was the breathlessness as severe. But I definitely was experiencing both symptoms.

And suddenly, I was very worried. For two days, I'd really been under the assumption that I had merely contracted a cold virus from my grandchildren, as usual, despite having read that COVID-19 often consists solely of or begins with mild cold symptoms that could develop into respiratory symptoms—respiratory symptoms that I now was most certainly experiencing.

The remainder of the day Saturday and Sunday, I felt the tightness and pressure in my chest increase until I became breathless upon the slightest exertion. My normal temperature is 97.6, exactly a degree below the average normal, and I had been conscientiously taking my temperature since my walk to the mailbox. My temperature had never gone above 99.1, so the equivalent of just over 100. However, I never recalled having a fever with what had begun as such a mild cold. The only time I felt any better was with my feet up and my torso reclined. With this development, my North Carolinian daughter, who is a scientist, and my mom, being a mom, both urged me to get tested. The local hospital, less than ten minutes from me, had begun offering curbside testing that weekend. But I really didn't feel well enough to go anywhere. I was also concerned that because I did not have a cough or a temperature elevated more than just a degree and a half, they would not test me. I thought I could imagine what kind of line there'd be now that testing was available for the first time.

Only I really hadn't been able to imagine the line. Sometime during the night Sunday, I woke up in a pool of sweat; even my hair was wet. Had a fever I was unaware of broken? Monday, I awoke feeling better except for the mild headache. I sterilized our thermometer, the same very old one I'd used when our girls were young, and asked my husband, whose normal temperature is 98.6, if he would take his temperature with it. When it beeped and I pulled it from his mouth, the readout showed 97.1. The thermometer was 1.5 degrees off. So my temperature, in fact, had been elevated by 3 degrees. Oops. Even though I felt better, I became more worried.

I thought my husband, after running downtown Sunday afternoon when no one was in the Ford Building, the site of his office, to pick up more work and his computer camera to use for Zoom hearings, was in for the long haul of isolation with me. But late Monday morning, he announced that maybe he should make one more grocery run and, oh, by the way, he did need to go back to his office to proofread the documents he'd left for his secretary to type when he'd gone down on Sunday. Here is who I knew would be at his office: his sixty-year-old secretary, whose husband had had one of his big toes amputated in the last year for out-of-control diabetes, and one of the two other attorneys with whom my husband shares space—a liver-transplant survivor. Just lovely.

As soon as he left, I called his secretary to warn her that I'd been sick, possibly with COVID, and for her own safety, she should stay the hell away from my husband. Then I figured I'd better get tested. I tried repeatedly to get through to Beaumont's coronavirus hotline, provided by the local hospital offering the curbside testing, to find out how to go about this. No one picked up.

I had intended to wait for my husband to get home, thinking I'd get my phone charger from his car before I left, but at 5:30, I gave up. I pulled out of my driveway at 5:32 and by 5:40 was at Royal Oak's Beaumont Hospital. I found the end of a line I assumed was for COVID-19 testing because I had never seen any sort of line before in the hospital parking lot. The line of cars was so long that I could not determine how it wound around or where it ended. I had with me my cell phone, but not my phone's car charger, a filled water bottle, but no Clorox wipes—and not enough hand sanitizer to make safe use of the porta-potty that I eventually spotted (after all, I was in line with scores of people like me, all of whom suspected they were carrying COVID-19). Also no food, no book to read, no laptop on which to work. I would never have guessed, pulling up behind the last car in line when I arrived at the testing site, how late it would be before I left.

Five and a half hours later, after racking up more points on the Duolingo French app on my phone than I ever had in one day before—stopping only when my phone's charge was down to 3 percent—I finally was second in line at the first station of six at the curbside clinic. At that point, the passengers in the car in front—this car had been in front of me the whole time—were sent on their way without being tested. They apparently did not qualify. I moved up and had my vitals taken. My temperature was normal. Uh-oh. Next, I was interviewed by a tall, gangly physician's assistant who, with his hospital gown blowing around him in the wind, determined that I was eligible for the test. (Why? The symptoms I related? My age? What?) Then I was registered, swabbed once in each nostril for influenza A and B, RSV, and COVID-19, braceleted with a barcode mirroring the one attached to my test vials, and finally discharged after receiving several pages of further instructions. I pulled away from the hospital at 11:30 and was home by 11:40.

I had a midnight dinner of chili with a glass or two of Cabernet and went to bed at 12:30, sleeping until 9:00 the next morning.

I awoke with even the headache gone. I suspect I will remember for the rest of my life the extent of my gratitude, as I sat on the edge of my bed with my feet on the cool hardwood floor, when I realized that I felt normal. Perfectly normal.

What does this story in the time of COVID have to do with a silver maple tree? The day I was tested, March 16, Michigan's Governor Gretchen Whitmer's Executive Order 2020-9 had closed down restaurants, cafés, coffee houses, bars (including Irish bars, of course; it was the day before St. Patrick's Day), taverns, brewpubs, distilleries, clubs, movie theaters, indoor and outdoor performance venues, gymnasiums, fitness centers, recreation centers, indoor sports facilities, indoor exercise facilities, exercise studios, spas, and casinos. The day after I was tested, the day I was relieved to feel normal again, was St. Patrick's Day. At the end of perhaps our first St. Patrick's Day together without a Guinness toast, my husband and I decided to go out for a walk.[2]

This was my first time outside since my breathless walk to the mailbox had so alarmed me. We walked west on our boulevard, which this day appeared even more beautiful to me, and cut up south into the neighborhood to Waterworks Park, where we sat atop a picnic table, our faces tipped up to Michigan's March sun, and FaceTimed with our grandchildren in North Carolina.

---

2 How many "COVID-inspired" end-of-the day walks have we, as of March 17, 2022, taken in the past two years?

Then, as we walked through the park toward home, I noticed a large tree just outside of the fenced tennis courts. Suddenly, I was outside of myself and our world's current crisis because at that moment I noticed an attribute that just the spring before I would have identified as this tree "being in bud." To me, this phrase would have indicated that the buds of the new *leaves* were becoming visible in advance of opening up. "In bud" to me would have referred to the time just before the tree "leafed out."[3]

But I knew more about trees this day than I had the year before. Paying attention to what I was seeing, I knew this tree, by the architecture of its trunk, to be a silver maple, a member of the tree species that my neighbor to the east has at the apex of her curved driveway. And this silver maple was not "in bud." It was *flowering*. One long branch was curved down right before my eyes as if to show me. The tree's red and yellow flowers struck me at the moment as intricately wrought, exotic. How had I ever missed them in all the years of my life?

In my journal on March 17, 2020, the date of this walk, of this noticing, after learning more about the flowering of silver maples, I wrote:

> *The silver maple is, in fact, one of the first trees to bloom in the spring here in the eastern United States, here in Michigan, here in Oakland County, here in Royal Oak, here in the Forest Heights neighborhood, my neighborhood. Where I am still living. As in: where I am still alive. It's the first tree I've seen this year, the only tree I see, flowering here now.*
>
> *This silver maple is blooming in Michigan the same week that COVID-19 is beginning to bloom in the Detroit tri-county area,*

---

3 Later, when I googled the phrase "tree in bud," I discovered that the first seventeen hits of my search referred to a term in radiology: "a finding on a CT scan that indicates some degree of airway obstruction," which might suggest a cause of breathlessness.

of which Royal Oak is a part. This day when I noticed the silver maple flowering is St. Patrick's Day, almost two months after the first U.S. case of the novel coronavirus (SARS-CoV-2) was confirmed on January 21, 2020, one week after Michigan confirmed its first case, and the day after I was tested for the virus. The day I recovered from whatever I had and felt perfectly normal. Such immense gratitude!

As far as I know, this silver maple—which I've *visited* in all its seasons since witnessing its flowering in March 2020—as far as I can imagine, had then, and has today, no idea of what's going on in the world of humans. I find this very comforting. We are only one part—granted, the most destructive part—of this planet. We are only one part of a much larger whole. In *The Songs of Trees*, David George Haskell writes:

Although tree trunks seemingly stand as detached individuals, their lives subvert this atomistic view. We're all—trees, humans, insects, birds, bacteria—pluralities. Life is embodied network. These living networks are not places of omnibenevolent Oneness. Instead, they are where ecological and evolutionary tensions between cooperation and conflict are negotiated and resolved. These struggles often result not in the evolution of stronger, more disconnected selves but in *the dissolution of the self into relationship* [emphasis added].

In this time of distancing, when individual survival means severing our networks of friends, family members, and colleagues in the world, it is reassuring to remember, as Native Americans well understood, that *all of life is networked*, not just humans. All living things on Earth are in relationship.

This pandemic most likely won't wipe humans off the Earth. Even if such human devastation were to happen in the near future, this particular silver maple would survive. Silver maples will continue to flower in late winter or early spring on planet Earth, regardless of COVID-19, with or without the presence of humans, with or without you and me.

12

Heartwood

The Sweetgum

(*Liquidambar styraciflua*)

My first grandchild, my dear granddaughter Avery Grace, was born on December 3, 2015. When we got the call, my husband and I speed-walked the two miles of pre-dawn DC streets from my oldest daughter's apartment, where we'd been waiting, to the George Washington University Hospital to attend the birth. We returned to Michigan to celebrate Christmas with my parents but made the trip to North Carolina in January to help Meagan get settled in her new apartment with her husband and to celebrate Avery Grace's first-month birthday.

On that January visit, hoping to get Avery Grace to nap by walking and singing her to sleep in my arms for the first time, I walked us away from the other three occupants of the apartment into the guest bedroom. In the course of completing a very small L-shaped circuit around two sides of the double bed, I paused and looked out of the third-story window facing east. A birdfeeder hung from the porch frame of a first-floor apartment a distance from my daughter's place. Birds were flying to and fro but were hard to see well from so far away. Also in my line of vision, in front of the same apartment building but closer, was one lone tree. This full-crowned deciduous tree was smaller than the tall straight pine trees in the Duke Forest that filled the view from all the other apartment windows, which faced north.

I was trying to remember the lyrics, find my way to the tune of "Summertime" as I periodically looked out of the window into the wintry afternoon. Eventually, I turned so that Avery Grace was facing the window. At some point, I realized that a very alert Avery Grace appeared to be actually looking out the window. She seemed to be focusing on the same tree I'd noticed planted between the two apartment buildings. I walked away from the window and then, after another few tight circuits, back, to confirm her interest.

It was a very gray day. Was it just the natural light framed by the window she was turning to, as a plant would, perhaps? Then I looked closer at the singular tree on which she seemed so focused. On the branches of the tree, hundreds of small balls swayed gently in a breeze. Could it be the motion of the balls? She was just five weeks old. She couldn't possibly be seeing the motion of those balls on that tree so far off in the distance, could she? And if she were, how was she interpreting this sight? What message was the tree sending? What message might she be receiving?

Her apparent interest in whatever she was seeing out that window snagged my own curiosity. What was the name of that tree with little balls that stay on through the winter? We had one back home in Michigan on the edge of our front yard. Later that evening, after my sweet granddaughter was asleep, the tree's name came to me: sweetgum. I didn't know then that the tree belonged in North Carolina, but not in Michigan; the sweetgum tree is a southern tree.

In March 2015, when I came back to Durham for another visit, I joined my daughter and Avery Grace for their daily walks on the trails in the Duke Forest. Here on the forest trail, from within the front carrier my daughter wore, Avery Grace gazed up past her mom's face, up and up the long straight trunks reaching to evergreen tops far away in the blue sky. As I tried to parse the subject of her interest, this tree became a focus of my attention, too. I couldn't remember ever seeing a tree with such a long straight trunk ending in a peculiar bristly bottle-brush of needles far above the rest of the forest canopy. What were these trees with which Avery Grace appeared so fascinated? Along the trail, we came to an interpretive sign identifying the trees as loblolly pines (*Pinus taeda*). My daughter and I theorized that the name might refer to their resemblance to lollipops: the long straight stick, the ball-shaped evergreenery topping it. I didn't learn until later that "loblolly" is a common word in the southern states for a mire or mudhole. Mud-hole pines? Yep, it turns out that the loblolly pine is found primarily in lowlands and swampy areas.

It had become clear to me that Avery Grace, the daughter of a particularly curious and observant mother—who had grown from a child exhibiting these two traits to become both a scientist and an artist—seemed to have a special interest in trees. And I wondered, why does Avery Grace appear to bestow such interest—which appeared so intense to make me imagine love—on trees? At the point when I first asked the question on paper to myself, when she was fifteen months old, she wasn't telling. But now, with Avery Grace in her fifth year, I wonder about the timing.

A book I'd written about Great Lakes islands was in the process of being published while Avery Grace and I watched the sway of the sweetgum balls that first winter day alone together. Avery Grace—her birth, her being, me becoming a grandmother—compelled me for the first time to consider what I might write next. Her apparent regard for trees made me curious enough to learn about the two species toward which her attention had first gravitated: the sweetgum and the loblolly pine. Her interest and my love for her initially translated into a fierce notion to write the text of a picture book about trees and dedicate it to Avery Grace.

I had never heard of a loblolly pine tree before Avery Grace, and all I had known of sweetgum trees was that the one out my window had particularly beautiful multi-colored leaves in the fall and little balls hanging from it during the winter that became a spiny hazard to bare feet in the summer after they'd fallen.

In the beginning of my search for facts about either of "Avery Grace's trees," I consulted the Cat in the Hat's Learning Library *I Can Name 50 Trees Today!*, a book Avery Grace—with her mom's help, of course—had given me for my sixty-third birthday after I'd shared my interest in writing a book about trees. The flyleaf of my copy of this kids' book about trees bears the inscription: "Happy Birthday, Grammy MoMo! Love, Avery Grace." While the loblolly pine didn't make it into that book, drawings of the habit, bark, and leaf of the "Sweet Gum" (written as two words in the book) are shown. The sweetgum leaf is held aloft by the character of Sally's brother in one hand; in his other hand is a star. The sweetgum pictures are accompanied by rhyming text about leaves:

> *Like your ears, some have lobes,*
> *which means that they are*
> *shaped a lot like your hand,*
> *or a mitten, or a star.*

The sweetgum's star-shaped leaves blaze with wide variations of beautiful color in the fall; sometimes many colors appear on one individual leaf: yellow, orange, red, purple. But the most interesting feature of the trees is their unusual-appearing dry fruit. One-inch brown balls covered in tiny spiny structures, they sway on long stalks that hang from odd corky-winged twigs off short gray horizontal branches. While one landscaping book from an earlier generation warns against planting a sweetgum near walks to prevent turned ankles—which speaks to the hardness of the balls—I know them intimately from the sharpness of their little spikes pressing into my bare feet on the way to my front border garden. I recently picked one of the balls from the many scattered on my January lawn. Under my hand magnifier, its pairs of spiky horns are open, beak-like, on opposite sides of dark irregular little empty cavities, which the preceding year would have been sealed shut, containing the tree's seeds.

My pursuit of trees was briefly interrupted in 2018. I did write a second book and dedicated it to Avery Grace and her brother, Caden Daly, who had joined the family that year, but it wasn't a picture book; it was a juvenile nonfiction book, and it wasn't about trees but about the Great Lakes. And then, when I returned to trees, the book became something else, became what this is.

Sweetgum trees are not common to Michigan, but here, nonetheless, one is growing alongside my neighbor's gravel driveway. Across the drive from this sweetgum is an eastern white pine (*Pinus strobus*). While the eastern white pine is not a loblolly pine, it is a relative of those trees in Avery Grace's forest. The white pine reaches over the drive south to the sun and provides a lovely dark green backdrop for the sweetgum, especially in the fall when the sweetgum radiates its colors. Come winter, I can't see the bobbing ornaments on the sweetgum without thinking of my dear granddaughter, who is responsible, after all these years, for returning me to trees.

From our respective windows—655 miles apart as the crow flies—we look out to different individual trees but to the same stars, the deep heart of our connection steady and strong.

13

Massacre in the Grove

The American Beech

(*Fagus grandifolia*)

More than four years after it is over, after it cannot be undone, I still stop breathing, hold my breath, when the memory stirs. What I exhale: rage, sadness, guilt.

The day I began trying to tell this story, I was overcome by a disabling anxiety—which at first I didn't recognize. That first day, I started searching my cell phone for photos to pinpoint dates for a timeline . . . and found myself instead culling through personal photos from the previous seven years. Distraction. Once I got back to the task at hand, I was surprised to find myself hungry for lunch two hours early, apparently needing a break. That evening at dinner, I poured myself a second glass of wine.

With new resolve the next day, I went looking for the pertinent documents on my laptop . . . only realizing, after almost an hour had passed, that I had somehow gotten caught up in reorganizing the document files in my computer directory. I knew what I most needed to do was go down to the basement to gather the journals from those four years. I did get down the stairs but never made it to the bookshelf where they reside . . . instead finally packing holiday decorations, which had been down there in piles for almost two months, away in their red plastic tubs.

Day 3, I just didn't make it to my desk.

And this inertia six years after it all began, over three years since the massacre occurred. Am I able to tell this story?

Breathe.

For the first few months after we moved to Royal Oak's Vinsetta Boulevard in July 2006, my husband and I took our mugs of coffee out into the soft summer mornings of our backyard to take in early birdsong with our caffeine. Even now, this memory of moisture-laden air caressing my arms and shoulders under the neighborhood's canopy of trees transports me to a magical otherworldly place.

Experiencing this sensation in our backyard, on our block, can *only* happen in memory now.

For over a decade after we moved here, through August 2017, the western portion of a grove of American beech trees—in which the houses of our block of the Forest Heights subdivision were nestled—was what I saw from the long wall of windows in our bedroom as I pulled up the shades after sunrise. The silhouette of this beech canopy was the last outdoor sight I took in before lowering the shades every evening. During the nights, owls called into my dreams from this grove.

Because beech trees stand so straight and tall, they are what come to my mind when I think of the Standing Nation.[1] Like elephants, beech trees are magnificent creatures in silvery-gray skin, beings who

---

1 Many Native American tribes refer to trees as members of the Standing Nation. Robin Wall Kimmerer, an American Distinguished Teaching Professor of environmental and forest biology and a member of the Citizen Potawatomi Nation, has written, "Traditional cultures . . . recognize that human people are only one manifestation of intelligence in the living world. Other beings, from Otters to Ash trees, are understood as persons, possessed of their own gifts, responsibilities, and intentions. This is not some kind of mistaken anthropomorphism. Trees are not misconstrued as leaf-wearing humans but respected as unique, sovereign beings equal to or exceeding the power of humans" ("Hearing the Language of Trees," in *The Mind of Plants: Narratives of Vegetal Intelligence*, ed. John C. Ryan, Patricia Viera, and Monica Galiano [Santa Fe: Synergetic, 2021], https://www.yesmagazine.org/environment/2021/10/29/hearing-the-language-of-trees).

live together in community. Who often live *hundreds of years* together in community.

The first sign of a threat to this community of beech came toward the end of February 2014 in the form of a postcard in my mailbox. Sent from the Zoning Board of Appeals for the City of Royal Oak, the card notified neighbors within three hundred feet of 2833 Vinsetta Boulevard of a public hearing on March 13, 2014. A realtor and his partner, as "Petitioners and Owners," were requesting that the Zoning Board of Appeals "overturn the Zoning Administrator's determination that the proposed land division does not comply with the definition of lot width in order to allow the petitioner to create 4 separate lots at 2833 Vinsetta Blvd."

Turns out the new "neighbor"—who had purchased the 1,875-square-foot 1947 ranch home on Royal Oak's iconic boulevard from Diane for $317,000 on February 22, 2013—was, in fact, a realtor who was planning to demolish the house he'd purchased a year ago and *subdivide the one residential lot into four building lots*. In February 2014, there was one house and a portion of a grove of mature beech trees on that lot.

And no chemical residue. For twenty-eight years, Diane had used no chemicals inside her house or outside in her yard. Mr. Realtor, apparently wanting to make sure she accepted his offer because he was the kind of potential buyer she'd want to sell to, had claimed in a letter to Diane that he needed to purchase a chemical-free lot for his epileptic golden retriever.[2]

The day we got the postcard, circa February 20, 2014, I took Baron, my elderly beagle, out for a walk past the address in question, trying to imagine four houses where there now was one. I was walking by the house four doors west of mine, right next to Mr. Realtor's house, when the woman who lived there, whom I'd never met before, pulled up and went to the mailbox to collect her mail. I walked up her drive

---

2 As one online reviewer of Mr. Realtor put it: "Terrible that you lied about your sick dog when u [*sic*] bought 2833 [V]insetta only to tear it down."

and introduced myself to her (Libby), asking if she'd gotten a postcard from the city. She looked at the pile of mail in her hand. She had. This was the first spark of a long and very expensive fight.

Libby, her husband Steve, their next-door neighbor Gary, and I went door-to-door the next Saturday, a very snowy day, canvassing neighbors to get promises to show up at the public hearing, promises from neighbors on both Vinsetta Boulevard and Webster Road, the street to the north that faced the backyard of Mr. Realtor's lot.

The standing-room-only public hearing on March 13, 2014, at city hall had neighbors actually spilling out the door, down the stairs, and lining the halls, those outside the hearing room watching the proceedings via closed circuit monitors.

We won Round 1: Four lots would not replace the one.

Meanwhile, since submitting his original request for a variance, Mr. Realtor had purchased a *second* piece of property on Vinsetta Boulevard on December 19, 2013. This second house had not been listed for sale. Nonetheless, Mr. Realtor was able to buy it by literally—according to another neighbor who talked to the seller—offering a suitcase of cash containing $300,000 to the son of Mrs. M., the owner of 2825 Vinsetta Boulevard. Mr. Realtor told Mr. M. he planned to move his future mother-in-law into this second house to provide care for the children he and his fiancée intended to have. He was soon in possession of the 2,074-square-foot, 1947 ranch of a unique architectural style. This second house was right next to the house Mr. Realtor professed to be living in at 2833 while he allegedly claimed a second homestead in another Michigan suburb—where he was *actually* living—on his taxes as well.[3]

Once Mr. Realtor owned the property adjacent to his original purchase, he proposed to the City of Royal Oak a "mini-subdivision" of *eight* houses in place of the two homes and the over one dozen mature beech trees that were currently living on the two lots.

3 The source of this information was a Royal Oak city employee.

Here's a bit of good fortune. The parents of the woman who was on the west side of this second lot lived on our street too, on the other side of the next block west. They had lived there at least since the 1960s, and Bob S., a retired attorney, still had a folder dating from that time in a file cabinet in his garage that he pulled out and shared with me after dark one spring evening. From it, I learned that in the last century there had been a neighborhood association—Vinsetta Heights Property Owners Association—apparently formed expressly to create deed restrictions on what property owners could do with their property, after, perhaps (there is some evidence for this), another development fiasco. Without Bob, may he rest in peace, and his file, we never would have known.

We formed a board of directors and reinstituted the homeowners' association. At our first meeting we developed a two-part mission statement:

1. To act for and on behalf of lots in the Forest Heights Subdivision in the City of Royal Oak, Michigan and to enforce the covenants, conditions, and restrictions set forth in the Restrictions Agreement for said subdivision, as initially recorded on July 23, 1947, in Liber 2126, Pages 122–127 of the Oakland County Records, as well as the Amended Restrictions recorded on October 29, 1952, in Liber 2929, Pages 534–536 of the Oakland County Records.

2. To promote the common interests and welfare of the immediate community and protect its quality of life and character, in accordance with the restrictions of the property, zoning laws of the City of Royal Oak, Oakland County, and the general laws of the State of Michigan.

The first attorney we hired filed articles of incorporation for the Vinsetta Heights Property Owners Association (VHPOA) on March 18, 2014. With that, a three-and-a-half-year struggle, involving two hired and two volunteer attorneys and costing over $51,000—all raised from small individual donations of neighbors and the proceeds of five neighborhood garage sales—began.

Ultimately, and step-by-step, we were successful in ensuring that Mr. Realtor could not divide the two lots into eight lots, seven lots, six lots, or five lots.

But that's where our good fortune ended. At the end of 2016, Mr. Realtor was given the City of Royal Oak's blessing to subdivide the two lots into four building plots despite city commission members previously assuring the VHPOA they "had our back." Although two certified surveyors were willing to show that the measurements of the four lots did not meet the city's ordinances, just by the math on the resubmitted surveys alone—without even considering the actual measurements, which would likely also have presented a problem—it appeared the city could not pass up the additional forthcoming property tax dollars of a fourth lot, even though there really is only land enough for three lots.

However, the resulting public pressure led to additional public hearings before the planning commission on November 15, 2016, and January 10, 2017, both of which were standing-room-only events. On the eve of Valentine's Day 2017, the Royal Oak City Commission did pass a resolution to amend the zoning ordinance so that such a development deviation, such a neighborhood disaster, could not happen here again.

The amendment came too late for this particular beech grove.

On April 12, 2017, with the threat of bulldozers approaching to remove the houses, feeling both panicked and depressed as I tried to tamp my anxiety down, I wrote a spell, a prayer, in my journal:

An Arboreal Spell

This morning, I will write a spell. The screech owl at dusk above us on Bicycle Hill was, certainly, a harbinger. The cross Norma witnessed spread across the sky on her Saturday night walk home from the Shrine[4] *may well have been a portent. But this will be a prayer. What is a prayer if not an alignment? An alignment of forces for the Good.*

Long, long ago, here in this very place, a creek ran, Red Run, between banks through forest. I call upon the river now imprisoned underground to wash away the greed, the lies, the evil that has come to this place we call Forest Heights, we call Vinsetta Boulevard, we call home.

Today, I call upon the giants by whom I am surrounded: Sycamore and Honey Locust, Silver Maple and Oak, and Eastern White Pine, Hawthorn, and Sweetgum, as well as the understory Ginkgo, Forest Pansy Redbud, and Weeping Cherry. And Beech, dear, dear Beech.

While we, neighbors, move through our morning routines— workouts and showers, breakfasts and news, good-byes and commutes—I will write a spell, I will send a prayer up through your branches, just budding. Using the antennae of trunks to align the forces of Good.

I call upon the Trees to hear the words I write upon the remains of one of their kind, to draw from the earth and pull from the air: Justice. How things are to be now and forevermore. Recognize our covenant with the land and let it be unbroken.

On this week leading up to the Christian Easter, the Resurrection, please be our stalwart champions. Pass the message through your branches. Send the message from your roots through our feet and into our lungs.

We breathe out, you breathe in; you breathe out, we breathe in. Birdsong to bind the human will around this constellation for Good.

Thy will be done.

So be it; may it be so.

---

4 The National Shrine of the Little Flower Basilica Catholic Church, located at Twelve Mile Road and Woodward Avenue (M1) in Royal Oak.

Neither my words, secular or sacred, nor any magic I might control—any more than the actions we took or the money we spent—was strong enough to make a difference, to save the beech community.

On April 26, 2017, the two houses on the two originally plotted lots, which were—on paper—protected by deed restrictions and which were sheltered in among the beech community—were demolished. The two building lots were staked into four narrow, long plots of land. In order for the developers to make their investments profitable, they would need to build skinny, long houses that entirely filled each of the four lots. They would need to cut down the part of the beech grove reaching into the sky from these lots.

These beeches originally grew in a grove on the banks of the Red Run, getting their start before the south branch of the creek was put underground in the 1920s, before the subdivision of Forest Heights was platted in 1915, before Royal Oak was incorporated as a village in 1891, before H. Wood farmed his forty-two acres straddling the Red Run here, before Royal Oak became a township in 1832, before the first settlers arrived in 1820, before Royal Oak was given its name on one of the surveying expeditions led by territorial governor Lewis Cass in 1819.

The first week of August 2017, as the days dawned, the shapes of the majestic trees rose up, stepped out of the retreating night. One of those summer mornings, the air was still soft and caressed human skin with the beeches' exhalations for the last time.

The week chain saws massacred the portion of the beech community on those two lots, I was out of town in Estes Park, spending a week at a cabin under evergreen trees next to the rushing Big Thompson River—miles away from any American beech tree—on a long-anticipated vacation with sixteen members of my and my husband's family, including my dear twenty-month-old granddaughter, Avery Grace.

As far as I know, the beech trees were not even used for their beautiful wood but were chipped up and trucked away.

When I returned home, it was many, many days before I could walk or drive by the devastation left in place of the beautiful trees. The first photo shown here was taken in the summer of 2017 after the two houses had been demolished but before the trees were cut. The second was taken in the spring of 2022, four and a half years after the trees were cut, after the still-vacant fourth lot had changed hands three times.

One opening into the northwest corner of the former beech grove between Vinsetta Boulevard and W. Webster Road and between Marywood Drive and Beechwood Drive. Beeches are slow growing and live for three hundred to four hundred years. The two largest ones in this photo were not, by far, the largest beech trees of the grove. Notice that all of the saplings surrounding these two trees are also beeches.

"**$245,000** Vacant lot available for sale. . . . Build your custom dream home atop this hilltop setting facing prestigious Vinsetta Blvd. Lot is approximately .32 acres and 52' x 295' in depth with mature beach [*sic*] trees & dual road frontage."* This last lot sold on March 19, 2021, for $409,000. On April 20, 2022, fencing materials were dropped off on this fourth skinny lot to enclose it so that the building of a house could commence.

*   The developers knew the trees were "mature beech trees" because at the public hearings this was part of our neighborhood's argument against destruction of the natural area. However, they apparently didn't know how to spell the species' name and went with its homonym.

But before the beech trees were cut, I did learn what had caused the summer softness of the air in the neighborhood. In one growing season, one mature hundred-foot beech tree has about two hundred thousand leaves and can take in, through their roots,[5] eleven thousand gallons of water from the soil, releasing this into the air again as oxygen and water vapor through a process called transpiration. Together the four lots measure over an acre and a quarter, and that land was once home to at least a dozen mature beeches of that stature with—hard to say how many: one hundred? more?—smaller beech trees, with many, many saplings crowded together in families below, in the understory, as they would be in an undisturbed forest. The softness in the air was from the large amount of water and oxygen this community of beech trees was exhaling.

When I learned about transpiration, my thoughts went to the mature beech straddling the east property line of our backyard. This beech tree is the farthest southeastern remnant of the beech grove as I've known it. Yesterday, I walked around the block and counted all the beeches I could find, mapping their locations. Seventeen scattered beech trees remain on our double-length block, between the beech tree in our backyard and Bicycle Hill (also known as Marais Park). All of the seventeen are within the yards of eight of sixteen contiguous residential lots. While on this walk, it dawned on me for the very first time that just as I have been mourning the trees cut from the two large residential lots, surely, over the preceding century, many other beech trees were cut and mourned by other humans as well as by their remaining community of beech trees.

When our Vinsetta house was built in 1956, it was on a lot that had been shaved from a much larger lot, a split that may have, given the timing, been a part of the development that prompted the formation of the Vinsetta Heights Property Owners Association and the original

---

5 Beeches are monoecious, bearing both male and female flowers on the same tree. Hence my use of "their" as a nonbinary singular pronoun here.

1947 VHPOA deed restrictions being conveyed to those lots in the neighborhood whose owners agreed with and would sign on to them. This would have been after a developer bought my neighbor's 1933 Cape Cod from the widow of the original owner—the only house on our entire side of the block in 1936—and split the one large lot into *nine*. Many beech trees in the grove must have been cut in that development scheme. Even before the first house was built in the neighborhood, the streets surely displaced members of the beech community as well. Houses on Vinsetta are built into the former banks of the Red Run,[6] which now runs through a fifteen-foot diameter pipe in the center of the boulevard. Those banks certainly held more members of the grove. And before that, this land was settled by a farmer. As farmland, this land changed hands at least once, but in 1872, H. Wood farmed forty-two acres with the Red Run running through his acreage. Did this beech grove serve as his woodlot?

Each beech tree exhaling hundreds of gallons of water every day? I can't imagine what being in this long-gone larger grove must have felt like before the arrival of the streets and houses, or the quiet of the grove before the arrival of landscaping companies with blowers removing the fallen leaves of the relatively few remaining trees.

While reading everything I could find about the transpiration process, I was stopped by this:

Scientists from three institutions . . . listened more closely—literally. They registered a soft murmur in the trees. Above all, at night. At this time of day, most of the water is stored in the trunk,

6   "Run" means a small stream; it's a word that the settlers to Royal Oak, Michigan, primarily from New York but also from New England, brought with them. The Red Run is a sub-watershed of the Clinton River watershed, which via the Clinton River drains to Lake St. Clair and through the Detroit River drains into Lake Erie and eventually the Atlantic Ocean. When the neighborhood of Forest Heights was being developed, the Red Run became part of a large district storm and sanitary drain system.

as the crown takes a break from photosynthesis and hardly tran-
spires at all. The trees pump themselves so full of water their trunks
sometimes increase in diameter. The water is held almost completely immobile in the inner transportation tubes. Nothing flows.
So where are the noises coming from?

When this long-gone beech grove was intact, could the beech tree with
whom I now share land hear the murmurs of the other members of their
community at night? Did they murmur back? Had the mycorrhizal fungal mycelium from the most recently decimated portion of the grove—
five residential lots down—reached as far as to the roots of the beech tree
that is my backyard neighbor? How did those murmurs and that underground network affect the lone beech in my yard? How has the silencing
of those murmurs, the severing of that network, affected my backyard
neighbor the beech tree?

Asking these questions caused my emotions to shift from rage at
the developer and the city's greed, from my guilt that I hadn't done
more, from deep and abiding sadness at the loss of the beech trees,
whose habits in all seasons were breathtaking, whose canopy at all
times of day was magnificent . . . to trying to imagine what such a loss,
piled on the earlier losses of family, friends, community members, must
have meant for my arboreal neighbor.

What would the loss of community mean for the beech who lives
between my neighbor's backyard and mine, this beech who once lived
in a beech grove stretching at least a double block before there were
blocks to constrain it?

What *must* such loss mean to my neighbor the beech tree?

The night after I ask these questions, I listen hard in the night for
murmurs of the beech tree across the yard from my bedroom's French
doors. I hear none.

But in the morning, on the doors' threshold, like a letter delivered,
a single gold beech leaf.

14

Rocky Mountain High

The Colorado Pinyon

(*Pinus edulis*)

On my first visit to my youngest daughter's new house in Denver, I had noticed the tree as a green shadow through a steamed-up bathroom window. On this subsequent trip, after I'd been at the Cherry Bean Café to read and write while Caitlin was at work, I walked back to her house on the street behind hers, so I could check out the demolition of a brick bungalow that was happening that day. From the street I used to get around the block back to her house, the shape of this tree of the green shadow, just one yard over from the side street, stopped me. With my phone's camera, I snapped a picture of this stalwart bristly evergreen emerging from behind a plethora of overhead electrical wires. Now I had a photo to enlarge. That was the start of it.

Putting a name to the evergreen tree next door to Caitlin and Andrew's Denver house took me a few days, days that included a search for Caitlin and Andrew's binoculars and the discovery—given that I was without my tree books from home—of arborday.org, which among other bits of tree information provides a wonderful online tree identifier, "Tree Identification: *What Tree Is That?*" This illustrated, step-by-step guide branches through a series of yes and no questions toward the species' name of any tree you'd want to identify.

Like the loblolly pine of North Carolina, the state where my other daughter, Meagan, and her family live, Caitlin's next-door neighbor's evergreen tree looks very foreign to the eyes of a Michigander. Evergreen trees in Michigan woods and forests—specimens of different pines, larches, hemlocks, firs, spruces, cedars, cypress, and junipers—are prevalent both in our national and state forests and as landscaping accents. But to someone from Michigan, this Colorado evergreen tree stands out. The tree is much bristlier than anything in my neck of the woods, bristly around each branch like the contents of the Fuller Brush man's cases he opened in the 1950s on the living room floor of our Detroit house: bottle brushes, toilet brushes, all kinds of brushes. A bushy, bristly tree.

What originally led me off the trail of correctly identifying this tree became clear when I realized, from a second-floor vantage point over the privacy fence, that the brick bungalow next door had an addition tacked onto the back. It appeared the addition came after the tree was established. The tree must have held a special place in someone's heart—not only had it been allowed to continue growing, it also appears that the tree may have prescribed the dimensions of this addition. However, as a result of its proximity to the house, the tree's lower branches had been removed. This, in effect, had removed the "gnarl" from the tree, "gnarliness" typically being one of this species' main features. Even from my position on my daughter's third-floor balcony, the tree, rising up from the other side of a six-foot privacy fence, was still taller than I was, and from there, I could see some twisting—some gnarl—in its upper branches, which added to its full bristly habit.

I had intended to find a Colorado tree to identify on our hike to North Table Mountain on Saturday, figuring there'd be trees on the mesa—I was wrong—but there were trees along the trail. However, by the time I'd made their passing acquaintance, my curiosity had been snagged by trying to figure out what that landscaping remnant back in the neighborhood was. I started reading about conifers.

Later that afternoon, a great wind came through. Saturday morning, when I went to let their dog NOTAM[1] out, there on the back deck was a gift, a key: a very small, odd pinecone.

That night I heard—or dreamed I heard—an owl calling from what I now knew was a Colorado pinyon.

Caitlin Skye, my dear youngest daughter, lives so far away that some of the trees growing there are different from those growing around me. When I am overwhelmed by sadness, by the pain of missing her, by the long distance away she is, so far from the Great Lakes, on the other side of the Mississippi River and into the Rocky Mountain region that, in this time of COVID, I've not been in her physical presence for over a year ... It's then that I think back beyond my grandparents' branches of the family tree to my great-great-grandparents, most of whom left their homes across the Atlantic Ocean to come to this country and start a new part of the family story. Those ancestors left parents and grandparents behind, never to see them again. No Zoom or FaceTime sessions, no long-distance telephone calls, just the possibility of writing letters, and the probability of long spaces in between letter and reply.

How did the physical distance between both my daughters and me come to be? When my daughters finished their undergraduate education under either Michigan or Ohio trees, they both ended up living in a state other than Michigan. At one time, while they were in graduate school, they both lived in North Carolina, still in the eastern United States but southeast from Royal Oak's USDA Hardiness Zone 6a to Durham, North Carolina's Hardiness Zone 7b,[2] a move of one (10 degrees Fahrenheit) zone south; more exactly, this is considered a move of three (5 degrees Fahrenheit) sub-zones. Trees used for landscaping there include more magnolia, rhododendron, and azalea,

---

1 NOTAM (pronounced "*no*-tum") means "notice to air missions"; both Caitlin and her husband are pilots.

2 The thirteen U.S. hardiness zones are based on the average annual extreme minimum temperature during the past thirty-year period determined by the U.S. Department of Agriculture (USDA).

all of which grow much larger and appear much happier than they do in Michigan. But it is the forests that look the most different to me. Loblolly pine trees—tall straight trees with all their branches at the top, a perfect bottlebrush habit—are the dominant species in the Duke Forest in the Durham area.

After graduating from Duke's law school, my younger daughter moved back to the Midwest, to Chicago, for her first job, and then on to Denver (Hardiness Zone 5b), where, to balance her intense work-life, she's enjoyed the outdoors over the last five years in very different landscapes from those in which she grew up. In 2017, she and her husband bought a second home in Leadville, Colorado, where they trained to compete to earn Leadman/Leadwoman status.[3] Known as the Two-Mile-High City, Leadville is the (incorporated) city with the highest elevation in the United States (10,152 feet) and is in Hardiness Zone 4b (the average annual minimum temperature is –25 to –20 degrees Fahrenheit).

The view at the end of their street in Leadville is of Mount Massive, the second-highest summit of the Rocky Mountains of North America and the state of Colorado; the highest summit, Mount Elbert, only 12 feet higher at 14,440 feet, is just south of it. Both mountains are part of the Sawatch Range and the Mount Massive Wilderness. There, in addition to the Colorado pinyon, are the evergreen trees Coloradans know as bristlecone pine, limber pine, lodgepole pine, ponderosa pine, Colorado blue spruce, Engelmann spruce, Douglas-fir,[4] subalpine fir, white fir, and Rocky Mountain juniper. Deciduous narrowleaf

---

3   The Leadman Race Series consists of a progressive series of five endurance events, each completed within a specified time cutoff, over two months, all held in the nation's highest city: the Leadville Trail Marathon, the choice of the Silver Rush 50-mile run or 50-mile MTB (mountain-bike race), the Leadville Trail 100 MTB (a 100-mile MTB), the Leadville 10K Run (the day after the 100 MTB), and the Leadville Trail 100 Run (a 100-mile trail run).

4   A Douglas-fir was the second species I identified on another Colorado trip; there is one growing in the corner of the tiny front yard on 6th Street in Leadville. The best identifying factor according to Arbor Day Foundation's *What Tree Is That?* (if you can see a cone): "See the 'mouse' scurry for cover between the cone scales!" Exactly.

cottonwood, plains cottonwood, and quaking aspen crowd the mountain slopes as well.

But those trees were all just dark shapes on dark mountains in the hours before dawn on August 18, 2019.

We'd flown out Wednesday, the 14th, so I could acclimate first at Denver's mile-high elevation in order to prevent the altitude sickness I'd experienced on our trip up in March 2018, when we went directly up to Leadville upon landing.

In August 2018, Caitlin had successfully completed the first two of the four necessary races that preceded the one-hundred-mile run: the trail marathon and the fifty-mile run. She was on her way to qualifying for Leadwoman status, but then, during the one-hundred-mile bike trail race the Saturday before the run, she missed a time cutoff around mile 70 and was pulled from the course. She walked the 10K run the day after, but on the day of the Leadville Trail 100 Run, she fell at mile 9, hurting her leg, and although she made it sixty-five more miles—to mile 74—she could no longer run or, for that matter, walk at that point. After having to abort the run, she had been in a cast, completed a lot of physical therapy, and tried some alternative therapies before beginning to run again, then train, and finally compete.

In 2019, when we had boarded our flight, I texted Caitlin to tell her we were on our way and was alarmed when she responded that she was at a doctor's office, not a place Caitlin is commonly found. She reported she'd been tired Sunday night, woke up feeling sick Monday morning, and felt worse Tuesday, so she headed to a doctor in Leadville to be checked out, given that the race was just three days away.

My husband, Craig, and I were up in Leadville in time to accompany Caitlin to pick up her race packet for the Leadville Trail 100 Run at the Lake County High School on Friday, a hot, sunny day. That night, in the two-bedroom, 980-square-foot house, all of us who had volunteered to be members of Caitlin's support crew tried to fall asleep early, alarms set for 3:00 a.m. Craig, from whom she gets her athletic ability, and I were the only "newbies" to the race. Caitlin's husband Andrew is an ultra-runner who, having completed all five events, won the title of Leadman in 2018 and may aim for it again in 2021.[5] Andrew's parents Carol and Dan (Dan has run marathons with Caitlin and Andrew) had crewed for Caitlin and Andrew in 2018, including Dan serving as a pacer running alongside Caitlin—as did Caitlin's friend Paul and her sister-in-law Sarah—in the second half of the race for ten-mile stretches. This year, Caitlin would also have three pacers in different legs after mile 50 of the race: her friend Emily, father-in-law Dan, and husband Andrew.

Very early the morning of August 17, Andrew added the refrigerated items to the cooler they'd packed the night before, while Caitlin posed for photos in her running shorts, to which was pinned her bib number, 820. She strapped on her hydration vest containing two bottles of water while the rest of us bundled up in layers against the 31-degree cold; temperatures for the runners over the next thirty hours would be all over the thermometer, between 23 and 73 degrees, depending on elevation as well as where the sun was in the sky. At 3:30 a.m. we all walked uphill less than two blocks from her Leadville house, crossing Pine Street, to the starting line. In addition to us, most of the 831 entrants, also with crew members in tow, were funneling onto 6th Street. The best-known ultra-run on Earth, also known as The Race Across the Sky (because it's run in the mountains), was about to begin.

With the shot of a gun at 4:00 a.m., the over eight hundred runners from all over the world began taking off—Caitlin crossed the starting line at 4:00:09—heading west under the "Leadville Trail 100 Run" banner at the head of 6th Street, headlamps bobbing cheerfully in time to their confident strides in the dark. If today were to end like all the other race days since the race began in 1983, fewer than

---

· 5 Andrew came in 62nd out of 678 runners in the 2021 Leadville Trail 100 Run with a time of 24:43:39, improving his 2018 time by just over 3.75 hours.

half the runners would make it back, running east under what would then be the finish-line banner within the thirty-hour cutoff time. By 4:02, I was struggling to keep sight of Caitlin's back as she ran under a streetlight and headed out of town, running toward the challenge of climbing and descending 15,600 feet on an out-and-back course over rugged trails and dirt roads, on which she'd be traversing elevations ranging from 9,200 to 12,620.

Now began the scramble for us, half her crew, to pile into Andrew's truck and catch her at the first ascent of the race. We drove around Turquoise Lake on a gravel road, parked in the dark at the bottom of a steep trail, and watched for her to come up the road in the dark, in the midst of a much smaller group of bobbing headlamps; she had pulled ahead of the crowd significantly already. Because this was not an aid station, few other spectators were there. We cheered her on as she left the gravel road and headed onto a steep uphill trail going into the forest in the dark.

Then we scrambled back into the truck, north up the east end of Turquoise Lake and west along its long north shore to May Queen, the first official aid station of the race. The full moon was fading behind evergreen trees on the mountain across the trail from us when we arrived. Before 6:00 a.m., we were jockeying for a good spot along the asphalt trail, 12.6 miles out from the start. Here, the runners were filing through the spectator-lined asphalt trail one at a time, some with their headlamps still lit. At 6:10 a.m., Caitlin grinned in recognition of our enthusiastic ringing of cowbells as she passed between the markers that picked up the electronic chip in her bib, recording her as having crossed that first checkpoint in the race. She was still running a little fast, doing ten-minute miles. She slowed to a walk, but barely stopped as we helped her quickly select energy snacks from the canvas wagon we'd brought and offered her all we could in the way of encouragement. The sun was due to rise at 6:20 a.m., but by then, Caitlin was long gone in the cold dark, with miles to go.

It was beginning to warm up at 8:17 when Caitlin passed under the inflatable structure at the Outward Bound aid station at mile 23.5 (just 2.7 miles shy of a marathon). Here the trail crosses a wide field of grass, a favorite habitat of prairie dogs, whose holes are famous for twisting runners' ankles. She stopped for a can of Coke and a handful of chips. Emily, a running friend who would later serve as her pacer, was at this stop. Andrew, wearing his Leadville Finisher zip-up, walked through the station with Caitlin as she headed back out, offering his counsel.

We were in two vehicles for the day, and while Andrew saw her at the Half Pipe aid station, 29.3 miles out, Andrew's parents, Craig, and I didn't see Caitlin again until Twin Lakes, which is both the (approximate) 40- and 60-mile marker. Caitlin reached Twin Lakes at 11:24, sat down for the first time, and took off her socks. Emily and her husband Ryan, also a runner, taped her toes while Caitlin munched on snacks. Emily worked on her quad muscles with a tiger-tail roller while Caitlin had a mini-Coke, and Ryan put her socks and shoes back on. Within ten minutes, she was back on the trail with Andrew walking alongside, giving her more encouragement and advice. The next time we'd see her, she would have been through the hardest part of the race and would be more than halfway through. We watched Andrew wish her well and then she headed out, amid a dwindling line of runners, toward the tree line and on to Hope Pass, the crux of the race, alone. In the four hours between her departure from and her return to Twin Lakes, clouds billowed above the mountains, a wind gusted up, pushing at the awnings crew members had set up, and the temperature dropped as the sun sank behind a mountain, leaving a pink glow framing the mountaintop's darkening silhouette.

Before her return to the Twin Lakes aid station, Caitlin would wade across four or five ice-cold streams at the course's lowest elevation (9,200 feet), some of which, this year, were as deep as mid-thigh, make her way up the Hope Pass vertical climb, stop at the Hope Pass aid station (some racers have named it the "Hopeless" aid station), where the llamas who bring the supplies to this point graze, just below the 12,600-foot summit of Hope Pass, climb back down, cross the Continental Divide, and reach the race's halfway point at Winfield (elevation: 10,200 feet), where Emily would be, waiting to pace her from mile 50 back, inbound. And then turn around to climb back up and down the same steep vertical pass and cross the same four or five icy streams.

Despite Emily's pacing and coaching, Caitlin arrived at 8:10 p.m. in rough shape. Her quad muscles and IT-bands[6] had seized up; the pain in her knees was "killing" her. Given the icy water, the twice up and down of the steep ascent and descent of the pass, and the thin air, this should have been no surprise. This was the only time she expressed any doubt about continuing, about finishing. While others got her into dry socks and shoes, Craig and I massaged her thighs. I asked her how she'd feel, afterward, if she stopped now. She appeared to make a mental shift, suited up for the dropping temperatures, hydrated, downed more snacks, and within fifteen minutes was on her way.

I am telling you all this so you can get a feel for what this race demands of a runner, and so you can imagine, perhaps, being a spectator who is the mother of a beloved runner. You need to have some understanding of this if you are to understand what happened next.

Just over twenty-four hours into the race, the crew members who were not sleeping or pacing Caitlin were in a truck headed back to May Queen, now the last official aid station. Had it been light, we would have seen the Mount Massive Wilderness stretching out below us for almost fifty square miles. But it was pitch black, except for the lights of mostly pickup trucks, coming and going, occasionally illuminating the forested foothills rising high from both sides of the narrow gravel road.

---

6 The iliotibial (IT) band is a long piece of connective tissue that runs along the outside of your leg from the hip to the knee and shinbone.

We got out of the truck, lifted out the cooler and the canvas wagon of snacks and supplies, and, loaded up with everything else we needed, started off toward the trail to await Caitlin. But I'd forgotten to bring my gloves and hat from the truck, and it was very cold.

I find myself going back to the truck to retrieve them alone. A lot of other people, so many people, had been pulling in when we arrived, but now absolutely no one is around. Just a long, dark row of empty parked pickups. Having been up now for over twenty-five hours, relatively active, and, of course, worried the entire time about Caitlin, I may be in a bit of an altered state of mind. So there's that to take into consideration.

All I know is this: on my way back to the truck, the forest rather suddenly leans in from each side of the road. I stop, not sure what is going to happen next. I feel like I have stepped into a dream. I know night animals are on the move in this wilderness forest: mountain lion, black bear, moose, elk, coyote, mule deer, mountain goat, porcupine, opossum, skunk, bat, and owl.

And so is my youngest daughter.

Stopped now, listening, I feel the soles of my feet through my hiking boots take root in the ground, as deeply as the roots of any of the pine, spruce, or fir. The trees lean in even closer. Time slows. I become aware on some wordless level of seismic signals. Of underground streams, fissures of steam, the static of fossil layers, subterranean mountains, slabs of rock plummeting, plates drifting, magma rising. After what feels like a very long time, I realize I've been holding my breath and take in a deep breath of the rich, calming scent of evergreen.

But before I can snap out of whatever trance has fallen over me, I realize I am aware of another breathing surrounding me. Is this what trees transpiring sound like? I don't have time to figure it out. In the breathing forest, I feel an expectation, a waiting, a listening. Outside of me.

I automatically send a fervent prayer straight up into dark tree shapes toward the cold stars . . . And immediately, I know that isn't where the listening is coming from. I redirect my prayer, deep down, through the soles of my feet to the massive network of roots, warm beneath the forest, the same network that Caitlin's feet are pulsing over—to the keepers of a closer knowledge, an older wisdom—a prayer to be with my fleet-footed, forest-running daughter, to keep her safe, to keep her strong.

Then suddenly at that moment, I snapped back from wherever I'd been. I realized I could entirely miss Caitlin coming through May Queen. She'd think I'd abandoned her at the race and had gone back to her house to sleep. Without locating our truck to get whatever it was I'd thought I needed, I turned and started back up the steep gravel road at a fast clip to catch up with the rest of the crew.

And that was when I felt it. For the first time in that long day—maybe since the first time I learned she was going to give the race another try—I felt both excited and relaxed. I was certain Caitlin and I were both where we were supposed to be and that everything was going to work out exactly the way it was meant to. I remember consciously wishing I could hang on to this unfamiliar feeling forever. Moving through that dark forest, I no longer felt alone; I felt like I had been heard and was seen. And it was abundantly clear to me, at the time, that whatever I was sensing was coming from the trees I was passing.

Trying to ward off the stitch developing in my side, I focused on a long-ago memory that just floated up to me, a memory from when I was very small, a "preacher's kid." My dad was the director of a summer church camp and my mom was the camp's arts and crafts instructor. One night my mom and some other people were taking me some-where; my dad was already where we were going. It was the first time I remember walking through woods in the dark. After what felt like a long walk, we came to a very large clearing with many people in it. A bonfire was roaring, the biggest fire I'd ever seen; it made me anxious.

The stars were silent but very sharp and too close; they scared me. A huge circle of campers, all much older than me, and their counselors were singing the hymn "Fairest Lord Jesus." The sound of their voices in the nighttime was heartbreakingly sweet and more than a little spooky. I recognized the song but was too young to join in, so maybe that is why I noticed the trees.

No one else seemed to be paying any attention to the trees surrounding us. The trees were leaning into the clearing in a friendly way, and had I understood the concept, known the word, I would have said they were the most reverent beings at the clearing that night. I was too young to explain, but I understood that the trees were very solid and somehow knew something important, I don't know what, but were helping me keep steady amid the intense emotional clamor of fire, stars, singing. They were keeping me safe from the hot and sharp and sweet of it. Later, the trees brushed their leaves against me as we went back through the woods to our cabins. Tired, with someone carrying me, I watched their comforting shapes go by in the dark as if in a dream.

I couldn't recall the last time I'd thought of that childhood experience in the clearing, probably the last time I heard "Fairest Lord Jesus" sung. But I was remembering it now, and at this very moment, on this Rocky Mountain road in the midst of forest, gratitude welled up again. Feeling a bit self-conscious, which was immediately overridden by a feeling of obligation, I whispered, "Thank you" up into the forest from the steep road. Tonight, I'd unexpectedly had the burden of the emotional clamor around my daughter's safety and success taken from me by something much larger and older than I, rooted in the ground, reaching for the sky.

The Japanese have a word for these unexplainable experiences: *Yūgen*. This word suggests "that which is beyond what can be said." "Mysterious grace." Those moments in life where what one is feeling transcends description. "*Yūgen* does not . . . have to do with some other world beyond this one, but rather with the depth of the world we live in, as experienced with the aid of a cultivated imagination."[7]

In my lifetime, I have been fortunate to experience moments of mysterious grace, the inexplicable synchronicity of human life, and sublime experiences of subjectivity and wonder . . . among others, at that campground clearing and in this mountain forest.

The rest of the race was exciting and fun. We cheered our racer on at two more unofficial spots as the sun rose in the midst of unbelievable beauty before heading back to the Leadville house. Shortly before 8:18 a.m. on August 18, 2019, Caitlin, wielding walking poles, crested the hill at the end of her street paced by Andrew and Dan. Her husband and father-in-law both fell away, while her dad and I hustled down 6th Street with her, tears in our eyes.

When she reached her house, just a block and a half from the finish line, she dropped her poles, grabbed the leash of a very happy NOTAM, and they both took off, joyfully running. Less than twenty-eight and a half hours after the gunshot had started the hundred-mile trail race, Caitlin—her smile oh, so wide—crossed the finish line running, triumphant.[8]

Minutes later, with the morning sunshine warming the mountain chill from our faces, we were all sitting on lawn chairs out in the street in front of Caitlin's mountain cabin, eating doughnuts while watching

7   More recently, I've heard the slang word *tadow* redefined by the Jamaican American musician and singer Masego as alluding to such moments as these. Tadow, according to Masego, "[e]xpress[es] the inexplicable synchronicity of human life and the sublime experiences of subjectivity and wonder that English language cannot adequately describe." Masego (Micah Davis) and FKJ (Vincent Fenton, aka French Kiwi Juice), *Tadow*, directed by Joe Wiel, *YouTube*, May 24, 2019, https://www.youtube.com/watch?v=szQdvAzGNwE. Some sources suggest "tadow" may have originally come from a combination of the exclamations "ta-da" and "wow."

8   Averaging seventeen minutes a mile for 100.4 miles, Caitlin Skye Barr finished at 28:26:27, coming in fourth among women in her age group, tenth in her total age group, twenty-fourth out of seventy-two women, and was number 174 overall out of the 386 runners who finished in under thirty hours.

other racers make their way to the finish line. I found myself thinking about my experience the night before in the dark mountain forest. What exactly had happened there?

In the morning-after memory, it felt like an extraordinarily vivid dream. And oddly, the more I thought about it, the more the experience seemed somehow tangentially connected to the bristly green shadow outside the steamed-up Denver bathroom window a couple of years earlier. The Colorado pinyon appearing outside the window had led me on a hunt that had resulted in my first successful identification ever of the species of an unknown (to me) particular tree. Had paying all that attention to one domesticated Colorado pinyon made me more easily open to some sort of tree energy or tree communication present in the mountain forest two and a half years later?

Everything I'd been reading about tree intelligence suggested that trees communicate with one another, *not* with humans, but after I got back home, I came across Peter Wohlleben's thoughts on the matter:

> And who knows, perhaps one day "the language of trees" will eventually be deciphered, giving us the raw material for further amazing stories. Until then, when you take your next walk in the forest, give free rein to your imagination—in many cases, what you imagine is not so far removed from reality after all!

Had what I experienced "just" been my imagination?

Researchers have long suggested that human imagination exists thanks to a widespread neural network in the brain. A tree's roots form a very wide spreading network in the soil. Both of these networks, human and arboreal, are sensitive and attuned to their environment. František Baluška from the Institute of Cellular and Molecular Botany at the University of Bonn is of the opinion that "brain-like structures can be found at [the] root tips [of trees]. In addition to signaling pathways, there are also numerous systems and molecules similar to those found in animals."

Could some sort of transfer of energy or communication occur between these two networks when they come in contact? For a minute, I flashed on the memory of the tenderness of my feet balancing on the roots of northern white-cedars while I was wrapped in their shade on the shore of Houghton Lake. As I was experiencing it, the event of the night before had reminded me of the church-camp-bonfire-in-the-woods. And then last night's experience in the mountain forest. Three very distinct times in my life I have been aware of having some sort of an exchange that, to put it most simply, felt like I was receiving a direct, specific message from trees. Despite not involving words, these messages felt as if they had been received just fine.

I looked around at my daughter and her support team chattering with each other and cheering as each racer passed us. Words, sounds. How else might I characterize these tree messages, which had neither? The subject of all three of the messages seemed to be related to me receiving reassurance. While the first that I remember felt like an unexpected but reassuring good-bye, the other two occurred when my state of mind involved anxiety.

We do know a fair amount about the effects trees have on our physical and mental and emotional states. Scientists have shown that *shinrin-yoku*, the Japanese practice of "forest-bathing"—sitting in or walking through a forest—lowers human blood pressure, pulse, and heart rate variability:

● Trees reduce human blood pressure levels.

Scientific studies published in English and Japanese were reviewed, considering all published, randomized, controlled trials, cohort studies, and comparative studies that evaluated the effects of the forest environment on changes in systolic blood pressure. A subsequent meta-analysis was performed, and twenty trials involving 732 participants were reviewed. Systolic blood pressure of the participants in the forest environment was found to be significantly lower than that of those in the non-forest environment. Additionally, diastolic blood pressure of participants in the forest environment was significantly lower than that of those in the non-forest environment.

- Trees improve human cardiovascular health.

A review of 364 scientific papers yielded 14 studies that met the criteria for inclusion in this scientific review. When the studies were synthesized, the researchers concluded:

> Forest bathing interventions were effective at reducing blood pressure, lowering pulse rate, increasing the power of heart rate variability (HRV), improving cardiac-pulmonary parameters, and metabolic function.

Other studies have shown that being in forests can improve our immune system, decrease stress, and improve mood.

Are the positive effects of trees on our bodies and emotions the result of us pulling the oxygen-rich air of the forest into our bodies with our breath? Is it our response to being exposed to the bacteria that makes up the forest microbiome? Is it our pleasing experience of visually scanning the fractal patterns found in the forest—the repeating of the branching of trees, for instance? Is it the essential oils—the conifers' phytoncides—we're smelling? Maybe it is the combination of all these things, perhaps along with other forest characteristics we've yet to discover, that makes our hearts happier and that also gets to the heart of who we are as humans in communion with our environment, an environment that trees—our first home—represent.

Mount Massive Wilderness covers 30,540 acres of trees. Science writer Jim Robbins isn't the first person to point out that "across cultures and across time, trees have been revered as sacred, as living antennae conducting divine energies."At three thousand trees per acre, that's over 91.5 million antennae connecting earth to sky. Were the trees picking up something from me? Could those trees, in community, sense my daughter's feet running through the night on the trails between them? I have no idea of the answer to either of those questions. I do know those trees profoundly influenced my emotional state as I entered their community that night.

That morning after I turned from my wondering about what had happened in that mountain forest back to enjoying watching my healthy and happy daughter smile as we began to think about getting some sleep—even I'd been awake for thirty hours by then. Like us humans, most living organisms adapt their behavior to the rhythm of day and night. Plants are no exception: flowers open in the morning; some tree leaves close during the night. Scientists from Austria, Finland, and Hungary are using laser scanners to study the day-night rhythm of trees. As it turns out, trees go to sleep too.

As I prepared for bed that morning with the sun moving higher in the sky, I felt fortunate that the trees of the mountain forest had been awake for me during the long night.

Whatever it was that had happened.

15

In Memoriam

The Eastern Redbud

(*Cercis canadensis*)

Just outside my front study window is a 'Forest Pansy', a cultivar of an eastern redbud tree that we planted about four feet too close to our house. The eastern redbud is one of my two favorite Michigan flowering trees. So much to admire in all four seasons. The tiny clusters of purplish, pointillistic flowers abloom on the bare, almost-black branches in spring. Beautiful broad, green hearts of leaves in summer. The pale yellow of the tree's fall attire. And the horizontal architecture of their graceful branches in the winter.[1]

The redbud is a tree connected to family members on both sides of the Dunphy-Daly family tree. The common eastern redbud grows wild, blooming early in March in North Carolina, where my dear eldest daughter and son-in-law, three of my four precious grandchildren, and some of my favorite cousins live. My dad always liked this tree but bemoaned the need to pull up its prodigious seedlings. I remember my dad, his fair Celtic skin burning on sunny Saturdays, his freckled hands—the hair on their backs and fingers lightened to a golden red

---

1 Redbud flowers are bisexual, having both female and male parts, so they/their/them pronouns are appropriate.

and speckled with dirt from my parents' Northville gardens—pulling out redbud juveniles. This is a never-to-be-repeated scene, except in memory, now that my parents have moved to a condo, where their only plants are grown in pots and my dad must use a walker to move between rooms.

The fast-growing redbud is an understory tree, one that can grow in the shade cast by larger companions. The redbud tree I had planted out front is shaded by the sycamore and two of the three honey locusts planted in or at the edge of our yard. On Pelee, between our cottage and the lake, there is a redbud that receives more sun. This eastern redbud was planted for us by our Pelee Island friends Ron and Lynn in memory of Craig's mom, Georgette Agnes Daly (née Yezbick). Planting a redbud tree in memory of a loved one is a Pelee custom. And my mother-in-law certainly was beloved.

In the beginning, however, my mother-in-law did not take the same shine to me that her youngest daughter, her middle son, and her husband had. My husband's youngest sister, Lanny, at age twelve, introduced me to my husband-to-be, suggesting he walk me to the neighborhood park to show me where I could walk my dog. And that, quite simply, was that—no looking back. However, despite the fact that Craig's girlfriend of seven years had recently left him, his mom seemed to view me as the interloper. I felt an undercurrent of suspicion, of what exactly I don't know—my motives, perhaps—in the tone of her voice, in the words she chose when speaking to me, and in how she watched me. While Craig was still in law school when I met him, I had already been successful in my first job out of college. After six months at the advertising agency Ross Roy, Inc., I was the first woman to whom the agency offered a junior account manager position. When I declined, I was promoted from an account administrator position to copywriter, the position to which I'd aspired before being hired. If I had been interested in wealth, I'd have not made that choice. A gold digger I was not.

My husband and I met when I rented the upper flat next door to Craig's parents' house, the house in which Georgette had grown up with her seven siblings and had inherited from her dad. Craig and the three oldest of his five siblings had lived at that house, too, in their early years. When I met him, Craig lived on the other side of his parents' house in a house owned by his ex-girlfriend's father; she had recently moved out of this upper flat they had shared. I could see his bedroom window from mine, across the roof of his parents' one-story house. I was surprised the morning after the first night he stayed over at my flat to watch him, from that same window while I was getting ready for work, go to his parents' side door and invite himself to breakfast. As far as I knew, he didn't generally eat breakfast with them. Had they seen him leaving the back door shared by my flat and the lower flat, where his brother and his family lived? I suspected they—more specifically, his mother—wouldn't think he had been visiting his brother's family at that time in the morning. What would she think? Why did I suddenly care so much?

When we first moved in together, we rented a lovely Detroit upper flat with leaded-glass windows across Woodward from Palmer Park. We soon invited Craig's parents for dinner. When we showed Craig's mom our shared study, his mom wondered aloud where, in our two-bedroom flat, his bedroom was, not understanding that we were sharing a bed as well as a flat.

It was almost three years before I felt that Craig's mom approved of me. Craig and I did happen to get married three years after we had met, but that wasn't what instigated the change in my relationship with his mom. The change came about when we started sharing books, beginning with her lending me her hardcover copy of *Sophie's Choice* by William Styron, published the year we were married. Craig's mother was an avid reader. She had paperbacks stuffed in shelves under a half wall that divided their front-door entrance from the living room, and she was a regular visitor to the Ferndale Public Library.

In the first book she lent me, Sophie, a Roman Catholic survivor of Auschwitz, forced to decide, chose her son's life over her daughter's. I have wondered if Georgette may have been her father's favorite, and have been of the opinion, over the years, that my husband may also have been—at least in some respects—Georgette's favorite. From a young age, smart cookie that he was, my husband insisted on accompanying his mom grocery shopping every Friday after his dad brought home his paycheck. These trips meant time alone with Mom. She confirmed his story that he in fact would throw a temper tantrum if she didn't take him with her. My husband still likes to grocery shop, and now that there are just the two of us and he has taken over most of the cooking, I'm grateful he's the one who shops for our household.

When I first met Georgette—or "Gee" as she was called by most family and friends, and eventually by me—besides still having two children at home and helping raise two grandsons, she was working as a reading aide at Harding Elementary School, the school directly across from her house on Grayson Street, where three generations of the Yezbick-Daly family had attended school: she and her seven siblings, all of her six children, and her two nephews. She had graduated from Lincoln High School in Ferndale in the class of 1939 but apparently did not have the opportunity to go to college. She was a voracious reader, however. She began helping other children learn to read while her two youngest children were still enrolled at the school where she worked. One family story is of Gee telling her youngest son, Kevin, who was in one of her reading groups, that he wasn't to call her "Mom" in that setting. I suspect she wanted to feel more professional in her workplace.

Only much later did I learn she had wanted to be a writer. She shared a piece with me, immaculately typed, double-spaced, on six pages of thin typing paper and kept in a clean manila folder, that she'd written about her first, and only, trip to Lebanon, from where her parents, Joe and Anna (née Joseph) Yezbick had emigrated maybe fifteen years before Georgette was born. My sister-in-law Noreen guesses that her mom may have been inspired to document this trip after reading an account of another Ferndale family's roots in either the *Crow's Nest*, the Ferndale Historical Museum's newsletter, or the local paper, Royal

Oak's *Daily Tribune*. Noreen recalls her mentioning she wanted to do something similar, to write about her roots.

At the time Gee gave me her travel memoir to read, I was teaching fiction workshop, business writing, and advanced prose courses at Oakland University. I was still years away from becoming a writing workshop facilitator outside of a university setting and from discovering that I had a knack for and enjoyed coaching other writers of fiction and nonfiction and editing their work. I read Gee's piece solely in my role as her daughter-in-law, looking for clues as to who she'd been before she became a wife and mother, trying to understand how she had, at the late—by 1947 standards—age of twenty-six, married a handsome member of the local "Irish Gang" who had only an elementary-school education and anger issues that increased with age. My father-in-law was the son of a (purported) alcoholic of Irish descent who as a youth had starred in the Ziegfeld Follies and who, after marriage and the birth of three children, deserted his family. I read Gee's piece to see who *she* was—and who she thought she was on her way to becoming—as she approached young womanhood, ten years before she married.

I was not reading her untitled piece of writing as a writer—or considering her a writer—nor was I considering her level of craft. My mistake.

The account begins:

When I was fifteen years old, my parents decided to make a trip to Syria,[2] their homeland, after a thirty-year absence. I persuaded them to take me along, so on May 3, 1937, we left [from the] Michigan Central Depot for New York.

2 In the first half of 1920, Lebanese territory was claimed as part of Syria; Lebanon did not declare independence from the French Mandate, under which it was considered one of six states, until 1943. Syria did not officially recognize Lebanon's sovereignty until 2008.

Perhaps to simplify her account, she didn't mention that her younger sister Lucille, age four then, also accompanied their parents. I wonder now who was looking after their five other siblings during this trip (the eighth of the siblings was born after it). The trip lasted six and a half months, with the four not sailing back home from Naples aboard the *Conte di Savoia* until November 18.

In her six-page version of this trip, Georgette Agnes Yezbick establishes herself as both an adventuresome teen and an observant writer. The Yezbicks went by overnight train to New York City and enjoyed the sights there for four days, including riding a subway for the first time and visiting:

- The Empire State Building
- The Bronx Zoo
- Van Cortlandt Park (in the Bronx)
- Rockefeller Center (which was not completed until two and a half years after their visit although most of the nineteen-building complex had been completed two and a half years earlier)
- NBC Studios, where they went on a tour
- Radio City Music Hall, where they saw Janet Gaynor in *A Star Is Born* (the first of the four movie versions), which had premiered in New York exactly two weeks before. They also saw the first newsreel taken at the scene of the Hindenburg disaster that happened that day, less than one hundred miles away.

I conjecture that Georgette Yezbick, like many teenage girls, might have imagined herself in Gaynor's place. She was, after all, in the midst of doing something exciting, adventurous, and more than a bit glamorous.

Four decades later, in the years that I was included in Christmas Eve celebrations on Grayson Street—beginning with my first year with Craig, an event at which his ex-girlfriend also appeared, but for the last time—Gee, of naturally dark hair and eyes, would don a long, gold, sparkly evening dress and dangling earrings, hairspray her blond waves, and put in her blue-tinted contact lenses before the party began—a gracious hostess who was more than a bit glamorous. The fragrance of the perfume she wore only for special occasions filled the small kitchen along with the clacking of her bracelets as she concocted Santa's Surprise punch (the surprise being a liberal addition of peppermint oil), put out shrimp cocktail, and took smoking calf livers wrapped in bacon out of the oven.

These treats were set out with her wonderful Lebanese dishes, which were, during the rest of the year, served alongside her baked kibbeh—made with ground turkey instead of lamb, so my husband and I, and later our daughters, who didn't eat red meat, could eat it, too. On Christmas Eve, as on special Sunday dinners, we looked forward to a plate of hummus (Gee's fingernails, frosted with pale nail polish, peeled the skins from the chickpeas, the trick to achieve ultimate smoothness), a puddle of melted butter in the middle, a sprinkle of paprika across, and served with warmed fresh Syrian bread; tabbouleh, with fresh chopped mint from the garden strip along her childhood home next door; my favorite, which we called na'eesh—Syrian flatbread topped with olive oil and the Middle Eastern spice mix za'atar—dried oregano, marjoram, thyme, sumac, and toasted sesame seed—and baked; and finally ma'amouls purchased from Oasis Gourmet Cuisine, the Royal Oak bulk store and catering service owned by Halim and Lamia Zahr where Gee purchased ingredients for her fine Lebanese cooking.

The Yezbicks departed New York City for Naples on Saturday, May 8, 1937, sailing third class on the Italian ocean liner SS *Rex*. In her travel memoir, based on the diary she kept during the trip, Georgette set down the chronology of their transatlantic crossing and the next six months, which were split between the seaport of Beirut, where her father was born, and the village of Chartoun, about twenty miles from Beirut and up in the mountains, where her mother had been born and where her grandfather was, at the time, mayor and owner of the village's bread oven.

The details of her full account, beginning with her departure from Detroit, are both sensory—they didn't get much sleep because the train was "crowded and jolty"—and informational, once they arrived in New York City—she was "duly impressed" by the subway going sixty-five miles per hour and the visibility from the Empire State Building being seven miles the day they were atop it.

But today, it is her stories—and how she envisioned who she was in her youth, who she might become—that jump out at me reading her account:

- Her story of losing sight of her parents in Van Cortlandt Park, being chased by some boys, ending up in tears surrounded by a crowd, only to be rescued by a policeman who—most thrillingly—rode her on his motorcycle until she found her parents.
- Her story of being amused by the plight of seasick fellow passengers on their rough second day at sea until she was one of them: "The fresh air on deck helped and a kind steward gave me a lemon to suck on."
- Her story of being the only girl her age aboard the ship and so being spoiled by the ship's crew, who allowed her to enter the first- and second-class areas to watch the dancing and attend the movies, despite the fact that her family was traveling third class. Her last night onboard, she was invited up to first class to go dancing for an hour.
- Her mature first impression of Naples: "horses and buggies and endless soldiers . . . Mussolini's pictures were everywhere, and he seemed to be idolized by most of the people."
- Her story of being "awakened by considerable noise outside

our portholes upon docking at Alexandria, Egypt and [looking out,] we were shocked to see men in what appeared to be their nightgowns. . . . On the dock a regular show was put on for our benefit with acrobats, a magician and a strong man who could bite huge nails in two with his teeth. . . . After each performance, they looked up expectantly, and we threw down coins for them." She may have been sailing in third class, but at that moment, she was a wealthy American showering "foreigners" with money.

● Her first impression of Lebanon was of its "picturesque stone houses and winding stone stairways leading from one plateau of houses up to the next, the homes being built up and down the numerous mountains."

● Her story of their time spent at the seashore: "We . . . rented a cottage which consisted of woven mats set up all around on top of a small brick building. We could raise the mats for light and ventilation. At night we spread mattresses on the floor to sleep." In the evenings, "we would gather with our neighbors around a huge bonfire to sing songs, dance and tell stories. The dancing was done alone, and as one [dancer] finished, he or she would pull someone else up to take his place. By adding a little boogie-woogie to the simple steps, I became a success and in great demand."

● Her stories about her American wardrobe: "I wore my slacks, which attracted quite a bit of attention as the girls had never seen anything like them before. The French girls in the city were more modern, but even they didn't wear them. The girls were very interested in my clothing, and everything was closely inspected, particularly my underclothes which were much different than their cotton homemade ones. . . . A custom at the seashore was that the men would go in swimming together and the women waited until they were through before going in. . . . Also, the women didn't wear bathing suits, just an old dress . . . in the water.

Needless to say, my bathing suit was a sensation, and when I even dared to swim with the men, all were convinced I was Satan's handmaiden herself."

● Her story of marriage proposals: "My dad and numerous uncles told me there had been many bids for my hand, as it is the custom for a suitor to speak to a male relative. However, I rightly suspected that the proposals were made with the hope of coming to the States, as most of the young men only seemed to live for the day when they could."

Later on in life, after Gee had retired from her job as a reading aide, she took lessons in hula dancing, the storytelling dance of the Hawaiian Islands; sang, attired in a long blue evening gown with sequins, in annual lip-sync concerts put on by the local senior citizen organization; and volunteered weekly at the Ferndale Historical Museum, piecing together the stories of others. Gee was known in the neighborhood—and thanked in the local newspaper's letters to the editor column for picking up the litter in Harding Park where she daily walked Misty, her Yorkie.

Gee also helped me. On Thursday afternoons, she came over to our house to watch my youngest daughter, Caitlin, after school, providing me with one full, uninterrupted day of work as a freelance instructional designer, creating training programs. Between the end of the school day and my husband's homecoming, Grammy Daly and Caitlin would read stories, play gin rummy, and color together. My husband says that most of his good attributes came from his mom; I'd agree.[3]

---

3 In fairness, however, it was Craig's dad who agreed to let me rent the flat, despite me having a young dog, the first such exception ever granted to a renter; Shannon the Irish setter responded to the kindness while I was at work all day—when she wasn't barking—by chewing up the floor covering and balusters of the railing on the large front balcony of the flat.

For the first sixteen years of raising our family, we lived just across Woodward Avenue, seven minutes away from my in-laws. In 2000, we moved more than half an hour away to a farther northern suburb. My husband visited his parents on his way to or from work, but Caitlin and I only saw the Dalys on the occasional weekend. In 2006, after six years away, Gee was so very happy to learn that we were moving back to a southeastern Oakland County community neighboring hers. Her often-difficult husband, Donald Vincent Daly Sr., had died over a year before on April Fool's Day. A practicing Catholic all of her life, Gee was still afraid to die and held my husband's hand while they watched old black-and-white movies together. As she got closer to the end of her life, Gee welcomed our beagle, Baron, up on her bed.

Georgette Agnes Yezbick was born on September 2, 1921, moved to Grayson Street in Ferndale, Michigan, when she was five, lived there for eighty years, and died there on the Fourth of July 2006. We moved to our new home in the area three weeks later. She never saw the house we moved into and still live in now. I always thought she'd like the house and am surprised by how often I think of her here.

The Argentinean poet Antonio Porchia included the aphorism "One lives in the hope of becoming a memory" in his *Voices*. Between raising six children of her own and helping raise our two nephews, between preparing three meals a day and doing laundry for up to eight people, between working out of her home after her youngest started school, and keeping very busy in her retirement, I doubt my mother-in-law took much time to think about becoming a memory, but she did set her own memories down in writing, first with a fountain pen in the 1937 green leather-covered yearbook she used as a diary on her trip to Lebanon as a teenager and then, when she was older than I am now, in her well-composed and neatly typed travel memoir based on that diary. Beyond her early diary keeping and her later writing, she was a very memorable person for how much she gave to others.

I wonder what else might she have written if her life had been different? If she had had fewer people to care for or more help, if she had had more time for herself and some encouragement? What other stories did she harbor? What else might she have shared? What stories of hers were left untold?

Frequently, when I look out to Lake Erie from our Pelee cottage, especially when the sun is setting, my eyes come to rest on the eastern redbud planted in Gee's memory. A perfect tree for her. Its spring "bling" in the bare landscape reminds me of Gee's festive entertaining. Throughout the growing season, I admire the redbud tree's leaves, those elegant hearts stirred by the breeze off the lake. After the pale-yellow leaves fall in the autumn, I am struck anew by the tree's graceful habit—and by just how much I miss Gee.

16

Puzzle Pieces

The Japanese Zelkova

(*Zelkova serrata*)

After recently coming across some baby photos of my oldest grandson that prompted the memory of a day that was both terrifying and, perhaps totally unrelated to the fear, marked a beginning, I went searching for the first entry in a journal I had received for my birthday several years ago:

11/20/18, 10:30 a.m.
Duke University Plaza
Durham, North Carolina

This is to be the year of the tree book. I have a plan for getting at least a first draft of a book proposal—which I first began in March 2017—done by the end of the calendar year, in the next six weeks. Which will force me to figure out what the book is about.

Well, yes, trees. But what about trees? This afternoon—or maybe yet this morning—I'm going to return to trying to answer this question.

For now, I have sun on my shoulders, a large peppermint tea before me, and Caden Daly, my six-month-old grandson, sleeping peacefully next to me in his stroller. Caden's been sick, and I keep checking on him because several minutes ago, just as we were walking past the Duke University Chapel, he started coughing.

And by the time I'd stopped the stroller to check on him more closely, he'd stopped breathing. Stopped breathing completely. Was this a "breath-holding spell"?[1] I was all too familiar with and frightened of these spells, having witnessed several such episodes with his older sister.

But could I be sure that was "all" it was? He'd had croup. What is one supposed to do when a baby with croup coughs and stops breathing? I didn't know. I had absolutely no idea what to do.

Everything slowed down while students, professors, and a tour group streamed by us. I could hear the hissing of air expelled by the brakes of a bus pulling up somewhere behind us on the street we had crossed just minutes ago.

His mother was in her office and too far to get to, to be of help in time. It was just the two of us here. He needed help right now.

Panicked, I blew on his face, gently and then more forcefully, over and over.

After what seemed an unbelievably long time, he startled and started breathing again.

And so did I.

My dear, dear sweet boy.

How is it that I'm a grandmother? My grandchildren are as

---

1 A breath-holding spell is when a child holds his or her breath, generally as a result of being startled, in pain, frustrated, or angry. The spell can result in the child passing out for up to a minute. In the most extreme cases, the child may have a seizure, although if this happens, it does not cause any long-term harm or put the child at risk for a seizure disorder. Breath-holding spells happen in up to 5 percent of healthy children from six months to six years old. They're most common when kids are six to eighteen months old, and they tend to run in families. Children outgrow the spell without any treatment. ("Breath-Holding Spells," reviewed by Amy W. Anzilotti, MD, Nemours Kids Health, https://kidshealth.org/en/parents/spells.html [accessed 4/01/22].)

dear to me as my two own daughters, but somehow everyday life with daughters—or maybe some sort of protection from one hormone or another—made such intense love bearable. I've met my grandchildren—who live far away from me—at an intersection in our lives that makes these relationships both more enjoyable and more terrifying; I understand so much more about the fragility of life.

Trying to get my heart back to beating its normal rhythm again after the stopped-breath episode, I start to sit down under what I recognize to be some species of oak. But then I notice, all around us, a species of tree I don't recognize. A row of them is planted across the way with tables and chairs set up underneath. I move to one of those tables to get a closer look. And then, I just sit there, breathing, grateful.

When I can actually see what I'm looking at, I notice that the bark of the small trees resembles pieces from a puzzle yet to be assembled. The trees' branches are releasing showers of gold and brown leaves on the puffs of a small breeze. I take four or five photos of the bark, the branches, the leaves, the seedpods.

I wonder what Grandma and Grandpa Klotzbach would think of me carrying around this little thin box, taking up about the same square-inch area as a three-by-five index card and containing both a phone and a camera. I visualize Grandma's pink wall phone standing out against the kitchen wallpaper and the heft of the beautifully handmade wooden boxes in which Grandpa kept and carried his cameras and other photographic equipment. No matter where I am, I am always able to make a phone call or snap a photo. And I have what amounts to a library of information at my fingertips—no need for either the big heavy green antique globe on its stand in their den or the well-worn set of The Book of Knowledge. *On this same box, I can even type notes about what I see, research, discover.*

I check that Caden is still breathing and arrange his stroller so his face is shaded. I wonder what would surprise me, if I could know it now, about his world when he enters his sixty-sixth year in 2084.

May he have a long happy life full of love, rich and deep like the love I feel for him today.

I pick up three leaves from this mystery tree: a cream, a pink, and a brown one. And then, looking at the tree's patchy trunk, do a minute of quick research on my phone. Could these unfamiliar trees with "puzzle-piece" bark be one of the South's ubiquitous crêpe myrtles perhaps? This was exciting—a southern belle!

A bright green lizard scuffles around in the trees' leaves caught up in the vine on the railing next to me, and I'm distracted by trying to get a good photo on my phone. Such a beautiful vivid green.[2]

As I've sipped my cooling peppermint tea, the sun has gotten hot. Thoreau wrote, "Write while the heat is in you." I feel myself coming back to my self here and now. Time to try to capture what has started simmering in me . . .

I remember turning to a clean page of my journal, smoothing flat the gutter of the pages' spread, taking a deep breath, and beginning—finally—by jotting down a list of analogies that had been drifting through my ramble of thoughts about trees for a while now:

At points in our history, the following statements were not *considered "fake news" items:*

- *Women are not intelligent enough to vote.*
- *Black males are subhuman.*
- *Children born "different" with physical or mental disabilities and "senile" elderly people, those who suffer from dementia, should be shut away from the world.*
- *Animals experience no emotions.*
- *Fish feel no pain.*

---

2 This bright green lizard was a male green anole, one of thirteen species of lizards found in North Carolina.

I glanced at my sleeping grandbaby and then let my gaze rest again on the tree trunk closest to me. Puzzle pieces. How to express my line of reasoning most simply?

These statements have all been scientifically disproven. The last statement, the one about fish not feeling pain, is the statement most recently disproved, at least fifteen years ago.

The actual characteristics or capabilities of women, blacks, disabled children, seniors with dementia, animals, and fish have not changed over time. However, the scientific—fact-based— understanding of each of these groups has changed. This revised understanding has resulted, in some cases, in changes in our human institutions and, in many cases, in changes in our individual behavior toward members of these groups of other living beings with whom we share the planet.

Caden was beginning to stir. I looked up from the page and pushed his stroller further under the shade cast by our companion tree's canopy, willing him to continue to breathe peacefully in his sleep for a few more moments. My eyes sought out and rested yet again on the trunk of my nearest new arboreal friend across the table from me. All the puzzle pieces.

I suspect humans from earlier times and other places may have divined some of the characteristics and capabilities of our oldest companions—our tree friends—who have provided us with food, shelter, medicine, fuel for our fires, building materials, images and materials for our art, beauty, of course, and shade, as well as the fractals we see, the phytoncides we smell, the forest biome we breathe in; these last three, researchers in this century have determined, reduce the effects of depression, anxiety, and stress and increase our sense of well-being.

I pulled up on my phone a note containing a line of reasoning almost a century and a half old, written down by one of the most distinguished scientists of his time, best known for his contributions to evolutionary biology. Charles Darwin wrote:

> The course pursued by the radicle [the primary root] in penetrating the ground must be determined by the tip; hence it has acquired such diverse kinds of sensitiveness. It is hardly an exaggeration to say that the tip of the radicle thus endowed, and having the power of directing the movements of the adjoining parts, *acts like the brain of one of the lower animals; the brain being seated with the anterior end of the body, receiving impressions from the sense-organs, and directing the several movements* [emphasis added].

I had loaded my suitcase for this trip with five books on plant communication, perception, and intelligence, all written within the last six years. Each of these books is full of research that cracks the paradigm of how we've thought of trees, at least in my lifetime. Just the titles of these books open doors to a new way—at least for us in modern times—of thinking about our oldest friends:

- *The Hidden Life of Trees: What They Feel, How They Communicate—Discoveries from a Secret World*
- *What a Plant Knows: A Field Guide to the Senses*
- *Brilliant Green: The Surprising History and Science of Plant Intelligence*
- *The Revolutionary Genius of Plants: A New Understanding of Plant Intelligence and Behavior*
- *Thus Spoke the Plant: A Remarkable Journey of Groundbreaking Scientific Discoveries and Personal Encounters with Plants*

All the puzzle pieces.

I turned back to my journal, formulating the crux of my wonderings in two questions:

How long will it take before what we already know about trees—what humans may once have understood intuitively and what has recently been scientifically proven—is understood, accepted, heeded? Will it be in time?

Caden gave a little gasp as his eyes opened and briefly tracked the tree's dangling seedpods playing in the breeze above him before he started to fuss. My beginning had ended for now. I packed us up, and we headed back to my daughter's office at Duke University Nicholas School of the Environment so his mom could feed him. I left the shelter of these new southern tree friends—who I was pretty certain were crêpe myrtles—directing a smile down at my sweet wide-awake grandson, his eyes on my face. I felt such gratitude as I watched him breathe like he had never stopped. Both of us were breathing easy now—me for having made a small start at figuring out what about trees I might write.

Two years later, I decided to write about the crêpe myrtle as a North Carolina tree that, at the time, I believed didn't grow in Michigan, any more than the Colorado pinyon does. I first wanted to confirm that the species really didn't grow up north. The late-in-the-season blooming quality of the crêpe myrtle tugged at a memory. The August before I sought respite with Caden under the shelter of the puzzle-piece trees, I'd driven past some trees covered in white flowers on the median strip of Eight Mile Road between Inkster Road and Beech Daly. I'd never known a flowering tree to bloom in southeastern Michigan after the catalpa trees finished in July. What could these trees be?

When I mentioned these mystery trees to my mom, she said there was a very sweet-smelling, white-blossomed tree blooming the same week in August near their church. I couldn't safely get across the multi-lane road to the trees I'd spotted on the median strip, nor had I made the drive to my parents' church, so I'd never figured out that puzzle.

Now, I wondered if I was wrong in thinking that, just because I'd never made her acquaintance in a neighbor's front yard, this southern belle never crossed the Mason-Dixon Line.

I found out easily enough. The common species of crêpe myrtle that grows in the South is *Lagerstroemia indica*. Cultivars of this species are not hardy enough to be grown in Michigan. But there is another species, the Japanese crêpe myrtle, *Lagerstroemia fauriei*, a larger tree with smaller white blossoms and larger leaves, that was introduced to the United States in 1956 and has hardier cultivars that can be grown farther north. Turns out some hardy varieties of this species can be grown in Hardiness Zone 6b. Southeastern Michigan falls in Zone 6a, for the most part, but the area of this region closest to the Detroit River, made more temperate by its proximity to the water, is Zone 6b, so definitely a possibility. In its introduction to this Japanese crêpe myrtle, the U.S. Forest Service suggests that the tree's upright, vase-shaped crown makes it well suited for street tree planting. Word is, though, with respect to northern climes: "They will probably die back to the ground over the winter, then resprout in spring." The large trees on the median strip of Eight Mile Road do not die back to the ground in the winter, so I'm not convinced I've figured out that particular puzzle.

Regardless, the common crêpe myrtle is a southern tree with a Michigan connection through the Japanese crêpe myrtle species. I guessed that was even better. Until it wasn't.

In my wallet, I had been carrying one of the small leaves that had showered down upon Caden and me that sunny day on Duke's West Campus Plaza. Every time I saw it, I felt the relief of my return to the subject of trees wash over me. I'd signed a contract almost exactly a year before my November afternoon with Caden to write a juvenile nonfiction book on the Great Lakes, which is dedicated to the only two grandchildren I had at the time, Avery Grace and Caden Daly. The drafting of the little book had involved full days of writing, every day of January and February 2018. Then, in March of that year, I helped my mom close Painter's Place, her studio and gallery of fifty years in Northville, Michigan, and next I packed and moved my elderly parents from their home of forty-two years to a condo; these two physically and emotionally exhausting major life events had taken up March through October 2018. My afternoon spent with Caden under the trees on the West Campus Plaza at Duke University marked a return to considering trees.

Trees had first come to me as something I needed to write about in April 2016, just before my island book had been launched in June; I'd committed myself to the idea at 2017's Notable Night. However, I recently came across the single phrase "Tree Nation" on a page of a little idea journal of mine dated September 29, 2015, and later in the same little notebook, on November 24, 2015, I had written: "Documenting with stories and photographs members of the Standing Nation." So, after carrying the seed of the idea around with me for three years, it had felt good to write that journal entry sitting under the trees with my grandson. And then to be reminded of my commitment by carrying the puzzle-piece tree's leaf with me.

While doing research on the common crêpe myrtle, I went into my closet to find the wallet with the leaf in it. During the first eleven months of the pandemic, on my sole drive once a week to pick up and deliver groceries to my parents, I had been carrying a different, larger wallet as I no longer really needed to carry a purse for the one errand. I eventually found my pre-pandemic wallet. The two-inch-long leaf was still in it, and a beautiful little leaf it was. Next to where I'd stashed the wallet were a number of paint strips I'd picked up from a paint store while we were trying to decide on a new trim color for our bedroom. On Benjamin Moore Paints' "parchment" palette, I identified the leaf's particular color as "hex." The name didn't really match my idea of my southern belle's arboreal charms. I held the leaf up and admired its satiny sheen in the sun, then focused on the leaf's evenly spaced serrated margin, such a perfect saw-toothed pattern.

Wait. A serrated margin? Neither species of crêpe myrtle—*lagerstroemia indica*, with its oval rounded leaves, nor *lagerstroemia fauriei*, with its oval pointy leaves—bears *toothed* leaves. In fact, the tree is called crêpe myrtle because its flowers look like crêpe paper and its leaves look like those of the evergreen flowering plant commonly called myrtle. I have copious amounts of myrtle providing groundcover in my Michigan yard, and the leaf I held in my hand looked absolutely nothing like any myrtle leaf I'd ever seen.

Of course, I'd found the leaf before I knew much of anything about tree leaves. I was clueless then about leaf attachment, leaf venation, leaf margins. Truth be told, at that beginning point in this project, I had been pretty much clueless about most facts concerning trees. All I knew was that I'd always been inexplicably drawn to trees and was beginning to feel compelled to write about my relationships with them.

Since the year before meeting the puzzle-piece tree with Caden in November, I had for the first time, in 2017, (1) identified a tree using a tree guide; and (2) identified a tree that didn't grow in Michigan—the Colorado pinyon. So it is probably no surprise that I was romantically imagining making the acquaintance of a southern tree on a jaunt with my grandson, a second gift after he started breathing again. But if the puzzle-piece tree, as I was back to calling it, wasn't a crêpe myrtle, what on Earth was it?

I have an actual leaf and photos of the bark on the trunk, the branches shot from underneath the tree, and of the "rosary-bead" sprigs of dried seedpods that I can pull up on my phone. Looking at it today, I would never mistake the tree for a crêpe myrtle. With what I'd learned in the last two years about trees, it didn't take long to peg an accurate identification: the Japanese zelkova, or *Zelkova serrata* (the species name "serrata" specifying the saw-toothed nature of the tree's leaves). Non-native to the United States, the Japanese zelkova is a member of the elm (Ulmaceae) family, a member that is both resistant to Dutch elm disease (the Zelkova serrata 'Village Green' cultivar is also known as the "Japanese keaki elm") and featured as one of forty-one "recommended alternatives to ash trees for Michigan's lower peninsula." Now that I compare my photo of the Japanese zelkova's *splotchy* bark with images of the *streaky* cream and fawn bark of the common crêpe myrtle, I see that while both are beautifully mottled, the result of the trunk's bark exfoliation looks significantly different. In addition, other than being a similar shade of brown, the Japanese zelkova's dried 3-D heart-shaped seedpods do not look like the flower-petally crêpe myrtle seedpods at all.

The Japanese zelkova, briefly a southern belle imposter to me, is a hardy replacement for two American trees—the elm and the ash—lost recently enough that our cities and towns, our landscape and our imagination, still feel their absence. So definitely a tree worth paying homage to today. And this puzzle piece of a tree is the impetus that finally got me writing about trees and helped push me to learn more.

Meanwhile, having gotten more familiar with the true southern belle, the crêpe myrtle, I realize now that when my oldest daughter, Meagan,[3] moved to Miami to earn her master's degree in marine biology, I had a serious look at—but didn't identify—my first crêpe myrtle in the landscaping of a parking lot. I was intent on identifying the bird perching in the tree instead, which turned out to be my first sighting of a mockingbird, Florida's state bird. Turns out, mockingbirds are known to nest in crêpe myrtles.

Meagan's next relocation was to North Carolina's Duke University to earn her PhD at Duke's Marine Lab. In 2009, on the coastal island of Bogue Banks, also known as the Crystal Coast, she invested in a beach townhouse to live within a short drive to the lab and easy

---

3 Meagan is the mother of my grandchildren Avery Grace, Caden Daly, and Tyler James, my youngest grandchild in Durham, who was born during the pandemic (as was Cameron Gerrard—born in Denver to my youngest daughter, Caitlin—the youngest of all my grandchildren).

walking distance of the wide, replenished ocean beach, which stretches for miles. From her second-floor balcony, to the northeast, across the Allen Slough to Money Island Bay, she could see Bogue Sound and to the south, the Atlantic Ocean stretched to the horizon, the two bodies of water less than half a mile apart at this point of the skinny coastal island. Crêpe myrtles grow at both ends of the Atlantic Beach Causeway Bridge that connects the island to the mainland. When she and Jason married in a June wedding at the Watson House and Gardens of Emerald Isle, at the other end of the long island, crêpe myrtles were in full bloom the length of the island.

Over the two decades I've been visiting my oldest daughter, first in Florida and then in North Carolina, at the beach house, at her apartment, and at her house in the Triangle Area, crêpe myrtle trees have continued to fascinate me. To my northerner's eyes, regardless of the season, they appear exotic.

On the other hand, the trees that seem to contain, to project, the most "tree-ness" to me when I consider deciduous trees are maple, oak, beech, and ash—trees well represented in Southeast Michigan's onetime virgin forests of maple, oak, beech, ash, hickory, chestnut, and the four of those species with whom I have shared land.

Do each of us humans make connections with trees on some level, conscious or otherwise? Jean Shinoda Bolen, in her 2011 book *Like a Tree: How Trees, Women, and Tree People Can Save the Planet*, suggests that people like me—and probably people like you, since you're reading this book—are "tree people." While I believe that trees and those humans who support them—"tree people"—may save our planet, I also believe that developing and fostering relationships with trees is one of the things that makes us truly human. After all, our species has been dependent on trees since humans first appeared on the planet—first when we were safe up in their crowns, and then under their sheltering canopy.

Imagine for a moment that all we needed to do to start solving the puzzle of the many personal and planetary challenges facing us—to make things right for ourselves, for the trees, for the Earth—was to listen to the murmurs of the trees more often, more carefully.

The evolutionary ecologist and public science communicator and pioneer in the field of plant bioacoustics Dr. Monica Gagliano suggests one approach:

> When we learn to listen to plants without the need to hear them speak, a language that we have forgotten emerges; it is a language beyond words, one that does not wander or pretend or mislead. It is a language that conveys its rich and meaningful expression by bypassing the household of our mind and directly connecting one spirit to another.

First, take a deep slow breath, remembering where the gift of oxygen for that breath has come from.

Then listen.

What do *you* hear?

Appendix A

The Trees

1. Maple

How do I know that our neighbor's tree—which we could observe from my dad's upper study window of our bungalow parsonage on Tracey Street in Detroit—was a maple?

My memory of its seeds gives the genus of the tree away. Maple seeds are individually enclosed in a distinctive thin-skinned, winged fruit, known as keys or samara. After my introduction to TREE, in my preschool years, I often picked up these "helicopters" from the sidewalk beneath the Dombrowskis' tree.

Let's consider what species of maple that tree most likely could have been. In the maple family (Aceraceae) of about 125 species, there are at least eight species native to the United States and Canada:

- **Sugar maple** (hard maple or rock maple)
- **Silver maple** (soft maple or white maple)
- **Red maple** (scarlet maple or swamp maple)
- **Black maple** (hard maple or rock maple)
- **Striped maple** (moosewood)
- **Mountain maple** (moose maple)
- **Oregon maple** (big leaf maple)
- **Boxelder** (ashleaf maple or Manitoba maple)

But to complicate matters, several other species of *non-native* maples populate American city streets and suburban yards:

- **Japanese maple** (*Acer palmatum*)—Native to Japan, Korea, China, eastern Mongolia, and southeast Russia, Japanese maples were first introduced to England in 1820. The Arnold Arboretum of Harvard University, the oldest garden and arboretum intended for public use in the United States, planted its first Japanese maple on March 1, 1880. The 'Bloodgood' Japanese maple was introduced into the United States before World War II. It is a cultivar named after the Bloodgood Nurseries in Flushing, New York, America's oldest nursery.
- **Sycamore maple** (*Acer pseudoplatanus*)—Also known as planetree maple, this is a native of northwest/central Europe and Asia. The sycamore maple was brought to the northeastern United States via the horticultural trade as a street and parkland tree. At the beginning of the twentieth century, the University of Connecticut recorded the tree seeding itself from planted trees in natural areas. The sycamore maple is now naturalized in at least twelve states but, because of its invasiveness, is prohibited for sale or planting in several states.
- **Norway maple** (*Acer platanoides*)—Native to most of Europe and Asia, this maple species was introduced to the United States from England in 1756 by John Bartram, the first native-born American botanist, as an ornamental shade tree. Relatively unknown until the mid- to late 1800s, the Norway maple became one of the most popular urban trees by the end of the twentieth century.

Several varieties of maple were planted on Detroit streets in the first third of the twentieth century. I'm guessing that the maple who helped me learn the word *tree* was probably a Norway maple, as it was not only the top maple species planted in Detroit but also the top tree species currently represented in the Detroit canopy, comprising 18 percent of the local urban forest.

Norway Maple

Family: Maple (Aceracae)

Scientific name: Acer platanoides

Native range: Native across Europe—from Norway to Caucasus and northern Turkey—and Southwest Asia. Widely planted as an ornamental shade tree across the United States, in particular in Hardiness Zones 4–7.

Preferred habitat: Humid temperate regions. Once revered as a good "street tree" because of its tolerance of city smoke and dust, it "escaped" along roadsides, so it is now considered an invasive tree in wooded areas.

Lifespan: 60–200 years.

Typical size: Fast-growing; 40–60 feet tall (some grow as tall as 100 feet), with a crown up to 70 feet wide and a trunk diameter of 1–2 feet.

Habit: Widely rounded crown of dense foliage, shallow roots.

Bark: Gray or grayish-brown; becoming rough and furrowed in narrow ridges.

Flower: Usually dioecious—male and female on separate trees—but can be monoecious. Buds large (over $3/16$ of an inch) reddish, husky, and blunt; large flowers $5/16$ of an inch wide with 5 greenish-yellow petals on a 1–2-inch-long green stalk in inconspicuous upright or spreading clusters in early spring before leaves. The wind pollinates the female flowers with the pollen of a male flower from a different Norway maple.

Leaf: Opposite attachment, 4–7 inches long and wide. Leaf is broader than tall and palmate, with 5 angular lobes and slender sharp ends; the shallow lobes and edges with scattered long teeth; 5–7 main veins from a notched base. Bright green with sunken veins atop, paler and hairless beneath. Turns bright clear yellow in autumn. Long petioles (leaf stalk) with a bitter milky sap at the end when broken off from the twig, a good way to identify the species.

Fruit/seed: 1½–2 inches long; paired keys (also known as samaras/samarae) with long wings and a flattened body, spreading widely, green-yellow, sometimes with pink blush, pendulous clusters hanging on long stalk; appear in June, mature in summer, fawn-colored in autumn.

Harvested wood: Hard and strong: pale cream in color. Can be seen with curly or quilted grain. Used for veneer, paper (pulpwood), boxes, crates/pallets, musical instruments, turned objects, and other small specialty wood items. Not often grown commercially because of problems associated with gray squirrels, who strip the tree's bark.

More information:

- Norway maples are no longer recommended for planting because of their invasive traits.
- The tree is also prone to girdling roots; the Norway maple in my front yard is choking itself.
- At one time, considered to be the most disease- and insect-resistant of the maples, but Asian long-horned beetles—large, aggressive, wood-boring insects that prefer but do not limit themselves to maples—were first discovered in the United States in 1996 by their "bullet holes" in Norway maples in Brooklyn. The pesticide imidacloprid, a nicotine-based system neurotoxin injected into a tree's vascular system, is considered effective in destroying the pest.
- Norway maples have also proven to be susceptible to verticillium wilt, anthracnose, and tar spot. Verticillium wilt was

first discovered on Californian crops in 1995. The soil-borne fungal blight affects over 300 plant species, and no effective treatment exists. Mulching trees with chips from infected trees is thought to be providing a transmission vehicle for the fungus, which is taken up by the roots. I have a growing concern for the Norway maple in my front yard experiencing crown dieback, a symptom of verticillium wilt; for several years in the past, before I was aware of the threat, I mulched the tree with bagged woodchips.

2. American Sycamore

Family: Plane (Platanaceae)
Scientific name: Platanus occidentalis

Other names:
- American sycamore
- American plane tree (or American planetree)
     NOTE: *Platanus orientalis*, also called the Old World sycamore (Oriental sycamore or Oriental plane tree), grows from the Balkans in Eurasia to as far east, at least, as Iran and is one of the parents of the popular London planetree; the (American) sycamore is the other parent.
- Western plane[1]
- Buttonwood[2]

---

1 The American sycamore's European relatives are known as plane trees; the name "sycamore" in Europe is used for the sycamore maple species (*Acer pseudoplatanus*), aka false plane tree.

2 "Buttonwood" is the alternative name that Thoreau and many earlier naturalists knew the tree by; the fine grain of sycamore wood prevented it from splitting even when carved into something as small and thin as a button.

- Buttonball (or button-ball tree)
- Ghost of the Forest

And, in earlier times:
- "Wild fig-tree"[3] (the word *sycamore* comes from *sŷko*, or fig, and *mór*, or mulberry)
- Water beech
- Cotton-tree (because of hairy down on underside of leaf)

Native range: One genus of eight species, three are North American: the American sycamore, Arizona sycamore, California sycamore. The American sycamore grows in the eastern United States from southwestern Maine west to northeastern Nebraska and south into Texas, and along the Gulf of Mexico to northern Florida. "Sycamores seem to reach their largest proportions in the valleys of the Ohio and Mississippi Rivers." Hardiness Zones 4–9.

Preferred habitat: Moist soils of banks of streams, flood plains, edges of lakes and swamps, and on islands, or rich bottomlands in sun to partial shade, two traits that led William Cullen Bryant to write in his poem "Green River" (using the sycamore's alternative name "plane-tree"):

> *Yet pure its waters, its shallows are bright*
> *With coloured pebbles and sparkles of light,*
> *Clear are the depths where its eddies play,*
> *And dimples deepen and whirl away,*
> *And the plane-tree's speckled arms o'ershoot*
> *The swifter current that mines its root.*

---

3 Falsely so named; in the Far East (and in ancient times), the name "sycamore" is used for the sycamore fig tree (*Ficus sycomorus*).

Lifespan: 200–250 years.

Typical size: 60–120 feet, a large, stately, fast-growing tree, which can grow up to 70 feet in the first 20 years, and one of the largest broadleaf trees in Michigan. The sycamore is generally considered the most massive tree of the eastern United States. On rich bottomlands, it can reach 150 feet in height and 12 feet in diameter; the former champion tree was 15 feet in diameter. No eastern hardwood grows larger in terms of girth.

Habit: "Wayward," often with a massive, buttressed, single trunk and an oval-shaped, open, irregular wide-spreading crown of crooked branches and angular twigs.

Bark: The sycamore is most easily recognized by its striking mottled exfoliating bark, a feature that begins after the tree is 10 years old. Look for an "army camouflage" pattern of plates of smooth, brittle, and blotchy bark of olive green, brownish gray, reddish brown, flaking off from the trunk and branches in oblong, plate-like scales, and the exposed patches of creamy inner bark. Because the sycamore's bark is so rigid, it is unable to stretch to meet the size of the expanding trunk, and instead sheds its bark. The bark flakes off in irregular patches, often with oblong holes in the flakes, exposing the creamy, smooth layer below. Older trees tend to have dark, tough, thick, scaly bark at the bottom of their trunk and light and smooth bark on their branches.

Flower: Monoecious. Male (yellow) and female (red) flowers grow on different twigs in clusters that form a sphere. Wind-pollinated.

Leaf: Resembles a very large maple leaf. Deciduous, alternate, simple, palmately veined with 3–5 lobes with occasional coarse teeth, long-stalked, and large—often 10–12 inches long and 6–8 inches wide, but often as broad or sometimes broader than they are long. The tree's genus name, *Platanus*, most likely comes from the Greek *platys*, meaning "broad."

The underside of the leaf is paler than the dull light green top side. Both sides of the leaves sport a cream-colored fuzz on the veins, which is also on the tree's stems. This indumentum—the hair-like, fluffy covering—is released by wind or touch. One of my tree-care providers has compared the indumentum to fiberglass, as when it is inhaled, it can irritate the eyes, skin, throat, and lungs of people like him, who are sensitive to it.

Sycamore leaves are attached to their twig with a "plunger-like" petiole, which tents over next year's leaf buds.[4] In autumn the leaves first turn yellow and then brown before they wither and fall, characteristically pinwheeling as they head for the ground. If you pick up a fallen leaf and check out the end of the petiole, you'll see the space that this year's bud occupied when the leaf was on the tree.

Fruit/seed: The fruit forms from the female flower, and these ball-shaped dry round fruits are why the tree was named "button-ball tree." Non-edible for humans, the 1-inch round balls, hanging from long stems that allow them to engage in both dangly and bobbing motions, are composed of tightly packed—approximately 800—multiple seeds attached to tan hairs (that can cause irritation to human lungs), which fall into the seed category of "nutlets" called achenes. At the heart of the ball is a hard core of segmented pattern that vaguely resembles the outer ball but is not perfectly spherical and seems to serve as a hub for the hairs, which end in a seed. The sycamore—like the one in my front yard—has single

---

4 Nancy Ross Hugo, author of *Seeing Trees* (Portland, OR: Timber, 2011), makes the apt comparison of the structure to that of a candlesnuffer, with the bud being the flame.

seed balls, while those of the London plane (*P. acernifolia*), thought to be a hybrid of *Platanus orientalis* and *Platanus occidentalis*, hang in two or more per stalk. Seeds are scattered by wind and water.

Harvested wood: Sycamore wood is said to have a beautiful pattern. "The sapwood is white to light tan, while the heartwood is a darker reddish brown. Sycamore . . . has very distinct ray flecks present on quartersawn surfaces—giving it a freckled appearance. It is . . . sometimes called 'Lacewood.'" However, the wood is hard, heavy, and relatively weak; it warps when sawed into lumber. Its interlocked grain makes it difficult to work, but it has historically been used for veneer, paneling (including in Pullman train cars), tobacco and cigar boxes, fruit and vegetable baskets, barrels, pallets, crates, butcher blocks, furniture, piano and organ cases, and, of course, buttons.

More information:

- Some confusion appears to abound, even in a few scholarly sources and particularly with respect to the male flowers, about the difference between the American sycamore and the Sycamore maple (aka "planetree maple")—trees from two different genera.
- Sycamore seed balls (soft and larger) and sweetgum seed balls (hard and generally smaller) are not interchangeable when it comes to identification or use in craft projects.
- A fungal anthracnose disease may defoliate sycamores after an unusually cool, wet spring. When this happens, the tree puts out a second batch of leaves in late June to early July. The sycamore in my yard did this in 2021 after a cool, wet spring.
- Sycamores drop many pieces of their anatomy: male flowers, leaf stipules, bark, twigs, large leaves, seed balls (which, once split, distribute their seeds, each attached to a hair), and the

core of the seed ball, which looks like a similar, but harder, version of the outside. (I'm guessing it was the detritus of all of these parts that accounted for the "messy" aspect my mother forecast based on her grandma's experience.)

3. Oak

Over six hundred species of oak (*Quercus*) grace our planet.

In 2001, the oak tree was voted the favorite tree of the United States in a National Arbor Day Foundation poll, and in 2004, Congress passed and the president signed a historic bill making the oak the official national tree of the US. About ninety species of oak are found in the United States, most of which are categorized into either the red oaks (sharp-tipped leaf lobes) or white oaks (rounded leaf lobes) groups. (The third group of oaks are the live/evergreen oak group, which grow in Hardiness Zones 7–10, so not in Michigan.)

Oaks are "notoriously promiscuous." Oak hybrids abound in many areas, and they can confound the novice trying to sort them out. But not all oaks can cross with one another. The pollen of a scarlet oak (Q. coccinea) would suffer rejection at the stigma of a . . . white oak (Q. alba). These two oaks belong to different oak groups and there are just too many incompatibilities between their genes to allow reproduction.

Depending on who's holding forth, seven to eleven species of oak grow in at least part of Michigan:

White Oak Species

- White oak (*Q. alba*)—Throughout the Lower Peninsula and scattered in the UP

- Swamp white oak (*Q. bicolor*)—Southern half of the Lower Peninsula (aka "bicolor oak")
- Bur oak (*Q. macrocarpa*)—Southern half of the Lower Peninsula (aka "blue oak," "mossycup oak")
- Chinquapin/Chinkapin oak (*Q. muehlenbergii*)—Not common in Michigan; found only in southern quarter of the Lower Peninsula (aka "chinquapin," "yellow oak," "chestnut oak," "rock oak")
- English oak (*Q. robur*)—Introduced; native to Europe, northern Africa, and western Asia

Red Oak Species

- Northern red oak (*Q. rubra*)—Throughout Michigan
- Northern pin oak (*Q. ellipsoidalis*)—Scattered throughout the Lower Peninsula (aka "black oak," "hills oak," "Jack oak")
- Black oak (*Q. velutina*)—Southern half of the Lower Peninsula
- Scarlet oak (*Q. coccinea*)—"Local in Michigan" (aka "red oak," "black oak")
- Shingle oak (*Q. imbricaria*)—Southern Michigan (aka "laurel oak")
- Shumard oak (*Q. shumardii*)—Southern Michigan (aka "spotted oak," "swamp oak")

Given the descriptions of the oak species native to Michigan, my best guess—based on the memory of the Boundary Oak's habit, seared in my mind, of the shape of the leaves that we collected beneath it in the fall to iron between sheets of wax paper, and the fact that its acorns are the only ones to this day that look to me exactly how acorns should look—is that The Boundary Oak was a white oak.

White Oak

Family: Beech (Fagaceae)
Group: White oak (*Leucobalanus*)
Scientific name: Quercus alba

Other names:
- Stave oak (because the wood is outstanding for making the staves of the tight oak barrels used for aging wines, beers, distilled beverages like whiskey and brandy, hot sauces, and traditional balsamic vinegar)
- American oak (the name employed by the American beverage industry because it is the most predominant species used in making aging barrels)
- Northern white oak
- Southern white oak

Native range: Native to the United States: southern Ontario and extreme southern Quebec east to Maine, south to northern Florida, west to eastern Texas, and north to east-central Minnesota; to 5,500 feet or above in southern Appalachians. Sometimes referred to as the "classic eastern oak" and "our mighty oak." Hardiness zones 3–9.

Preferred habitat: Moist, well-drained uplands or lowlands, often in pure stands.

Lifespan: 150–250 years.

Typical size: 50–150 feet with a trunk 3–4 feet or more in diameter.

Habit: Single straight trunk with wide-spreading horizontal stout branches spiraling out—some gnarled and twisted—into a broad rounded crown.

Bark: Light gray, shallowly fissured into long scaly reddish plates or scales, often loose.

Flower: Monoecious. Female flowers are green-red and are at the tips of new shoots; male flowers are greenish-yellow catkins, 2–3 inches long, composed of many tiny flowers, ⅛ of an inch wide and near the tips of last year's branches. Wind-pollinated.

Leaf: Finger-like, 5–9 rounded lobes, 4–8 inches long and 2–4 inches wide, alternately attached, widest above middle and tapering at the base, lacking teeth, bright green above, paler below, often clustered at the ends of the branches. Fall: red/brown, often remaining attached until spring.

Fruit/seed: Green egg-shaped acorn, turns brown, ½–1½ inches long, light-gray cap covers upper third of edible nut, produced each fall, with large crops produced every 4–10 years (aka "mast years"). One tree can produce 2,000 acorns a year.

Harvested wood: Very important tree in the lumber industry. Wood used for furniture, flooring, whiskey barrels, crates, and much more.

More information:

● Susceptible to oak wilt, which can cause gradual death if not treated. While trees in the red oak group die quickly from the disease, white oaks can be treated for oak wilt. To prevent oak wilt, do not prune any oaks during the growing season.

4. Eastern White Pine

Family: Pine (Pinaceae)
Scientific name: Pinus strobus

Other names:
● White pine
● Northern white pine
● Soft pine
● Weymouth pine[5]

---

5 In England, where the eastern white pine was introduced in 1605 by Captain George Weymouth of the British Navy, an English explorer of Maine, where today the eastern white pine is the state tree.

Native range: Native to North America: Eastern North America from Newfoundland, Canada, west through the Great Lakes region to southeastern Manitoba and Minnesota and south along the Appalachian Mountains and upper Piedmont to northernmost Georgia. Hardiness Zones 3–8.

Preferred habitat: Dry and sandy to moist upland sites.

Lifespan: 200–250 years.

Typical size: This is the largest northeastern conifer, averaging 70–100 feet in height but may reach a height 150 feet; diameter 40 inches.

Habit: Single straight tall trunk with whorls of evenly spaced horizontal branches, one whorl added a year, and a broad, irregular crown.

Bark: Gray to brown and smooth when young, breaking with age into large broad scales that are separated by deep furrows.

Flower: Monoecious. Tiny female flowers are light green, tinged with red in small clusters near the top of the tree, and large cylindrical male flowers, up to 2 inches long, in larger clusters near the ends of branches behind the new growth, are yellow.

Leaf: 3–5 inches, soft, slender, flexible needles in clusters of 5; counting the number of needles in the clusters is the best way to identify the tree.

Fruit/seed: Green cones that turn brown when mature, whereupon they are 4–8 inches long, curved, resin-coated, with a pointed white tip on each cone scale.

Harvested wood: Used for construction, millwork, trim, and pulpwood.

More information:

- Many eastern white pine trees have been killed by white pine blister rust—caused by a fungus—which gradually girdles twigs, branches, or trunk, preventing water and nutrients from passing through the area.

5. Eastern Redcedar

Family: Cypress (Cupressaceae)
Scientific name: Juniperus virginiana

Other names:
- Red cedar (also known as eastern red-cedar or eastern red cedar)
- Eastern juniper
- Virginian juniper
- Red juniper
- Tennessee red cedar
- Pencil cedar
- Aromatic cedar
- Virginia red cedar

Native range: Native to North America: Eastern North America from southeastern Canada to the Gulf of Mexico and east of the Great Plains. Hardiness Zones 2–9.

Preferred habitat: The eastern redcedar is tolerant of many conditions: drought, extremes of heat and cold, poor dry soil, alkaline or acidic soils, dry rocky outcrops, wet swampy land, and wind.

Lifespan: Very long-lived; some individuals are older than 500 years. The oldest eastern redcedar reported was 940 years old.

Typical size: Grows to 25–50 feet in height; diameter 12–40 inches.

Habit: Pyramidal.

Bark: Shredding, vertically furrowed red bark.

Flower: Dioecious. Female trees produce light blue-green, egg-shaped, almost-closed conelets on short straight erect stalks and males produce yellow-brown pollen cones (aka strobilus) in large numbers at the tips of the branches.

Leaf: Scaly needles, 1–2 inches long with sharp pointed tips.

Fruit/seed: Seed cones known commonly as "juniper berries," the fruit is about the size of a pea and looks like a dark blueberry with a whitish bloom on it. Each cone contains 1–4 seeds and makes an appearance in fall on female trees.

Harvested wood: Redcedar wood is rot-resistant and known for its aromatic oil, a natural insect repellant. Those fragrant blocks of redcedar heartwood that you may have tucked between your folded wool sweaters (or items made of silk, cashmere, angora, or fur) deter moth larvae, seeking to fulfill their diet of keratin, from grazing on the clothing. The water-resistant, aromatic wood is used outdoors for fence posts and railroad ties, indoors for cedar closets, shoetrees, clothes hangers, and chests, and in perfumes and cosmetics. The red heartwood, drifting toward purple at times, particularly in contrast with the redcedar's pale sapwood, makes for a beautiful finished product.

More information:

● The eastern redcedar and the common juniper (*Juniperus communis*) varieties of juniper are vulnerable to a type of biotrophic fungus, a rust (*Gymnosporangium juniperi-virginianae*) that is known as "cedar apples" (aka "juniper rust"). It takes two hosts within a mile of each other: a juniper species and an apple or crabapple. Similar cedar rusts also affect hawthorn,

pear, quince, serviceberry, and any member of the Rosaceae
family, including Knock Out roses.

● All junipers have a very combustible resinous sap and should
not be planted where there is danger of wildfires.

6. Northern White-Cedar

Family: Cypress (Cupressaceae)
Scientific name: Thuja occidentalis

Other names:
● Eastern white-cedar
● Arborvitae/eastern arborvitae/American arborvitae
● Eastern thuja
● Swamp-cedar

Native range: Native to eastern Canada and much of north-
central and northeastern United States. Hardiness Zones
3–7.

Preferred habitat: Cool, moist, nutrient-rich sites, particularly
on organic soils near streams or other drainage-ways, or in
soil containing calcium carbonate, limestone. "While Cedar
is capable of growing with 'wet feet' it is also found in great
numbers on cliffs and in the sand dunes of western Michigan;
the commonality . . . being that both of these habitats are
inhospitable to most tree species."

Lifespan: Up to 800 years old; oldest known living specimen
over 1,300, but a dead specimen with 1,653 growth rings has
been found.

Typical size: 10–200 feet.

Habit: Dense pyramidal form.

Bark: Stringy-textured, reddish-brown bark.

Flower: Monoecious. Female flowers are in single egg-shaped green cones with 4–6 scales and up to ½ an inch long. Male flowers are short reddish-green pollen cones with brown tips. Both sexes' cones begin to develop in autumn and then grow further in late winter.

Leaf: Scale-like, 0.04–0.40 inches long in alternating crossing pairs in four rows along the twigs, creating fan-shaped branchlets of flattened sprays. Fragrant. Tasty to deer.

Fruit/seed: Pollen cones are small, inconspicuous, and located at the tips of the twigs. The seed cones start out similarly inconspicuous but grow to about ½ an inch long and mature in 6–8 months. They have 6–12 overlapping thick, leathery scales, with each scale bearing 1 or 2 small seeds with a pair of narrow, lateral wings.

Harvested wood: Lightweight, durable, easily split wood, which resists rot and decay; was used for canoe frames and railroad crossties in the past. Now used for fence posts and rails, shingles, siding.

More information:

- More than 100 different varieties of this tree are known.
- Widely cultivated as ornamental trees and used extensively for hedges.

7. Ash

Family: Olive (Oleaceae)

Scientific name: The hybrid of white ash and green ash is identified as *Fraxinus americana* × *pennsylvanica* (aka *Fraxinus pennsylvanica* × *americana*).

Of the native ash found across the Northeast and Upper
Midwest, there are two especially widespread, common species: white ash (*Fraxinus americana*) and green ash (*Fraxinus
pennsylvanica*, sometimes also called "red ash"). These two
species can be very difficult to tell apart, especially because
they hybridize.

> *Green ash may be confused with white ash, which is also
> planted in urban areas as a cultivated tree. The best char-
> acter[istic]s to look at to tell these species apart are the bark,
> the terminal buds and leaf scars on winter twigs, leaflet
> stalks, and fall colour.*

Other names:
- White ash, also called American ash
- Green ash, also called
    - Swamp ash and water ash because of its preference for
      wet soils
    - Red ash because at one time it was thought that green
      ash and red ash were two different species:

> *Red ash (Fraxinus pennsylvanica) and green ash (Frax-
> inus pennsylvanica var. subintegerrima) are nearly iden-
> tical except that the leaves, leaf stalks, flower stalks, fruit
> stalks, and twigs of green ash are almost hairless, while
> those of red ash have dense hairs.*

Native range: Both white and green ash trees are native to North
America, from Nova Scotia to Saskatchewan, south to Florida and Texas. Hardiness Zones 3–9.
Preferred habitat: White ash prefer well-drained upland soil
and sun; green ash prefer wet soils and grow along streams,

in lowland forests, and in shade. (Pelee Island has both environments.)

Lifespan: White ash: 150–200 years; green ash: 75–100 years.

Typical size: White ash: 40–80 feet in height; green ash: 50–60 feet; white ash: 2 feet in diameter; green ash: 1½ feet.

Habit: Single straight trunk (white ash: narrow, open, round crown; green ash: ascending branches and irregular crown).

Bark: Many deep furrows and interlacing diamond-shaped ridges (white ash: greenish-gray; green ash: brown).

Flower: Dioecious. Both female and male flowers have no petals and bloom in small clusters 2 weeks before leaves on separate trees and are cross-pollinated by the wind. White ash male flowers occur in tight clusters of 200–300 flowers on second-year twigs and are less than ⅛ of an inch across, their color from yellowish green to greenish purple. White ash female flowers occur in small panicles on second-year twigs and are similar to male flowers. Both green ash male and female flowers are very similar to white ash flowers of the same sex. Some studies indicate that male ash trees flower every year but female trees flower every 2 to 5 years.

Leaf: Pinnately compound opposite leaves with 5–9 leaflets branched off a central stalk (these branchlets also with an opposite arrangement).

The most distinctive features separating the species [of white ash and green ash] are presence or absence of papillae on lower leaf surfaces, depth of notch on apical margin of leaf scars, presence or absence of waxy flakes exfoliating from the epidermis of second season's growth, the angle between the plane of leaf scars and the twig axis, petiole length and the number of teeth on margins of leaflets.

Fall color is another identification clue: White ash leaves turn a bronze purple in the fall; green ash leaves turn yellow.

Fruit/seed: Samaras (aka keys/winged seeds) that hang in clusters from female trees.

Harvested wood: The strength, elasticity, and resilience of this hardwood make white/green ash wood (because of their similarities, both are generally sold as "white ash") particularly good for baseball bats, bows, tennis rackets, hockey sticks, snowshoes, and tool handles.

More information:

● White ash was the most abundant of all 16 ash tree species in the United States, but green ash was the most widespread of Michigan ash trees.

● White ash and green ash often hybridize, as they did on Pelee Island.

8. English Oak

Family: Beech (Fagaceae)
Group: White oak (*Leucobalanus*)
Species: Quercus robur

Other names:

● Common oak
● Pedunculate oak
● British oak
● European oak

Native range: Most of Europe, northern Africa, and western Asia. Hardiness Zones 4–8.

Preferred habitat: Moist soil, along roadsides and forest edges.

Lifespan: Can live for over 1,000 years!

Typical size: 80–115 feet tall; trunk with a diameter of 3–5 feet.

Habit: Short, stout trunk with wide-spreading branches and broad, rounded, open crown.

Bark: Silver in color; initially smooth but developing deep fissures with age.

Flower: Monoecious. The male flowers form greenish-yellow drooping catkins (known less technically as "those wormy things" and more technically as aments). Each little bump on the catkin is a flower. The catkins grow in large clusters. The red female flowers are very small and round. Both sex flowers grow on different parts of the same branch and are wind pollinated with pollen from other English oak trees. The flowers and leaves sprout together in April or May.

Leaf: Dark green above, pale blue-green beneath; 2–5 inches long and 1¼–2½ inches wide; shallow rounded lobes including 2 small ear-shaped lobes at base of the very short-stalked petiole.

Fruit/seed: Compared to other trees of the white oak group in Michigan, a longer acorn.

Harvested wood: Used extensively in the construction of cabinetry, furniture, boats, and wine and whiskey barrels and for interior trim, flooring, veneer, and firewood.

9. Eastern Cottonwood

Family: Willow (Salicaceae)

Scientific name: Populus deltoides

Other names:

- Common cottonwood
- Southern cottonwood
- Carolina poplar
- Necklace poplar (referring to the long, narrow line of catkins produced by both female and male trees resembling a string of beads)

Native range: Native to North America: eastern, central, and southwestern United States, southernmost part of eastern Canada, and northeastern Mexico. Hardiness Zones 2–9.

Preferred habitat: Found along streams, rivers, lakes, and in lowland areas and floodplains in rich, damp soil; planted for shade and to create windbreaks.

Lifespan: Short-lived, 50–200 years.

Typical size: Fast-growing; 40–80 feet high and a foot or two in diameter, but may reach 150 feet high and measure up to 7–8 feet in diameter. The eastern cottonwood state champion in Michigan in 2012 was in Emmet County, measuring 101 feet high with a crown average of 84 feet and a girth of 26¼ feet. At the time, the largest eastern cottonwood tree in the United States was located in Beatrice, Nebraska, with a girth of 37½ feet, a height of 88 feet, and a crown average of 108 feet.

Habit: Large tree with a massive trunk often forked into stout branches, wide-spreading open, irregular-shaped crown with rounded top and slightly drooping branches.

Bark: When mature, gray, thick with deep, flat furrows.

Flower: Dioecious. 3½-inch-long catkins: male flowers are red, and female flowers are yellowish green; early spring, but not until the tree is at least 15–20 feet tall.

Leaf: Deciduous. Large, smooth (hairless), pointed, sticky, buds flat against twigs. Simple, alternate leaves, thick and waxy, shiny dark green above and below, yellow in autumn. 3–6-inch triangular (the *deltoides* of its species name means "delta-shaped") with curved coarse teeth margins and having two glands where leaf blade connects to petiole. The long, flattened petiole causes the leaves to flutter on the slightest breeze, reflecting glints of sunlight off of their waxy surface.

Fruit/seed: Catkin-like fruit, 4 inches long, made up of many tiny (¼ of an inch long) egg-shaped capsules that split open into 4 parts and release seeds borne by the breeze on the tree's namesake "cotton."

Harvested wood: The fastest-growing species with commercial value in North America. The light, soft wood is used for boxes, crates, furniture, plywood, woodenware, matches, and pulpwood, particularly for paper manufacture.

More information:

🌰 See Donald I. Dickmann and Katherine W. Stuart, *The Culture of Poplars in Eastern North America* (East Lansing: Michigan State University, 1983).

10. Ginkgo

Family: Ginkgo (Ginkgoaceae)
Scientific name: Ginkgo biloba

Other names:

- Gingko (a different spelling pronounced the same way: "*ging*-koh")
- Maidenhair tree (called this in England because the leaves look similar to the native maidenhair fern that grows there)
- Duck's foot (historic Chinese name, so called after the leaf shape)
- Silver apricot (historic Chinese name, so called after the fruit)
- White fruit (most common colloquial Chinese name; silver apricot is the name most often used in writing)
- Grandfather-grandson tree (because only old trees bear seeds, it is the grandson of the planter who benefits from the precious "silver apricots" of the tree)
- Forty-crowns tree (the price the French botanist Pétigny paid for a ginkgo specimen in 1788)
- Tree of Peace
- Tree of Longevity

Native range: Native to China, *Ginkgo biloba* is the oldest tree species on Earth. The species has been unchanged for about 56 million years and fossil records show that it has been present for 270 million years, including during the entire Jurassic period (yes, alongside the dinosaurs). Darwin referred to the ginkgo as "a living fossil" because it is the only surviving species of the ancient Ginkgoaceae family. The ginkgo is thought to be a distant relative of the conifer. While fossils reveal that the ginkgo, at one time, flourished on all parts of the Earth, today this tree is extinct in the wild except for 167 trees discovered in 1989 in Zhejiang province in eastern China. The ginkgo was introduced to the West in 1730 and is planted in the eastern United States and on the Pacific Coast. Hardiness Zones 4–8.

Preferred habitat: A very hardy tree, it prefers deep, sandy, moist soil and requires full sun. Drought-resistant, it can also thrive in cold. It can adapt to soil pH, tolerate air pollution, and resist soil salt contamination. All of these attributes make it a good choice for urban plantings.

Lifespan: A ginkgo can live for 1,000 years; some ginkgo trees in Chinese monastery gardens are approaching 3,500 years old.

Typical size: A medium to large tree, a ginkgo reaches 65–115 feet, although some specimens in China are over 165 feet.

Habit: Straight trunk, upright, broadly angular conical/pyramid-shaped crown becoming widespread and irregular.

Bark: Pale grayish brown; vertically fissured when mature.

Flower: Both sexes of flowers emerge from a leaf shoot with leaves, but not until the tree is 20 to 40 years old (my tree has yet to flower; the oldest it could be is 19 or 20 this past May). The female flower is complicated: a solitary stalk, just under 2 inches long with two opposing ovules at the end of the stalk. The male flower looks like the head of a green stalk of grain, an inch-long catkin-like structure that sprouts in clusters. However, a strange phenomenon of "sex-switching" has been studied in ginkgo trees, where individual branches on ginkgo trees changed sex from male to female or vice versa. Pollination is wind-driven.

Leaf: A lobed simple leaf, about 3 inches wide and distinctively fan-shaped: two-lobed (may be deeply notched or barely at all), leathery leaves with diverging, but almost parallel, veins. Several leaves, spirally arranged, emerge from each shoot. Deep green in the summer, ginkgo leaves turn a very vibrant yellow in autumn and often all fall within a very short period of time, depending on the wind, often leaving a golden ring of heaped leaves around the tree.

Fruit/seed: After 15 to 20 years, female trees produce quite a prized fruit that looks like a small round apricot and contains a sweet nut. The possibility exists that the fruit of ginkgo trees fed dinosaurs in the Jurassic period. However, if the fruit is left to fall and rot, it becomes extremely malodorous, smelling of rancid butter, butyric acid, or vomit, depending on who is describing it. Because of this attribute, male plants are generally used for city and park plantings. Despite its weak toxicity, the "ginkgo nut" has historically been used in Chinese, Japanese, and Korean cuisine—it's said to taste like a pine nut—and has been used for oil and in medicine.

Harvested wood: The wood of a ginkgo is lightweight, brittle, and yellow. In China and Japan, where the wood is not so scarce, gingko wood was used for carving items, such as chess sets and chopping blocks, as well as for firewood.

More information:
- See *The Ginkgo Pages* (https://kwanten.home.xs4all.nl/), a website begun in 1999 by high school teacher and Netherlander Cor Krant, a website that has been recognized for its excellence by Peter Crane of the Yale School of Forestry and Environmental Studies at Yale School and author of *Ginkgo: The Tree That Time Forgot* (London: Yale University Press, 2013).

11. Silver Maple

Family: Maple (Aceraceae)
Scientific name: Acer saccharinum

Other names:
- Silverleaf maple (the underside of the leaves is silver)
- White maple

- River maple, swamp maple, water maple, and creek maple (all alluding to the tree's preference for a wet habitat)
- Soft maple (because its brittle branches break in windstorms, the species is considered one of the soft maples)

Native range: Native to eastern North America. One of the most common trees in the United States, with a range from southeastern Canada to north-central and eastern United States. Hardiness Zones 3–9.

Preferred habitat: Wet, along rivers and rich, moist soil of floodplains; can grow where other trees cannot, such as in poor and compact soil and even in hot, dry conditions.

Lifespan: Fastest growing of the maple species; may live 130 years or more.

Typical size: 75–100 feet. Can reach 50 feet within 20 years.

Habit: A short, thick trunk leading to forking main branches.

Bark: Silvery. On older trees, the bark is in long strips that often peel and curl at the ends.

Flower: Dioecious. Buds are reddish brown with large scales. Female flowers have red pistils and male flowers have greenish-yellow stamen; neither have petals. A silver maple tree can have only female flowers or only male flowers in one year. Silver maple is the first of the maples to bloom in North America, beginning as early as February and extending into May.

Leaf: 5-lobed; light green above and silvery white below.

Fruit/Seed: Develop in paired, light green samaras (aka keys) that are fully formed when leaves develop and that when mature (brownish-green) fall from the tree in early summer.

Harvested wood: Soft and brittle with a close, tight grain. The sapwood of maple trees is more commonly used than the heartwood. The sapwood of the silver maple ranges from almost white to a light golden or reddish brown, and it may have a curly or quilted grain pattern. The wood is used for veneer, paper (as pulpwood), boxes, crates, and pallets, musical instruments, turned objects, and other small specialty wood items.

More information:

> *The silver maple is closely related to the red maple (Acer rubrum) and can hybridize with it. The hybrid is known as the Freeman maple (Acer × freemanii). The Freeman maple is a popular ornamental tree in parks and large gardens, combining the fast growth of silver maple with the less brittle wood, less invasive roots, and the beautiful bright red fall foliage of the red maple.*

12. Sweetgum

Family: Witch-Hazel (Hamamelidacea)
Scientific name: Liquidambar styraciflua

Other names:
- American sweet gum
- Gum tree
- Gum-wood
- Redgum
- Sapgum
- Star-leaf gum
- White gum
- Liquidamber
- Satin-walnut

- Alligator-tree or alligatorwood
- Opossum-tree
- Hazel pine
- Copalm balsam
- American storax
- Bilsted (an "Americanism" dating back to 1755–65; origin uncertain)

Native range: Native to the eastern United States: extreme southwest Connecticut south through the east to central Florida and eastern Texas and as far west as Missouri, Arkansas, and Oklahoma, but only as far north as southern Illinois. It has been planted in California and cultivated in Hawaii. Hardiness Zones 5–9.

Preferred habitat: Tolerant of different soils and sites but classified as shade intolerant. It grows best on low, rich, moist, alluvial clay and loamy soils of river bottoms.

Lifespan: More than 150 years.

Typical size: 60–120 feet tall.

Habit: Straight trunk, conical crown that becomes a round and spreading canopy.

Bark: Gray, thick, deeply furrowed in narrow scaly ridges. The tree's dark gray-brown twigs have unusual, corky ridges that look like wings.

Flower: Monoecious. Flowers of both sexes appearing high in the tree from March to May, depending on latitude and weather. The spherical female flower structures hang down below the leaves containing masses of tiny yellow-green flowers. The male flowers rise up above the leaves on a thick stalk that contains clusters of very small red and green flowers in very large numbers.

Leaf: The simple, star-shaped lobed leaves are glossy green in summer. Their color variations of yellow, orange, red, and purple in autumn make this a popular ornamental tree. When the leaves begin to fall, they emit a pleasant smell that lasts until they are dry and shriveled. If a leaf is crushed, it smells like turpentine.

Fruit/seed: The spiky "gumball" fruits are a woody brown spherical cluster of *compound* seed capsules, 1–1½ inches in diameter with openings in the surface that release one or two seeds from each capsule. Each ball may hold more than 50 seeds. The fruit ripens in the fall (September–November) and often persists on the tree throughout the winter.

Harvested wood: Sweetgum wood can achieve a high polish and is second only to oaks as a timber tree among hardwoods. It is an important lumber crop in the American South, but because its wood is not strong, it is generally used in combination with other woods as a veneer or in the production of plywood. Veneer is used for crates, baskets, and interior woodwork. Lumber is used to make boxes, crates, furniture, interior trim, and millwork. Also used for crossties and fuel, with small amounts used for fencing, excelsior, and pulpwood.

13. American Beech

Family: Beech (Fagaceae)
Scientific name: Fagus grandifolia

Other names:
- Common beech
- North American beech

Native range: Native to North America: Nova Scotia west to southern Ontario, west to Wisconsin, and south to eastern Texas and northern Florida. Hardiness Zones 4–9.

Preferred habitat: The sandy loam of well-drained bottomlands or rich, moist uplands; shade tolerant. Grows with oaks and maples in mixed deciduous forests but is often found in pure stands.

Lifespan: 350 years or more.

Typical size: Slow-growing, typically 60–80 feet, but can grow to 125 feet.

Habit: Broad, spreading crown up to 60 feet wide.

Bark: Smooth, ashy gray.

Flower: Monoecious. The reddish female flower develops in pairs on the ends of new twig growth. The male flowers are small, yellow, drooping catkins. Pollination is wind-driven.

Leaf: Dark green, toothed, elliptical leaves, up to 6 inches long, turn gold and then brown in the autumn.

Fruit/seed: Beechnut (aka mast): a three-sided sweet nut enclosed in husklike seedpods that look like small burrs, singularly or in pairs; at the most three nuts to pod.

Harvested wood: Light reddish wood is durable underwater and is valued for tool handles, wood pulp, baskets, flooring, inexpensive furniture, and shipping containers.

More information:

● In a study published in the journal *Forest Pathology*:

Researchers and naturalists from Ohio State University and metroparks in northeastern Ohio report on the emerging "beech leaf disease" epidemic, calling for speedy work to find a culprit so that work can begin to stop its spread. Already, the disease has been found in 11 Ohio counties, eight Pennsylvania counties and five counties in Ontario, Canada. It's characterized by dark-green "bands" that appear between the veins of the trees' leaves and provide the first hint that the tree is diseased. In later stages, leaves become uniformly darker, shrunken, crinkly and leathery. Affected limbs stop forming buds and, over time, the tree dies. Young trees seem to be particularly vulnerable.

14. Colorado Pinyon

Family: Pine (Pinaceae)
Scientific name: Pinus edulis

Other names:
- Pinyon pine
- Piñon
- Two-needle piñon

Native range: Native to southwestern North America: Arizona, New Mexico, Colorado, Nevada, and Utah; also native to the desert mountains of California, east to New Mexico and Texas and north to Wyoming. Hardiness Zones 5–9.

Preferred habitat: Open woodlands, alone or with junipers on dry rocky foothills, mesas, and plateaus, at 5,200–9,000-feet elevation.

Lifespan: Long-lived; may exceed 600 years.

Typical size: A small, slow-growing tree: 15–50 feet tall, with a diameter up to 24 inches.

Habit: Gnarly and spreading, tending toward bushy; its crown is nearly as wide as the tree is tall.

Bark: Gray, smooth, and thin when young; red-brown, rough, and furrowed into scaly ridges at maturity.

Flower: Monoecious. Male cones are red, cylindrical, and in clusters of 20–40 near the ends of branches. Female flowers are solitary, purplish, and at branch tips.

Leaf: Evergreen needles: short (1–2 inches long), stout, and stiff, in clusters of two.

Fruit/seed: It takes 15–25 years for a tree to produce seeds, and then they are produced only once every 4 to 7 years, depending on rainfall. Short, stubby 1–2-inch cones don't mature until September of their second year (18 months). Each cone contains 10–20 "large" (½-inch) tear-shaped, ivory-colored, oily, edible seeds. Pinyon nuts are seeds similar to pine nuts, but the mild flavor of the pinyon nut is considered superior to the nuts from all other pines.

Harvested wood: Fence posts and fuel. A common wood to burn in chimeneas, terracotta outdoor fireplaces, for its distinctive fragrance.

15. Eastern Redbud

Family: Legume (Fabaceae)
Scientific name: Cercis canadensis

Other names:
- Redbud (or red bud)
- American redbud
- Spice tree (local to Appalachia, where the twigs and flowers are used in tea and the flowers are fried to eat)
- Love tree (from its heart-shaped leaves)
- Judas-tree or flowering Judas (from the belief Judas Iscariot hanged himself from this species of tree after betraying Jesus)
- Mediterranean redbud (from the Mediterranean, this is actually a different redbud from the eastern redbud)

Native range: Native to eastern North America: New Jersey south to central Florida, west to southern Texas, and north to southeastern Nebraska; also New Mexico, to 2,200-feet elevation. Hardiness Zones 4–9.

Preferred habitat: Moist soils, along streams, hardwood forest edges; as an understory tree, can tolerate shade.

Lifespan: 75 years.

Typical size: A small tree, 15–30 feet tall; spreads to 25–35 feet in diameter; the trunk is 10–12 inches in diameter.

Habit: Irregular flattop with umbrella-spoke branches hanging down in a horizontal branching pattern.

Bark: Smooth and flat, dark brown to black; with age, becomes marked with shallow furrows and scaly ridges. "The inner bark has high concentrations of tannins, which have a wide range of medicinal uses; an infusion of the bark has been used as a febrifuge and cough suppressant, helping to treat colds, fevers, and influenza."

Flower: Not classified as monoecious or dioecious, a redbud is cosexual (as are dogwoods, magnolia, apple, cherry, pear, rhododendron, yellow poplar, and American elm). Cosexual trees produce single flowers with both fully functional male and female parts. Long-lasting pink to purplish-pink to magenta pea-like flowers blooming for 2 or 3 weeks before the leaves. The redbud is cauliflorous, which describes their unique flowering along the woody, bare branches and trunk.

Leaf: Broad, heart-shaped leaves with smooth margins, 2½–4½ inches, reddish in spring, dark green in summer, and light yellow in fall. (The 'Forest Pansy', one of the most popular cultivars, has leaves that begin as shiny reddish-purple, then darken to maroon—the more sun, the darker the color; in fall, the cultivar's leaves are a profusion of reds, purples, and yellows.) The redbud is unique among members of the

Fabaceae family (earlier and alternatively known as the Leguminosae family)—commonly known as the legume, pea, or bean family—in not having compound, stipulate leaves.

Fruit/seed: Flattened, dry, beanlike rosy pods (2–4 inches long) that mature to purplish-brown in summer. Pods may remain on the tree into winter. Each pod has 6–12 seeds.

Harvested wood: Very hard and dry, redbud wood is used in the production of decorative bowls, knife handles, gunstocks, and veneers. The heartwood of the tree is black.

16. Japanese Zelkova

Family: Elm (Ulmaceae)
Scientific name: Zelkova serrata

Other names:
- Keaki
- Japanese keaki elm

Native range: Native to Japan, Korea, Taiwan, and Manchuria, it was introduced into the United States in 1862. Hardiness Zones 5–8.

Preferred habitat: Full to partial sun. Grows in a wide range of soil textures, acidic to slightly alkaline, moist to dry. Can tolerate compacted soil but prefers moist, well-drained soils. Tolerates wind, drought, and air pollution.

Lifespan: One of the oldest and best-known Zelkova trees grows in Toyono Nose, Osaka, Japan, and is called the Great Zelkova Nomo. It is more than 1,000 years old and is a National Natural Monument.

Typical size: Large, good shade tree. Fast-growing in its youth, it may grow to 98 feet tall, averaging 60 feet high by 60 feet wide.

Habit: A short main trunk divides into many upright and erect spreading stems into a vase-shaped habit with a broad, round-topped crown.

Bark: Grayish-white to grayish-brown and either smooth with lenticels or exfoliating in patches to reveal orange inner bark.

Flower: Monoecious. Male flowers are ⅛ of an inch long, greenish, and clustered at the base of new lower leaves. A solitary or a few almost stalkless female flowers develop in upper leaves.

Leaf: 1¼–2 inches long, simple and ovate with serrated margins and alternatively arranged. Slightly rough. Dark green in spring and summer, changing to a mix of yellows, oranges, and reds in autumn.

Fruit/seed: Small (about ¼-inch diameter), ovate/kidney-shaped, wingless green drupes that ripen to brown in late summer to autumn.

Harvested wood: Referred to as "Keyaki," the wood of the Japanese zelkova is highly prized by woodworkers for its beautiful grain. It is also hard, heavy, and dense, making it strong and durable. It is used for interior decoration (flooring and moldings), sculpture, traditional ornamental craft pieces (particularly lacquerware, bowls, and trays), furniture and cabinetry, and boat building.

More information:

● *Zelkova serrata* is planted as a lawn or park tree for its attractive bark, leaf color, and vase shape. It is commonly grown as an ornamental tree and is a popular choice for bonsai. Highly resistant to Dutch elm disease, it also displays good resistance to elm leaf beetle and Japanese beetle.

Appendix B

The Old-Growth Forests of Michigan

"Downstate" (in the lower half of Michigan's Lower Peninsula)

- **Newton Woods** (Fred Russ Forest, Cass County, east of Dowagiac)—Of 280 acres designated for Michigan State University research, 40 are a forest of undisturbed old-growth mixed mesic hardwoods,[1] primarily oak-hickory, designated as a national natural landmark.
- **Warren Woods** (Warren Dunes State Park, Berrien County, north of Three Oaks)—A more than 300-acre national area with the last known stand of virgin beech-maple forest in southern Michigan, designated as a national natural landmark.
- **Toumey Woodlot** (Michigan State University's campus in East Lansing, Ingham County)—A 24-acre tract of beech-maple forest, designated as a national natural landmark.

---

1 "Mesic" means: of, relating to, or adapted to an environment having a balanced supply of moisture.

"Up North" (in the upper half of Michigan's Lower Peninsula)

- **Roscommon Virgin Pine Stand** (Au Sable State Forest, eight miles east of Roscommon, Roscommon County)—A 34-acre grove of virgin red pine, one of the best stands in the Central Lowland portion of the United States and typical of the virgin pine forest that once covered much of the upper-middle part of the Lower Peninsula,[2] designated as a national natural landmark.

- **Hartwick Pines** (Hartwick Pines State Park, north of Grayling, Crawford County)—White pines and red pines with some hemlock.

- **Interlochen State Park** (southwest of Traverse City, Grand Traverse County)—Michigan's first officially recognized state park, Interlochen was created to preserve a stand of virgin eastern white pine for future generations and was originally called Pine Park.

- **South Manitou Island** (Sleeping Bear Dunes National Lakeshore, in Lake Michigan, accessible by ferry from Leland in Leelanau County)—The island's Valley of the Giants is a grove of enormous old northern white-cedars.

- **Colonial Point Memorial Forest** (Chaboiganing Nature Preserve, Cheboygan County, near Burt Lake)—These 484 wooded acres are the site of the largest old-growth red-oak stand in the northern Lower Peninsula, with trees as old as 150 years.

---

2   The Central Lowland is a flat-lying region located between the Appalachian Mountains to the east and the Great Plains to the west, extending from the Canadian Shield in the north to the Atlantic Coastal Plain in the south.

In Michigan's Upper Peninsula

- **Tahquamenon Natural Area** (Tahquamenon Falls State Park, Paradise, Luce County)—One of Michigan's largest old-growth northern hardwood forests. Tahquamenon River is the river in Longfellow's poem "Hiawatha." The Upper Tahquamenon Falls area offers a glimpse of Michigan's pre-settlement forests: 1,500 acres of old-growth forest of American beech, sugar maple, eastern hemlock, and yellow birch. The four-mile River Trail parallels the Tahquamenon River between the Upper and Lower Falls, traversing through old-growth forest, giant cedars, and hemlocks.
- **Estivant Pines Nature Sanctuary** (southeast of Copper Harbor at the tip of the Keweenaw Peninsula, Keweenaw County)—Old-growth conifer-dominated forest, particularly white pine.
- **Sylvania Wilderness** (Ottawa National Forest, southeast of Watersmeet, Gogebic County)—18,000 acres of record-sized red and white pines as well as old-growth hardwoods.
- **Porcupine Mountains** (Porcupine Mountains Wilderness State Park, northeast of Ironwood, Ontonagon County)—Adjacent to Lake Superior, at approximately 60,000 acres, this is Michigan's largest state park and home to a 35,000-acre old-growth forest, known as the "'biggest and best tract of virgin Northern Hardwoods in North America,' and . . . certainly one of the largest relatively undisturbed northern hemlock-hardwood forests west of the Adirondacks," which contains stands of massive hemlocks, white pine, and northern hardwoods.

Notes

ix "my Great Lakes island book was in the process of being published" See *Great Lakes Island Escapes: Ferries and Bridges to Adventure* (Detroit: Wayne State University Press, 2016).

2 "The most beautiful" Arbor Day Foundation, *What Tree Is That? A Guide to the More Common Trees Found in North America* (Lincoln, NE: Arbor Day Foundation, 2016), 85.

3 "In the gardens of Europe" Julia Ellen Rogers, *Trees Worth Knowing* (New York: Doubleday, Page, 1917), 257.

15 "And a new day will dawn" Led Zeppelin, "Stairway to Heaven," *Led Zeppelin IV* (Atlantic Records, 1971).

25 "An oak can be very tough" Peter Wohlleben, *The Hidden Life of Trees: What They Feel, How They Communicate— Discoveries from a Secret World* (Vancouver, BC: Greystone Books, 2015), 70.

25 "White oaks, which can live 600 years" Nancy Ross Hugo, *Seeing Trees: Discover the Extraordinary Secrets of Everyday Trees* (Portland, OR: Timber, 2011), 202.

25 "*Quercus* [Oak's genus name] belongs" Harriet L. Keeler, *Our Native Trees: And How to Identify Them* (New York: Charles Scribner's Sons, 1905), 326.

25 "Windsor Great Park . . . contains" Simon de Bruxelles, "Queen Fells Beloved Windsor Castle Oak Trees to Rebuild a Ship Fit for a Saxon King," *Daily Mail*, March 9, 2019, dailymail.co.uk/news.

26 "Years ago, I stumbled across a patch"   Wohlleben, *The Hidden Life of Trees*, 1.

27 *"they who know the oak"*   *Online Etymology Dictionary*, etymonline.com (accessed 2/07/20).

27 "Plants use their senses"   Stefano Mancuso and Alessandra Viola, *Brilliant Green: The Surprising History and Science of Plant Intelligence* (Bologna: Island, 2015), 4.

30 "directly impacted by humans"   Anthony D'Amato and Paul Catanzaro, "Restoring Old-Growth Characteristics" (Amherst: UMass Extension and Massachusetts Chapter of the Nature Conservancy, 2007), 4, https://extension .unh.edu/sites/default/files/migrated_unmanaged_files/ Resource000429_Rep451.pdf.

30 "The earliest lumbering in Michigan"   Randall Schaetzl, "White Pine Logging: A Background," *Michigan: A Geography*, http://geo.msu.edu/extra/geogmich/loggingbackgrd.html (accessed 3/27/22).

34 "I worked on a middle-grade book about the Great Lakes" *All about the Great Lakes* (Indianapolis: Blue River, 2020).

34 "old-growth forest having dwindled"   L. E. Frelich and C. G. Lorimer, "Natural Disturbance Regimes in Hemlock-Hardwood Forests of the Upper Great Lakes Region," *Ecological Monographs* 61, no. 2 (1991): 95.

41 "Using Stan Tekiela's field guide"   Stan Tekiela, *Trees of Michigan Field Guide* (Cambridge, MN: Adventure, 2002).

43 "repeated infection of this pathogen"   Helga George, "How to Identify, Prevent, and Control Cedar Apple Rust," *Gardener's Path*, July 3, 2019, https://gardenerspath.com/how-to/disease -and-pests/cedar-apple-rust-control/.

43 "The damage done to the leaves"   George, "How to Identify, Prevent, and Control Cedar Apple Rust."

44 "When possible"   "Cedar-Apple, Cedar-Hawthorn, & Cedar-Quince Rust," *Chicago Botanic Gardens*, https://www .chicagobotanic.org/plantinfo/cedar_apple_cedar_hawthorn _cedar_quince_rust (accessed 6/30/20).

46 "here is the suggested two-pronged strategy"   Jackie Carroll,
     "What Is Cedar Hawthorn Rust: Identifying Cedar Hawthorn
     Rust," *Gardening Know How*, https://www.gardeningknowhow
     .com/plant-problems/disease/cedar-hawthorn-rust-disease
     .htm (accessed 12/20/20).

47 "recognized irritant . . . moderately toxic to birds"
     "Chlorothalonil," *PPDB: Pesticide Properties DataBase* (last
     updated 3/11/2021), University of Hertfordshire, Hatfield, UK,
     http://sitem.herts.ac.uk/aeru/ppdb/en/Reports/150.htm.

47 "in addition to being a skin, eye, and respiratory irritant"
     "Chlorothalonil."

47 "Chlorothalonil exposure was found to have an effect"
     Scott T. O'Neal et al., "Chlorothalonil Exposure Alters Virus
     Susceptibility and Marker of Immunity, Nutrition, and
     Development in Honey Bees," *Journal of Insect Science* 19, no. 3
     (2019): 14, https://academic.oup.com/jinsectscience/article/
     19/3/14/5497621.

47 "mancozeb is a combination of two fungicides"   "Mancozeb,"
     PPDB: Pesticide Properties DataBase (last updated 3/11/2021),
     University of Hertfordshire, Hatfield, UK, http://sitem.herts
     .ac.uk/aeru/ppdb/en/Reports/150.htm.

48 "The widely used fungicide mancozeb"   Marta Axelstad et al.,
     "Exposure to the Widely Used Fungicide Mancozeb Causes
     Thyroid Hormone Disruption in Rat Dams but No Behavioral
     Effects in the Offspring," *Toxicological Sciences* 120, no. 2
     (2011): 439–46.

48 "defined as a normal maternal thyroid-stimulating hormone"
     Isabelle Runkle et al., "Early Levothyroxine Treatment
     for Subclinical Hypothyroidism or Hypothyroxinemia in
     Pregnancy," *Frontiers in Endocrinology*, October 19, 2021.
     https://doi.org/10.3389/fendo.2021.743057.

48 "mancozeb is also highly toxic"   "Mancozeb."

48 "it has been found to be moderately toxic"   "Bordeaux
     Mixture," *PPDB: Pesticide Properties DataBase* (last updated
     3/11/2021), University of Hertfordshire, Hatfield, UK, http://
     sitem.herts.ac.uk/aeru/ppdb/en/Reports/150.htm.

48 "A nickname for a Bordeaux mixture-stained" Dan Koeppel, *Banana: The Fate of the Fruit That Changed the World* (New York: Plume, 2008), 108.

49 "Given that plants do not have pain receptors" Melissa Petruzzello, "Do Plants Feel Pain?" *Britannica*, https://www .britannica.com/story/do-plants-feel-pain (accessed 12/19/20).

49 "The simple answer is that" "Do Plants Feel Pain? Things to Consider," *PETA*, https://www.peta.org/features/do-plants -feel-pain/ (accessed 12/19/20).

49 "Itzhak Khait and his colleagues at Tel Aviv University" Adam Vaughan, "Plants Emit Informative Airborne Sounds under Stress," *NewScientist*, December 5, 2019, https://www .newscientist.com/article/2226093-recordings-reveal-that -plants-make-ultrasonic-squeals-when-stressed/.

50 "Both species are just two of the sixty-three" "Juniperus," *The Gymnosperm Database*, https://www.conifers.org/cu/Juniperus .php (accessed 12/19/20).

58 "pandemics rely on the introduction" Alberto Santini and Andrea Battisti, "Complex Insect-Pathogen Interactions in Tree Pandemics," *Frontiers in Physiology*, May 9, 2019, https:// www.frontiersin.org/articles/10.3389/fphys.2019.00550/full.

58 "The introduction of alien species" Roberto Danti and Gianni Della Rocca, "Epidemiological History of Cypress Canker Disease in Source and Invasion Sites," *Forests* (Multidisciplinary Digital Publishing Institute, April 15, 2017), as found in R. P. Keller, M. W. Cadotte, and G. Sandiford, *Invasive Species in a Globalized World: Ecological, Social, and Legal Perspectives on Policy* (Chicago: University of Chicago Press, 2014), 1–20.

58 "creates the conditions for a range of deadly pathogens" Katarina Zimmer, "Deforestation Is Leading to More Infectious Diseases in Humans," *National Geographic*, November 22, 2019, https://www.nationalgeographic.com/ science/2019/11/deforestation-leading-to-more-infectious -diseases-in-humans/.

58 "When forests or grasslands are razed"   Helen Briggs, "Covid: Why Bats Are Not to Blame, Say Scientists," BBC News, October 13, 2020, https://www.bbc.com/news/science-environment-54246473.

58 "a squirrel could travel"   Josh Swartz, "The 'Most Ambitious' Species Restoration Project in the World," posted on radio station WBUR's blog *Endless Thread* at https://www.wbur.org/endlessthread/2018/04/27/that-old-chestnut (accessed 1/11/21).

58 "The demise of the American chestnut trees"   George A. Zentmyer, "Origin and Distribution of *Phytophthora cinnamomi*," *California Avocado Society 1985 Yearbook* 69:89–96, http://www.avocadosource.com/cas_yearbooks/cas_69_1985/cas_1985_pg_89-96.pdf (accessed 1/12/21).

59 "PPR steadily killed the chestnut"   Jane Hodgins, "What It Takes to Bring Back the Near Mythical American Chestnut Trees," U.S. Department of Agriculture blog, July 29, 2021, https://www.usda.gov/media/blog/2019/04/29/what-it-takes-bring-back-near-mythical-american-chestnut-trees.

59 Sandra Anagnostakis, "Protecting Chestnut Trees from Blight" (Connecticut: Connecticut Agricultural Experiment Station, 1997).

59 "there are only 100 or so"   Hodgins, "What It Takes to Bring Back the Near Mythical American Chestnut Trees."

61 "This fungus was first reported in the United States"   "Dutch Elm Disease," *Life*, September 11, 1944, 59.

61 "The European elm bark beetles"   C. J. D'Arcy, "Dutch Elm Disease," *APS* (American Phytopathological Society), 2005, https://www.apsnet.org/edcenter/disandpath/fungalasco/pdlessons/Pages/DutchElm.aspx.

61 "Quarantining and sanitation efforts"   "Dutch Elm Disease." *Life*, September 11, 1944, 59.

61 "The first case of Dutch elm disease"   "Michigan History: How Detroit Lost Its Stately Elms," *Detroit News*, December 20, 2001.

61 "Of the estimated 77 million elms"   "New Varieties of Elm
    Raise Hope of Rebirth for Devastated Tree," *New York Times*,
    December 5, 1989.

62 "my cross-folded, laminated, tree-identifier leaflet"   Thomas
    Rosburg, "Trees in Your Pocket: A Guide to Trees of the Upper
    Midwest," in *A Bur Oak Guide* (Iowa City: University of Iowa
    Press, 2012).

62 "A concentration of [rock elms]"   Landmark Trees of Ontario,
    Facebook, November 9, 2012, https://www.facebook.com/
    LandmarkTreesOntario/photos/a.155316981273729.32695
    .146668978805196/172224482916312.

63 "Beech bark disease (BBD) has been killing"   Jennifer L.
    Koch, "Beech Bark Disease: The Oldest 'New' Threat to
    American Beech in the United States," *Outlooks on Pest
    Management*, April 2010, 64–68, a part of the USDA Forest
    Service Scientific Journal Publication series, https://www.nrs.fs
    .usda.gov/pubs/jrnl/2010/nrs_2010_koch_002.pdf.

63 "first introduced to the continent"   James J. Worrall, "Beech
    Bark Disease," *Forest Pathology*, https://forestpathology.org/
    canker/beech-bark/ (accessed 1/11/21).

63 "its geographic origin unknown"   Katy Mallams et al.,
    "Evaluation of the Status of Cypress Canker on Young
    Port-Orford-Cedar in Coos County, Oregon," *USDA
    Forest Service*, https://www.fs.usda.gov/Internet/FSE
    _DOCUMENTS/fsbdev2_026319.pdf (accessed 1/15/21).

63 "believed to have originated in"   Jennifer Juzwik et al., "The
    Origin of *Ceratocystis fagacearum*, the Oak Wilt Fungus,"
    Annual Review of Phytopathology 46 (September 2008): 13–26.

63 "first reported in the Upper Mississippi River"   "Oak
    Wilt—*Ceratocystis fagacearum*," *Invasive and Emerging
    Fungal Pathogens—Diagnostic Fact Sheets*, USDA Agricultural
    Research Service, https://www.nrcs.usda.gov/Internet/FSE
    _DOCUMENTS/nrcs144p2_002511.pdf (accessed 2/28/21).

63 "It can be carried by beetles"   Maya Hayslett, Jennifer Juzwik,
    and Bruce Moltzan, "Three *Colopterus* Beetle Species Carry the

Oak Wilt Fungus to Fresh Wounds on Red Oak in Missouri," *Plant Disease* 92, no. 2 (2008): 270–75.

63 "An infected tree is killed *within a few weeks*" Bill Cook, "Oak Wilt Disease," *Michigan State University Extension*, April 11, 2016, https://www.canr.msu.edu/news/oak_wilt _disease_1.

64 "Every part of the world has experienced" Stephanie Pain, "Why Tree-Killing Epidemics Are on the Rise," *Smithsonian*, September 28, 2020, https://www.smithsonianmag.com/ science-nature/why-tree-killing-epidemics-are-rise -180975917/.

64 "which came from northern Japan" "Japanese Beetle (*Popilla japonica*)," *Minnesota Department of Natural Resources Invasive Terrestrial Animals*, https://www.dnr.state.mn.us/invasives/ terrestrialanimals/japanese_beetle/index.html (accessed 1/15/21).

64 "feed on about three hundred species of plants" "Japanese Beetles in Yards and Gardens," *University of Minnesota Extension Yard and Garden Insects*, https://extension.umn.edu/ yard-and-garden-insects/japanese-beetles (accessed 1/15/21).

64 "native to Japan and first observed" "Hemlock Woolly Adelgid," *New York State Department of Environmental Conservation*, https://www.dec.ny.gov/animals/7250.html (accessed 1/15/21).

65 "has the potential to do more damage than Dutch elm disease" "Asian Longhorned Beetle," *USDA Animal and Plant Health Inspection Service*, https://www.aphis.usda.gov/aphis/resources/ pests-diseases/hungry-pests/the-threat/asian-longhorned -beetle/asian-longhorned-beetle (accessed 1/15/21).

65 "was first discovered in the United States" "Emerald Ash Borer," *Arbor Day Foundation*, https://www.arborday.org/trees/ health/pests/emerald-ash-borer.cfm (accessed 1/15/21).

65 "Since 2002, EAB has killed" "Michigan Information," *Emerald Borer Information Network*, http://www .emeraldashborer.info/state/michigan.php (accessed 1/15/21).

69   "he sought refuge at the Boscobel House"   English
        Heritage, "Charles II and the Royal Oak," https://www
        .english-heritage.org.uk/visit/places/boscobel-house-and
        -the-royal-oak/history/charles-ii-and-the-royal-oak/#:
        ~:text=Like%20many%20other%20houses%20belonging
        ,priests%2C%20known%20as%20priest%20holes (accessed
        3/30/22).

70   "Ah, this truly is a Royal Oak"   Owen A. Perkins, *Royal
        Oak, Michigan: The Early Years* (Royal Oak, MI: Royal Oak
        Historical Society, 1974), 15.

71   "get the story"   "Royal Oak's Acorns Come from Original
        Tree in England," *Royal Oak Tribune*, November 12, 1937, in
        Royal Oak Twigs and Acorns: A Book of History, compiled by
        David G. Penney and Lois A. Lance (Royal Oak, MI: Little
        Acorn, 1996), 259.

72   the acorns arrived   Owens A. Perkins, *Royal Oak, Michigan:
        The Early Years* (Royal Oak, MI: Golden Jubilee '71, 1971),
        16–18.

72   "MEMORIAL PARK & ENGLISH OAK GROVE"
        D. Penney, *Royal Oak Historical Tour* (Royal Oak, MI: Royal
        Oak Historical Society, 2001), 4.

73   "Two historic oak trees"   Donald Drife, "Historic Oaks
        Planted at Museum," *Royal Oak Historical Society Newsletter*,
        July 2021, 2.

74   "The last survey done"   Scott Daniel, Mike McConnell,
        "Royal Oak Moving to Protect Trees," *Royal Oak Patch*, posted
        June 19, 2017, https://patch.com/michigan/royaloak/royal-oak
        -moving-protect-trees (accessed 8/19/22).

74   "But a city report"   Royal Oak Planning Division, Royal
        Oak Community Development Memorandum, July 28, 2017,
        "Proposed Zoning Ordinance Text Amendments, Preservation
        and Replacement of Existing Trees," https://www.romi.gov/
        DocumentCenter/View/18484 (accessed 9/08/22).

78   "re-engaged Revolutionary ideals"   From the University
        of Pennsylvania Press's catalog description of Paul Douglas

Newman's book *Fries's Rebellion: The Enduring Struggle for the American Revolution* (Philadelphia: University of Pennsylvania Press, 2004), https://www.upenn.edu/pennpress/book/14088.html (accessed 4/24/22).

81 "In 2018, the top five countries"   Abby Budiman, "Key Findings about U.S. Immigrants," *Fact Tank: News in the Numbers*, Pew Research Center, August 20, 2020, https://www.pewresearch.org/fact-tank/2020/08/20/key-findings-about-u-s-immigrants/.

82 "Donald Trump will be remembered"   Rita Prasad, "US Historians on What Donald Trump's Legacy Will Be," BBC News, January 19, 2021, https://www.bbc.com/news/world-us-canada-55640427.

83 "Nature has its own ways of organizing information"   Pedro Cruz, John Wihbey, Avni Ghael, and Felipe Shibuya, "Stimulated Dendrochronology of U.S. Immigration, 1790–2016," part of an ongoing project with support by the College of Arts, Media, and Design at Northeastern University, https://web.northeastern.edu/naturalizing-immigration-dataviz/ (accessed 5/05/20).

95 "Greenmead Historical Park"   "Greenmead Farms," Wikipedia, https://en.wikipedia.org/wiki/Greenmead_Farms (accessed 9/21/16).

96 "This structure was built by Judge Alexander Blue"   "Greenmead Farms."

98 "Fred and Frank Wolfram purchased"   Suzanne Daniel and Kathleen Glynn, *Livonia Preserved: Greenmead and Beyond* (Charleston, SC: Arcadia, 2006), 78.

107 "In 1914, Woodrow Wilson signed"   "Celebrating Mothers," *Today in History* (Library of Congress, Digital Collections, May 9) (accessed 11/12/21).

108 "In 2014, saplings grown from the seeds"   "Hiroshima Ginkgo Tree Seeds Take Root in Manchester," BBC News, November 5, 2014, https://www.bbc.com/news/uk-england-manchester-29920359#.

110   "neither to rain nor to wind"   Howard Nemerov, "The
       Consent," in *The Western Approaches: Poems, 1973–1975*
       (Chicago: University of Chicago Press, 1975).

121   "Although tree trunks"   David George Haskell, *The Songs
       of Trees: Stories from Nature's Great Connectors* (New York:
       Penguin Books, 2017), viii.

126   "Like your ears"   Bonnie Worth, *I Can Name 50 Trees Today!
       All about Trees*, illus. Aristides Ruiz and Joe Mathieu (New
       York: Random House, 2006), 18.

126   "While one landscaping book"   Philip Chandler, Alan D.
       Cook, Gordon P. DeWolf Jr., Gordon E. Jones, and Katharine
       Widin, *Taylor's Guide to Trees* (Boston: Houghton Mifflin,
       1988).

138   "In one growing season"   USDA Forest Service, "Water &
       Forests: The Role Trees Play in Water Quality," 3, https://www
       .fs.usda.gov/Internet/FSE_DOCUMENTS/stelprdb5269813
       .pdf (accessed 4/11/22).

139   "Scientists from three institutions"   Peter Wohlleben, *The
       Hidden Life of Trees*, 58.

141   "*What Tree Is That?*"   Arbor Day Foundation, "Tree
       Identification: What Tree Is That?" https://www.arborday.org/
       trees/index-identification.cfm (accessed 2/28/21).

152   "*Yūgen* does not"   "Yūgen: Mysterious Grace," under
       "Japanese Aesthetics," *Stanford Encyclopedia of Philosophy*,
       https://plato.stanford.edu/entries/japanese-aesthetics/
       (accessed 11/13/21).

154   "And who knows, perhaps one day"   Peter Wohlleben, *The
       Hidden Life of Trees*, 245.

154   "brain-like structures"   Wohlleben, *The Hidden Life of Trees*,
       83, referencing František Baluška et al., "Neurobiological View
       of Plants and Their Body Plan," in *Communication in Plants*,
       ed. František Baluška, Stefano Mancuso, and Dieter Volkmann
       (New York: Springer, 2007).

155   "Scientific studies"   Yuki Ideno et al., "Blood Pressure-
       Lowering Effect of shinrin-yoku (Forest Bathing): A

Systematic Review and Meta-analysis," *BMC Complementary and Alternative Medicine* 17, no. 1 (2017): 409, https://www.ncbi .nlm.nih.gov/pmc/articles/PMC5559777/ (accessed 2/16/21).

156 "Forest bathing interventions"   Katherine Ka-Yin Yau and Alice Yuen Loke, "Effects of Forest Bathing on Pre-hypertensive and Hypertensive Adults: A Review of the Literature," *Environmental Health and Preventative Medicine* 25, no. 1 (2020): 23, https://environhealthprevmed .biomedcentral.com/articles/10.1186/s12199-020-00856-7 (accessed 2/16/21).

156 "Mount Massive Wilderness"   "Mount Massive Wilderness," Pike-San Isabel National Forests & Cimarron and Comanche National Grasslands, USDA Forest Service, https://www .fs.usda.gov/recarea/psicc/recarea/?recid=80753 (accessed 4/11/22).

156 "Across cultures and across time"   Jim Robbins, *The Man Who Planted Trees: A Story of Lost Groves, the Science of Trees, and a Plan to Save the Planet* (New York: Spiegel and Grau, 2012), xvii.

157 "At three thousand trees"   Lucas Ward, "Foresters Say Colorado Forests Are Too Thick," 9NEWS, July 19, 2005, https://www.9news.com/article/news/local/foresters-say -colorado-forests-are-too-thick/73-344718577.

169 "One lives in the hope"   Antonio Porchia, *Voices*, trans. W. S. Merwin (Chicago: Big Table, 1969), 13.

176 "The course pursued by the radicle"   Charles Darwin, assisted by Francis Darwin, *The Power of Movement in Plants* (London: John Murray, 1880), 572.

178 "They will probably die"   Teo Spengler, "Zone 6 Crepe Myrtle Varieties—Growing Crepe Myrtle Trees in Zone 6," *Gardening Know How*, https://www.gardeningknowhow.com/ garden-how-to/gardening-by-zone/zone-6/zone-6-crepe -myrtle-varieties.htm (accessed 2/08/21).

181 "recommended alternatives to ash trees"   Bert Cregg and
    Robert Schutzki, "Recommended Alternatives to Ash Trees
    for Michigan's Lower Peninsula," Michigan State University
    Department of Horticulture and Department of Forestry
    Extension Bulletin E-2925, July 2004, https://www.canr.msu
    .edu/uploads/resources/pdfs/recommended_alternatives_to
    _ash_trees_for_michigans_lower_peninsula_(e2925).pdf.

183 "When we learn to listen"   Monica Gagliano, *Thus Spoke the
    Plant* (Berkeley, CA: North Atlantic Books, 2018), 9.

187 "also the top tree species"   Kevin Sayers, "Urban &
    Community Forestry in Michigan," Michigan Department
    of Natural Resources, https://www.michigan.gov/documents/
    dnr/UCF_Presentation_-_FMAC_2016_2_510160_7.pdf
    (accessed 9/12/20).

188 "Norway maples are no longer"   J. Swearingen, B. Slattery,
    K. Reshetiloff, and S. Zwicker, "Norway Maple," in *Plant
    Invaders of Mid-Atlantic Natural Areas* (Washington, DC:
    National Park Service and U.S. Fish and Wildlife Service, 2010),
    https://www.invasive.org/alien/pubs/midatlantic/acpl.htm.

190 "Sycamores seem to reach"   Clarence M. Weed, "The
    Sycamore or Buttonwood," in *Our Trees: How to Know
    Them*, 5th ed. (1908; repr., Garden City, NY: Garden City
    Publishing, 1946), 185.

190 "Yet pure its waters"   William Cullen Bryant, "Green
    River," in *Poems* (Cambridge, MA: Hilliard and Metcalf,
    1821).

193 "The sapwood is white"   Eric Meier, "Sycamore," *The Wood
    Database*, https://www.wood-database.com/sycamore/
    (accessed 4/06/22).

194 "And, oaks are 'notoriously promiscuous'"   Hugo, *Seeing
    Trees*, 121.

195 "classic eastern oak"   Elbert L. Little, *National Audubon
    Society Field Guide to North American Trees: Eastern Region*
    (New York: Knopf, 1980), 382.

195 "our mighty oak"   Arbor Day Foundation, *What Tree Is That?*
A Guide to the More Common Trees Found in North America
(Lincoln, NE: Arbor Day Foundation, 2016), 33.

199 "Female trees produce" The Friends of the Wild Flower
Garden, "Eastern Redcedar," *Trees & Shrubs of the Eloise Butler
Wildflower Garden,* https://www.friendsofthewildflowergarden
.org/pages/plants/easternredcedar.html (accessed 4/16/22).

200 "While Cedar is capable of growing"   Clay Bowers, "The
Magic of Cedar," NO. MI HUNT/GATHER, February 20,
2018, http://www.nomiforager.com/blog/2018/2/7/the-magic
-of-cedar.

201 "a dead specimen"   Rocky Mountain Tree-Ring Research,
Inc. & the Tree-Ring Laboratory of Lamont-Doherty Earth
Observatory and Columbia University, "Eastern Old List,"
2013, https://www.ldeo.columbia.edu/~adk/oldlisteast/.

202 "These two species"   "How to Recognize Ash," *Monitoring
and Managing Ash (MaMa): A Citizen-Science-Driven Program
for Conservation and Mitigation,* http://www.monitoringash
.org/ash-id-information/ (accessed 1/10/21).

202 "Green ash may be confused"   "Red or Green Ash," *Canadian
Tree Tours,* https://www.canadiantreetours.org/species-pages/
Red_or_green_ash.html (accessed 1/10/21).

202 "Red ash *(Fraxinus pennsylvanica)*"   "Red or Green Ash."

203 "Some studies indicate"   The Friends of the Wild Flower
Garden, "Green Ash," *Trees & Shrubs of the Eloise Butler
Wildflower Garden,* https://www.friendsofthewildflowergarden
.org/pages/plants/ash_green.html (accessed 4/16/22).

203 "The most distinctive features"   Sylvia May Obenauf Taylor,
"Ecological and Genetic Isolation of *Fraxinus americana* and
Fraxinus pennsylvanica" (PhD abstract, University of Michigan,
1972), https://mbgna.umich.edu/wp-content/uploads/
ResearchDocs/Fraxinus_Taylor_1972_small.pdf.

209 "except for 167 trees discovered"   Jill Jonnes, "The Living
Dinosaur: Peter Del Tredici's Search for the Wild Ginkgo,"

Harvard Magazine, November–December 2011, https://www
.harvardmagazine.com/2011/11/the-living-dinosaur.

210   "a strange phenomenon of 'sex-switching'"   "Ginkgo: A
Sexual Curiosity," Oak Spring Garden Foundation's blog,
November 7, 2017, https://www.osgf.org/blog/2017/11/7/
blandy-ginkgo.

212   "Silver maple is the first"   William J. Gabriel, "Silver Maple,"
U.S. Forest Service Southern Research Station, referencing
C. S. Schopmeyer, "Seeds of Woody Plants in the United
States," *U.S. Department of Agriculture, Agriculture Handbook
450* (Washington, DC: U.S. Department of Agriculture, 1974),
https://www.srs.fs.usda.gov/pubs/misc/ag_654/volume_2/acer/
saccharinum.htm#.

212   "The sapwood of maple trees"   Slightly paraphrased from Eric
Meier, "Silver Maple," *The Wood Database*, https://www.wood
-database.com/silver-maple/ (accessed 4/7/22).

213   "The silver maple is closely related"   "Acer saccharinum,"
Wikipedia, https://www.wikiwand.com/en/Acer_saccharinum
(accessed 12/28/20).

216   "researchers and naturalists"   "Beech Trees Are Dying, and
Nobody's Sure Why," *ScienceDaily*, January 9, 2019, https://
www.sciencedaily.com/releases/2019/01/190109114758.htm.

219   "The inner bark has high concentrations"   Alexander Bryant,
"Wild Edible Wednesday 3/27—Eastern Redbud," *Sarcraft*,
March 26, 2019.

225   "biggest and best tract"   "Porcupine Mountains," *Michigan
Department of Natural Resources*, https://www.michigan.gov/
dnr/0,4570,7-350-79133_79200_31427-54024-,00.html
(accessed 2/28/21).

Further Reading

Tree Identification Guides

Arbor Day Foundation. *What Tree Is That? A Guide to the More Common Trees Found in North America*. Nebraska City, NE: Arbor Day Foundation, 2016.

Little, Elbert L. *National Audubon Society Field Guide to North American Trees: Eastern Region*. New York: Knopf, 1980. The National Audubon Society has also published *Field Guide to North American Trees: Western Region* by the same author.

Tekiela, Stan. *Trees of Michigan*. Cambridge, MN: Adventure, 2002. Tekiela has also published tree field guides of the trees of Arizona, the Carolinas, Colorado, Illinois, Indiana, Minnesota, Missouri, New York, Ohio, Pennsylvania, Texas, and Wisconsin.

On Trees' Senses and Intelligence

Chamovitz, Daniel. *What a Plant Knows: A Field Guide to the Senses.* New York: Scientific American/Farrar, Straus and Giroux, 2012.

Gagliano, Monica. *Thus Spoke the Plant: A Remarkable Journey of Groundbreaking Scientific Discoveries and Personal Encounters with Plants*. Berkeley, CA: North Atlantic Books, 2018.

Mancuso, Stefano. *The Revolutionary Genius of Plants: A New Understanding of Plant Intelligence and Behavior*. New York: Simon and Schuster, 2017.

Mancuso, Stefano, and Alessandra Viola. *Brilliant Green: The Surprising History and Science of Plant Intelligence.* Washington, DC: Island, 2015.

Thompson, Ken. *Darwin's Most Wonderful Plants: Darwin's Botany Today.* London: Profile Books, 2018.

Wohlleben, Peter. *The Hidden Life of Trees: What They Feel, How They Communicate—Discoveries from a Secret World.* Vancouver, BC: Greystone Books, 2015.

On How Trees Help Humans

Delorie, Oliver Luke. *shinrin-yoku: The Healing Art of Forest Bathing.* New York: Sterling Ethos, 2018.

Gilbert, Cyndi. *Forest Bathing: Discovering Health and Happiness through the Japanese Practice of shinrin-yoku (A Start Here Guide).* New York: St. Martin's, 2019.

Li, Qing. *Forest Bathing: How Trees Can Help You Find Health and Happiness.* New York: Viking, 2018.

Miyazaki, Yoshifumi. *shinrin-yoku: The Japanese Art of Forest Bathing.* Portland, OR: Timber, 2018.

Plevin, Julia. *The Healing Magic of Forest Bathing: Finding Calm, Creativity, and Connection in the Natural World.* Berkeley, CA: Ten Speed, 2019.

Williams, Florence. *The Nature Fix: Why Nature Makes Us Happier, Healthier, and More Creative.* New York: Norton, 2017.

On How Trees Help the Planet We Share

American Forests: americanforests.org.

Arbor Day Foundation: www.arborday.org.

EarthShare: Original page, "Tree Benefits," no longer active, but see https://www.earthshare.org.

National Wildlife Federation: https://www.nwf.org/.

U.S. Forest Service: https://www.fs.usda.gov/.

For Kids

Berne, Emma Carlson. *From Cone to Pine Tree*. Minneapolis: Lerner, 2018.

Burns, Diane L. *Trees, Leaves and Bark*. Illustrated by Linda Garrow. Minnetonka, MN: NorthWord Books for Young Readers, 2016.

Hopkins, H. Joseph. *The Tree Lady: The True Story of How One Tree-Loving Woman Changed a City Forever*. Illustrated by Jill McElmurry. New York: Scholastic, 2013.

Ingoglia, Gina. *The Treebook: For Kids and Their Grown-ups*. Brooklyn: Brooklyn Botanic Gardens, 2008.

Wirth, Victoria. *Whisper from the Woods*. Illustrated by A. Scott Banfill. New York: Green Tiger/Simon and Schuster, 1991.

Wohlleben, Peter. *Can You Hear the Trees Talking? Discovering the Hidden Life of the Forest*. Vancouver, BC: Greystone Books, 2019.

Worth, Bonnie. *I Can Name 50 Trees Today! All about Trees*. Illustrated by Aristides Ruiz and Joe Mathieu. New York: Random House, 2006.

A Sampling of Other Interesting Books about Trees

Beresford-Kroeger, Diana. *Arboretum America: A Philosophy of the Forest*. Ann Arbor: University of Michigan Press, 2003.

———. *The Global Forest: 40 Ways Trees Can Save Us*. New York: Penguin, 2010.

Bolen, Jean Shinoda. *Like a Tree: How Trees, Women, and Tree People Can Save the Planet*. San Francisco: Conari, 2011.

Fowles, John. *The Tree*. Boston: Little, Brown, 1979.

Halkett, John. *By the Light of the Sun: Trees, Wood, Photosynthesis and Climate Change*. Queensland, AU: Connor Court, 2018.

Haskell, David George. *The Songs of Trees: Stories from Nature's Great Connectors*. New York: Penguin, 2017.

Hugo, Nancy Ross. *Seeing Trees: Discover the Extraordinary Secrets of Everyday Trees*. Photography by Robert Llewellyn. Portland, OR: Timber, 2011.

Jonnes, Jill. *Urban Forests: A Natural History of Trees and People in the American Cityscape*. New York: Viking, 2016.

Merwin, W. S. *Unchopping a Tree*. Drawings by Liz Ward. San Antonio, TX: Trinity University Press, 2014.

Powers, Richard. *Overstory: A Novel*. New York: Norton, 2019.

Stafford, Fiona. *The Long, Long Life of Trees*. New Haven, CT: Yale University Press, 2016.

Stone, Christopher D. *Should Trees Have Standing? Law, Morality, and the Environment*. London: Oxford University Press, 2010.

Suzuki, David, and Wayne Grady. *Tree: A Life Story*. Vancouver, BC: Greystone Books, 2004.

Tudge, Colin. *The Tree: A Natural History of What Trees Are, How They Live, and Why They Matter*. New York: Three Rivers, 2005.

Acknowledgments

I am deeply grateful for the inspiration, encouragement, and assistance I have received from many people and numerous trees over the course of working on this project. Thank you to all who contributed to me being able to find and travel this particular path between my tree companions.

Those who contributed to my interest in writing about trees, especially:

William A. (Bill) Dunphy, my dad, who ushered me early into the lifelong pleasures of reading and writing and fostered a fascination with eastern redbud trees. .

Avery Grace Somarelli, my dear granddaughter, who in 2016, at five weeks old, first got me thinking about writing about trees, and who, with the help of her mom, picked out the Cat in the Hat's Learning Library *I Can Name 50 Trees Today!* to encourage me.

Jeanne Seymour, my walking partner of many years, who knew I was particularly interested in trees before I realized it myself, gifting me with the *DK Smithsonian Nature Guide to Trees* by Tony Russell at the end of 2012 with the note: "There are a lot of trees you and I encounter that I know you're curious about."

Family and friends who contributed their support to the development of this book, especially:

Craig Daly, my wonderful husband and first reader, who continues to create extraordinary dinners night after night and is always eager to go on tree-identifying adventures with me!

Caitlin Skye Barr and **Meagan Mná Somarelli Dunphy-Daly,** my dear daughters, who allowed me to tell their stories.

Caroline Dunphy, my mom, who first taught me "TREE" and regifted me a book from her childhood that resided on my bookshelf during the years I played in The Field: *Talking Leaves: How to Identify American Trees*, by Julius King (1934).

Karen, Noreen, and Lanette, my Daly sisters-in-law, who located my mother-in-law's written account of her trip to Lebanon for me and then lent me her diary, which I hadn't known existed.

Jason Somarelli, my son-in-law and a scientist, who first made me aware of plant neurobiology by recommending Stefano Mancuso's book *Brilliant Green* (2015).

Karen Klein, my dear artist friend of over twenty years, whom I was introduced to when she needed someone to write a poem about an alder tree for her handmade artist book *Thirteen × Twenty-Eight + One* (2003), the first tree project of which I was a part; who lent me a stack of thirteen "vintage" books on trees, including *Davey's Primer on Trees and Birds* (1905); and who made me aware of the landscape painter Charles Burchfield's journal entry of November 28, 1915, which includes the line "I have never learned to talk and have only listened to the trees."

Ron Tiessen, my Pelee friend, writer, and naturalist, who provided me with an explanation of white and green ash hybridization and who made a treacherous trek on a frigid day when ice was on the island's West Shore Road to confirm that the elm at the Anchor and Wheel Inn is, in fact, a rocky elm.

Kathy Wildfong, my dear friend and fellow adventurer, who has walked miles and miles with me, and who has cheered me along this path through trees.

Harah Frost, friend and fellow writer, who first read my chapter on the eastern cottonwood and suggested adding a section to each chapter in the book's first draft that considered particular tree concepts. Titled "Tree's Big Idea," these pieces can now be found at maureendunphy.com under *Divining, A Memoir in Trees.*

Leigh Lash, a fellow (and self-proclaimed) "tree nerd," who walked the woods of Harbor Springs with me and sent me links to tree articles and photographs she came across.

Rhonda Hacker, friend and fellow writer, for introducing me to the elm and catalpa trees she regularly greets on her local mail route and for her gift of *Poems about Trees*, edited by Harry Thomas (2019).

Mary Robertson, friend and fellow writer, who sent me photos of trees, gifted me a copy of her favorite tree book, *Whisper from the Woods*, by Victoria Wirth, illustrated by A. Scott Banfill (1991), and invited me to lead her book club's discussion on Richard Powers's *Overstory* (2018) before the meeting became my first to be canceled because of COVID-19.

Laurie Harris, Mindy LePere, Barbara Arnett, Loretta Polish, and **Gerry Flood,** all writing friends, who sent me articles about and/or photos of trees.

Members of my writing workshops over the last five years, especially the "Ladies of the Long Table," for their interest in my project and their generous contribution to the fir tree planted in memory of my dad.

Others who contributed their knowledge or skills to the project:

Singing Tree Detroit ("Detroit's favorite family-owned tree service") owners Kevin and Emily Bingham, arborists Evan and Dean, and the rest of the crew for all the care they've provided members of the grove in which I live and for bringing the 'Princess Emily' flowering dogwood with whom I now share land.

Mark Taormina, director of Planning and Economic Development, City of Livonia, for the aerial view photograph of The Creek in The Field where I played during my elementary school years, and for his answers to my questions about the area.

Julia Fletcher, appraiser, City of Royal Oak, who supplied me with early photos showing the trees planted in my current yard and who first told me of the Royal Oak Arboretum which, along with the adjoining Tenhave Woods, contains all but sixteen of the eighty-six tree species native to Michigan.

Don Drife, naturalist and former Royal Oak Nature Society president, for his correspondence on Royal Oak's English oak population.

Bob Muller, naturalist and program director, founding member, and former president of Royal Oak Nature Society, for his information on Royal Oak's Tenhave Woods, Cummingston Park, and Royal Oak Arboretum and his kind offer of a tour of the latter.

Vikki Munroe, who kept opening doors, helped me keep on track, sent me anything tree-related with which she crossed paths, and suggested that my island book was "just practice" for a more important project.

Ericka Mojica, personal trainer, who kept me moving instead of allowing me to become rooted in my desk chair and who shared her long-ago school project on trees with me.

Tim Travis, owner of Goldner Walsh Garden and Home in Pontiac, Michigan, who helped me select the right tree—the concolor fir—and his team who planted it for me to memorialize my dad.

Many thanks to the entire talented team at and connected to Wayne State University Press, especially:

Annie Martin, editor in chief extraordinaire, for her belief in this book, her support of me in the writing of it, and her help in shaping it; **Marie Sweetman,** acquisitions editor, who took over shepherding this book in the midst of the review process and was able to talk me out of the weeds via email one Friday afternoon before we had yet to talk on the phone, let alone meet in person; **Kristin Harpster,** for her spot-on editorial, design, and production decisions, her precision, and her patience; **Carrie Downes Teefey** for her care in directing the cover design and finding the right designer to manifest it; **Lindsey Cleworth,** who created the beautiful (perfect!) cover for this book; **Robin DuBlanc,** copyeditor *magnifique,* who was willing to accompany me on this second journey of ours together with her careful reading and thoughtful questions; her divining of my intentions was as astute when it came to trees as when it concerned islands; and proofreader **Jennifer Backer,** who helped polish the book with final edits.

I'd like to recognize a few others who may never know how much they helped with this book by providing facts or inspiration:

Stan Tekiela, author of *Trees of Michigan,* and **Elbert L. Little,** former chief dendrologist, U.S. Forest Service and author of the *National Audubon Society Field Guide to North American Trees: Eastern Region.* Both their books remained atop my desk—and helped me create appendix A—when other tree books were in stacks on my study floor.

The Arbor Day Foundation, whose book *What Tree Is That?* helped me identify the Colorado pinyon in Denver, the Douglas-fir in Leadville, and many trees in Michigan over the last five years.

Ösel, the band created by Michael and Stephanie Johnson, who recorded *Medicine Buddha Mantra* (2012), which served as my soundtrack for this book project.

Taya, my crazy tuxedo "writing kitty," who keeps me company.

Some other trees in my life, not featured in this book, for whom I am grateful and to whose murmurs I also listen:

Other members of the grove on whose land I live:

- Eastern flowering dogwood
- Honey locust
- Black walnut
- White poplar
- Paper birch
- American smoketree
- Bradford pear

More Pelee Island trees:

- Hackberry
- Hawthorn
- Weeping willow
- Boxelder (aka Manitoba maple)
- Common hoptree
- Kentucky coffeetree
- American basswood (aka American linden)
- Dwarf red-leaf plum

Other trees farther afield in time or miles:

- Russian-olive
- Crab apple
- Red mulberry
- Apple
- Loblolly pine

About the Author

Maureen Dunphy is the author of *Great Lakes Island Escapes: Ferries and Bridges to Adventure* (Wayne State University Press, 2016), which received the 2017 Michigan Notable Book Award, and *All about the Great Lakes*. Her writing has been featured in *Beyond the Lines: Writing What You Couldn't Say, Bear River Review*, and *Peninsula: Essays and Memoirs from Michigan*. She is the lead fiction editor for the literary journal *Clockhouse*. She facilitates writing workshops privately and for Springfed Arts and, through Dunphy Consulting Services, provides writing, coaching, and editing services for individuals and institutions. She has taught writing courses at Oakland University, the University of Windsor, and Oakland Community College. Dunphy earned a BA in English from Oakland University and an MFA from Goddard College in Plainfield, Vermont. She lives in the Detroit metropolitan area.